WHAT COPS KNOW

WHAT COPS KNOW

Cops Talk About What They Do, How They Do It, and What It Does to Them

Connie Fletcher

Villard Books
New York
1991

Villard Books is a registered trademark of Random House, Inc.

Library of Congress Cataloging-in-Publication Data
Fletcher, Connie
What cops know: cops talk about what they do, how they do it, and
what it does to them / by Connie Fletcher.
p. cm.
ISBN 0-394-57719-1
1. Police—United States. I. Title.
HV7914.F57 1991
363.2′0973—dc20   90-50226

9 8 7 6 5 4 3 2

First Edition

Book design by Richard Oriolo

**This book is for
Trygve, Bridget, and Nick.**

Preface

Cops know things you and I don't. It's knowledge crafted out of years spent on the street, sizing up and dealing with the volatile, cunning, confused, comic, tragic, often goofy behavior of human beings from every social, economic, and mental level, and it's knowledge won as a by-product of investigating criminal specialties such as homicide, sex crimes, property crimes, and narcotics. A cop who works traffic has peered deeper into the recesses of the human psyche than most shrinks. A cop who works homicide, or sex crimes, will tell you things Dostoyevski only guessed at.

What cops know isn't scientific, quantifiable, or statistical knowledge. It may even contradict what studies show, what experts say. It can't be proven with numbers or pinned down on a chart. The world that cops inhabit is hard to describe and hard to understand.

I became aware of the fact that police are privy to special knowledge, most of which they share only with other police— and sometimes with their families—when my sister Julie became a police officer ten years ago. Suddenly my family was given a glimpse of a world that was all around us and yet invisible to us. This world exists in Joe Wambaugh, cops say. It may also exist in some nonfiction where police are allowed to speak for themselves. It does not exist, police have told me, in Hollywood cop movies or TV cop shows—with the exception of *Barney Miller.* I have yet to meet a police officer who does not swear that *Barney Miller* captured what it's like to be a cop.

I set out to find out exactly what it is that cops know in two senses: the technical sense, or what cops know about crime, criminal behavior, and human nature; and the feeling sense, or the ways in which this knowledge shapes cops and changes them, setting them apart from the rest of us. It seemed to me that police fiction and nonfiction, including collections of police narratives, looked almost exclusively at the feeling side of being a cop, only glancingly and tantalizingly at the technical side, and never at both together. But the two sides—what cops know by virture of their experience and expertise and what this knowledge does to them—cannot be separated. You cannot separate knowing how to use a battering ram, sledgehammer, and guile to get into a dope house from what it feels like at the moment you come crashing through that door into the unknown; you cannot separate knowing how to process an accident scene that has a child fatality or a case of child sexual exploitation from what that knowledge does to you when you next see your own children. Deep knowledge may lead to deep pain. It also leads to deep insight and compassion.

During the course of three years, I met with 125 Chicago police officers for the purpose of finding out what they know. I met police officers off-duty, in restaurants and coffee shops, a few times in their own homes. I interviewed individual police officers and I interviewed partners, groups of officers from the specialized units, or tactical teams—teams of officers who specialize in undercover work in vice and narcotics.

I wanted to give them the freedom to say whatever they wanted to say without fear of ending up walking a beat in Lake Michigan. I also wanted readers to know that they could trust what these officers said, that I hadn't contacted a handful of police with little experience or concern for the truth (what police call "loose lippers"). The format I hit upon to satisfy both these goals was to identify the police who had shared their war stories, expertise, and insights with me at the end of each chapter by name and career sketch, and to have the chapter itself consist of the cops' own voices, undiluted and anonymous.

When I contacted police, I'd ask them for an hour; only 2 out of 125 stopped there. The average length of an interview was ninety minutes; many times, especially with partners and groups of officers, the interview would stretch to three hours. We'd close places down, reschedule interviews, and then meet again.

Mostly, I interviewed in eateries. This had its advantages: the turf is neutral and food fuels conversation. However, cops talking loudly and urgently in public places about crimes and criminals they have known can get a little odd sometimes.

I met with a longtime homicide detective one weekend morning at a famous Swedish pancake house on Chicago's North Side. The place was packed, the tables set almost on top of one another. As the detective described the details of a torso murder in which the limbless body was found stuffed in the bathtub ("The first thing you noticed was that the shoulders were flush with the front of the tub—that didn't look right—and then you noticed that the neck portion was right up against the faucet. No head. No arms. No legs. This was a smart murderer, a guy who knew what he was doing, leaving no identifiers.")—as he was describing this in homicidal detail, I noticed people at adjoining tables casting doubtful looks at their lingonberry pancakes.

One night, I met with an Area Six tac team, wise in the ways of dope addicts and dealers, in their favorite Chinese restaurant. I wanted to know what drugs they saw on the street; how much crack there was; if new, exotic drugs were showing up. Ten guys and two women were sitting around four pulled-together tables in a crowded Chinese joint; they'd shout over each other to be heard. "Coke!" "It's all coke!" "Coke is all we're seeing—it's coke!" "Everybody wants coke!" Suddenly, the guy next to me stopped everyone. "Will you look at this? Who ordered all these Cokes?" Twenty-four glasses of Coke sat in the middle of the table, brought over every few seconds by our harried Chinese waitress.

Most of the officers I interviewed work or have worked in Area Six, a police jurisdiction (further divided into the Eighteenth, Nineteenth, Twentieth, Twenty-third, and Twenty-fourth Districts) that runs, geographically, from the Chicago River to the Wrigley Building downtown to the northernmost edge of the city and from Lake Michigan west, roughly following the river and the Kennedy Expressway. Economically, socially, and criminally, Area Six encompasses everything. "Area Six is probably *the* most exciting area in the U.S. for a cop to work," says Lieutenant Jim Nemec of the Chicago Crime Lab. "It has so many sections of society in it—you go from processing a knifing in Cabrini-Green [one of the city's bleakest, most crime-ridden projects] to a murder of a rich old lady in a brownstone on the Gold Coast [the second wealthiest city neighborhood in the country, after New York's Upper East Side—just two blocks from the Green]. And Area Six always has the nuttiest crimes."

The 22.4 square miles of Area Six are crammed with lawyers; doctors; bankers; corporation heads; hillbillies; gangbangers; the middle class; and the underclass of pimps, prostitutes, pushers, the predatory and the wasted. The very rich and the very poor live cheek by jowl, lakefront high-rise by crumbling apartment house. Area Six is where predator meets victim every day; the area that, year after year (according to the CPD Statistical Survey), leads all other Chicago Police Department areas in sheer variety of crimes committed. Area Six, one of the most socially, economically, and ethnically diverse police jurisdictions in the United States, represents a microcosm of crime.

"Whatever your game is, you can find a playmate in Area Six," says Captain Robert Sheehan of the Eighteenth District. "I don't care what kind of nonsense you're into—prostitution, dope, gambling, bondage—you can find what you're looking for in Area Six."

Area Six is a microcosm of crime, but every police beat in the United States and every cop's tour of duty is a microcosm—not just of crime, but of life and of human nature. Police are the unrecognized ethnographers of our time. Detective Ted O'Connor of the CPD puts it this way: "Living in our society is like living in a very tall building. The rich live on the top floors. The poor live on the lowest floors. And only cops travel to all the floors. Only cops see it all."

Acknowledgments

Police represent a closed society. They mistrust outsiders and avoid journalists. I gained access to this world for two reasons: my sister is a police officer, which made me seem, I was told, more likely to understand than a total outsider, and I was fortunate enough to come in contact with a number of police officers who advised and encouraged me.

Chief among these is Captain Tom Cronin, who is one of only twenty police officers in the United States trained by the FBI in criminal assessment and profiling. Tom Cronin gave me invaluable counsel and referrals and the benefit of his considerable expertise throughout the course of my researching this book.

I was constantly stunned, during my research, at the generosity of the police I met. They gave freely of their off-duty time, responding to call-backs or requests for more information or referrals with "Anything I can help you with. Call anytime." Out of 130 requests for interviews, I met with five refusals. Not a bad average.

Several of the police officers' assignments changed during the course of this book. Probably more will change by the time this appears, but the expertise of the officers interviewed remains a constant.

None of this book would have been possible were it not for Tina Vicini, spokesperson for the Chicago Police Department, who gave me permission to contact Chicago police officers. And it wouldn't have seen daylight without the support and encouragement of my colleagues at Loyola University, especially Elaine Bruggemeier, Ed Rooney, Marti Thomas, Bren Murphy, and Jo Ann Fricke.

I want to thank my family for bearing with me. My husband, Trygve, did *not* get upset at my running out to talk to police at all hours. My son, Nick, listened patiently to vice cops and violent crimes cops during his last three months in the womb. My daughter, Bridget, was the most help of all in writing the book and keeping me company during pneumonia. My aunts Kass Thompson and Gen McGuire and cousin Pat LaVigne were strong supporters. My brother, Bob, my sister, Julie, and my sister-in-law Michele Fletcher have always stood by me and I thank them. And I'm always grateful for the memory of my mother and father.

Contents

WHAT COPS KNOW

THE STREET

One time we had a jumper; this guy jumped out of the nineteenth floor of the Lawson YMCA. He hit the ground, and his head hit, and the top of his head popped off, and his brain fell right out. And it was perfectly intact. I'm walking all around it; I can't get over how it's just a brain laying there, complete and perfect as can be. It's laying right on the gutter. It didn't splatter—it wasn't icky or anything. It was like somebody just *placed* a brain on the gutter. Like an egg yolk. It was just perfect.

So now the paramedics come. And this one paramedic goes, "Look at this brain! Do you think we should put it in the chest with ice?" I'm looking at him like, Sure, pal, go ahead and transplant this on somebody. I couldn't believe it. He was gonna take this brain to the hospital, to Northwestern Memorial Hospital, in a cooler with ice, like it's a kidney or a liver or a heart or something. This is a *brain*—who are they gonna give it to?

–Area Six beat officer

People don't like cops. People don't like us. *I* get a reaction when I see a cop—and I'm a cop. I'll be driving down the street in a police car. I look up, and there's a squad car in my rearview mirror. I think, What does this asshole want? What's he doing following me?

–former West Side tac officer

Twenty years ago, a newly ordained Catholic priest, just sent to his first assignment, a parish on Chicago's South Side, went to a backyard barbecue.

"I was still trying to learn the streets and the names of the people— even the Mass schedule and where the front door of the church was," says Father Thomas Nangle, now police chaplain to the Chicago Police Department. "It was exciting and disorienting.

"I went to a backyard barbecue one weekend, some of the parishioners invited me over, and at one point, an old Dodge pulled up in the alley, and two men got out and they came in and joined the crowd in the backyard. And I noticed they both had guns on their belts. And they had Banlon shirts on, blue jeans, and gym shoes, and both were carrying guns. I thought, Gee, that's kind of a cavalier attitude. Maybe I should go home and get my box of grenades or my dynamite sticks or something. Join the crowd.

"Later, I was introduced to these two guys. They were both tactical officers from the Sixth District at Eighty-third and Green. Anyway, we're talking, and the guys found out I was a new priest, the new kid on the block. They said, 'Well, you know, Father, if you want to get to know your parish, why don't you come and ride with *us* a few nights?' And as most American males would do, I jumped at the chance. They took me around and showed me the hot spots and the dangerous spots and where drugs were being sold and where the bad guys lived and hung around, and it was—I was fascinated by it. Just absolutely fascinated by it.

"These guys took me around several nights. We really hit it off. A lot of times, there's just a natural affinity between priests and police. I've yet to figure it out.

"We both deal with the evil in life—but the difference is, with priests, there's a big distancing from evil—priests only hear about it in the confessional and the office. For the priest, it loses about nine tenths of its impact and its, its *wham.*

"But with the police officers, with their experience of evil, there's an immediacy. They stand in it. They touch it . . . they taste it . . . they smell it . . . they hear it . . . they have to handle it. The priest only knows about evil intellectually; the cop knows it in his gut.

"One other thing about police—cops know things other people don't. Their experience is so rich. After a year or two on the job, there's nothing that a big-city police officer hasn't seen or handled. Nothing. Consequently, they feel that they can handle just about anything, because there ain't nothin' around that shocks them anymore."

It's called getting your street degree. Cops count this as far more valuable than any formal education. And it can only be earned on the street.

The cops who work the street are the first on any scene, whether they're the beat cars, responding to in-progress calls or situations, or the tac officers, who work plainclothes, crime patterns, and in-progress calls. Beat and tac officers are called "the real police," a cop term edged with contempt for police who have bypassed the street. As one Area Six cop puts it: "A lot of the guys who have risen to the top have never left the building. They're not the real police. Nobody should get to the top ranks who hasn't worked the street. Unless you've felt that trickle of sweat running down your back when you're running up and down stairs in the projects, unless you've felt that terror you get when you sense something horrible is about to happen, you're not the real police."

This chapter is made up of street scenes and street smarts gleaned from many of the cops interviewed for this book, but mostly from twenty-five officers—beat officers, tac officers, gang-crimes specialists, a field lieutenant, a district captain, a dispatcher, two ex-wagon men—who have spent most of their careers studying the street.

Retired Officer Edward Tansey, a legend among Chicago cops and a street historian, spent thirty-five years working a beat and the wagon in Area Six, never applying for higher rank because, as he says, "I never wanted to do anything else. You saw everything. You did everything—especially on the wagon—we delivered babies, transported corpses, handled drunks, whores, disorderlies. Everything." When Tansey retired in 1986, he was still working the midnights and, now seventy, says he'd come back on the force and the wagon and the midnights in a flash.

"The great thing about working the street," says one veteran, "is you don't have to go to war or to some jungle to have adventures. You have all the adrenaline, all the excitement, and still take a day off and go see the Bears.

"I remember, when I was in college, I had a summer job in the Loop. It always impressed me, seeing the armies of commuters coming out of their offices every night at five, fighting their way across the bridge to the train. It seemed like prison to me. From home to train to office to train to home. What did they ever get to see?

"After I joined the force, I realized these people were still coming out of the offices, sitting in the train, going home, sitting in front of the TV, *watching* the things that I was a part of. And it was all because of the magical star, that gave me the access to this world that nobody ever sees. . . ."

What follows in this chapter and every other chapter in this book is pure cop, direct, unedited, undiluted quotes. Quotation marks, except as they occur within the quotes themselves, have been omitted.

Practically *anything* can happen in the street. My partner and I stopped a fellow speeding down Lake Shore Drive; the ceiling's forty-five; this guy must have been doing a hundred.

"Stop that son of a bitch!" So we turn on the blue lights, pull him over to the side. And he ran back to the car—we didn't even get a chance to get out, this is how fast he came back to the car.

He says, "Look. I know I'm speeding. You've got to help me out." He says, "Please don't—I don't have time to get a speeding ticket. You see the girl in my car?" We say, "Yeah." "That is the greatest sexual experience I've ever had. She lives at the YWCA at Oak and Dearborn. If I don't get her back in five minutes, she's never gonna be able to go out with me again. I'd love to talk with you—if you stay here, I'll be back in ten minutes, you can write me up then, but I don't have time for this now"—he runs back, jumps back in the car—and *zooom!*—off he goes again at a hundred miles an hour.

We were stunned. By the time we realized what he had said, realized the absurdity of it, he was probably already pulling up in front of his girlfriend's joint.

My partner and I were driving one night, a guy flagged us down. He had a knife sticking out of the top of his head. All we could see was the hilt coming out. "Somebody stabbed me." "Okay, get in, get in, we'll take you to the hospital." He sat in the back of the squad; he had to keep his head tilted so he wouldn't hit the car roof. The amazing thing was, he was talking away, laughing, joking, didn't seem to hurt at all. Perfectly calm. He just couldn't sit normally. We take him to the hospital—he's out of the car, walks in, he's still talking to us normally.

They take him into surgery. We ask one of the docs, "Is he gonna make it?" The doc said, "The minute they take it out, he's dead." Just like that.

I don't know, I'd keep it in. Get a good barber.

I got a call to meet one of the wagon crews one night at a motel on Sheridan Road. They said, "You gotta see this one, boss." I walked into the motel room and went back to the bathroom. And in the bathtub was a man with his head, hands, and feet cut off. And I looked down, and he looked like a stuffed turkey. And I said, "Whoo. I have never seen anything like this." And they said, "That's why we called you."

My partner and I were in tac together, and we had a call one time of shots fired on Chicago Avenue. It's about four in the afternoon. Normally, a call like that, it's firecrackers or something or it's over before you get there. This particular thing stands in my mind because as we turned the corner off a side street, there's people out of their businesses and people on the sidewalk are all looking down, so we knew we had something serious. It looked like a parade, almost, because it seemed everything stopped as we were going by.

We pull up to the address, and it turns out to be a pool hall.

There are shotgun blasts in the front window of this place. As I'm getting out of the car, a guy comes running up out of there, running up at me like a maniac. So I put my gun on him right from inside the car, and I'm just holding on to him. And he's going—he's just frantic—"They killed a man. They're shooting in there," and all that.

So we take care of this guy and go into the pool hall. As we go in there, the pool hall is empty. The back door is swinging. The cigarette smoke is still swirling from the people running through it. I mean, that stands out in my mind. The smoke's still swirling from everybody trying to get out—you could just *see* it. Usually, in a pool hall, especially in a cheap place, they don't have a fan to suck the air out. This place, the smoke's just hanging there.

So the back door's swinging. My partner and I have got our guns out. We're moving through the pool hall. Now we see a guy laying on the floor. It looks like the shotgun had cut into his head and he had like a hood, you know, like it had taken the top of his head off. So we're both looking and we figure, he's DOA.

So my partner gets ready to call for the ambulance—I grab his hand, I hold him because the back door's creaking. He instinctively turns the radio off not to alert anyone inside to our presence. So we're getting ready—we figure, he's *gone.* Okay? We don't see any guns, so, you know, fuck him, we're gonna walk over him. But we're looking at this guy's scalp; it looks like a hood; the scalp is all exposed; he looks like Custer at the Last Stand. How can I put it? It was crinkled up, sort of like—crunched. Picture a very tight, small toupee and it's all crunched. Like an accordion. All corrugated. All crunched. That's the best way to describe it.

This guy looks like he's gone for us. He's just gone. So I whisper to my partner, "Fuck it, he's dead." We get ready to go down and go over to that back door. As we go over him to go to the back door, this guy grabs Al by the ankle. To me it looked like Al's jeans went *eeee,* like the Stooges—his pants legs are vibrating, his legs are shaking so hard. And his hair is like—*sproinggg!*

And the guy on the floor; he's got Al by the ankle, he goes, "I just want to know one thing. Am I gonna *liiive?*" He kept saying it. "I just want to know one thing. I don't want to know about the motherfucker who hit me. I just want to know one thing. Am I gonna *liiive?"*

So now Al calls for the ambulance, and we hit the basement. We're inching our way down the stairs, and we see pens at the bottom—I'm not sure if it was for cockfighting or dogfighting, it must have been dogs, because Puerto Ricans are into cockfighting, but blacks are into dogs—this was a black area—but they definitely had pens down there. So we're inching our way down, there's no lights, we can't find any lights, we figure we're gonna hit it. We get down there, and we got the radio on now.

The basement is empty except for some chairs and the dogfighting pens and a roll of carpeting. We start to walk out and we hear a very faint "Uh . . . Uh." "Did you hear something?" Silence. There it goes again. "Uh . . . Uh." We hear a moan. Now, we finally hear it. It's "Officer"—"Uhficer . . . Uhficer."

Now we got our guns out. We start inching our way toward the corner where we hear the voice. And we're like—we're already freaked; our hair is standing straight up already from the upstairs; Al's pants are rolled up to his knees—and we're moving toward this voice. We don't see anything but the rolled-up carpet. But the voice is coming from *inside* the carpet. And this carpet is tightly rolled, so tightly and so well, you'd never think anybody could be in there. I mean, tight. *Tight.*

What had happened, this guy got shot in the ass upstairs during the whole thing, ran downstairs for his life, gets inside the carpet, and *dweek!,* rolls himself up in it. But he couldn't get out. And there he was—in the carpet. That whole thing—it was like the last scene in *Carrie,* with the hand coming up from the grave. It was a good time.

I'm working Special Employment one time in the projects. Me and my partner are driving to this project, Rockwell Gardens. He really knows his way around there. I've never been there. As we approach it, we notice a gang fight. These goofs are shooting at each other. So we park the squad about a block away and try to sneak up on them. We get up to them, they spin around—now, they're shooting at us.

My partner takes off—I can just see his long legs carrying him off—"I'm going to 2840," he's shouting as he's running.

Now the problem is, any copper who works the projects knows all the buildings by numbers. They don't identify them by the number and street address—just by the number—in Cabrini-Green, if you say 1117, everybody knows you mean 1117 Cleveland. I don't know the numbers. I don't know the buildings. I'm trying to find where we are—these gangbangers are still shooting at me—I'm consulting my prostitution beat map; this is when I was in Vice, but I need a projects beat map—all the numbers are different.

So I'm running between all these huge buildings, lots of them, and I'm shouting into the radio, "I'm being shot at. I'm in Rockwell Gardens, but I don't know where." Dispatch is going, "Can you see any numbers?" "No, no, just buildings." I'm running and screaming into the radio. I've totally lost my partner. "Give us a street." I could see the lights over the expressway—"I'm near a highway." I'm getting so excited I'm totally forgetting where I am. Finally, I found my partner, we got cover, reinforcements rolled in, but I keep thinking, What the hell am I doing anyway, running around chasing a bunch of goofs into buildings?

I've been working Dispatch four years. One of the first things you notice when you come on is, police officers overmodulate when they get excited. They're talking in a rush, the voice goes up four or five octaves, they're hollering in the radio, but the radios are very sensitive—when you holler, it's hard to hear.

Say it's a chase. Tac guys, they're classic for this—we don't know where they are to begin with because they work undercover and they never tell you where they are. So all of a sudden—"Squad! I'm chasing a male black wearing a dark coat down the alley." "What alley? Where are you?" "I'm on Seventy-ninth Street between Marshfield and Paulina. Wait—Now, I'm going through the yard." "What yard?" "He just jumped over the fence, now, he's doubling back. Squad, I'm rolling."

Now the other cars want to know what's up, does he have a gun, four or five different units are coming in, asking information and giving it. Everybody's overmodulating. You say to the tac guy on the chase, "Six-Sixty-One Charlie, you have the air.

All other units—unless you have pertinent information, stay off the air. Six-Sixty-One Charlie, you have the air—go."

If you get somebody that's calm, that's a blessing. That happens about once a year.

I'll tell you the dispatcher's nightmare, it's when you know a car needs help and you don't know where it is. When I was brand new, I had just got in the Room, right around the Fourth of July, we got a call from a field unit working the Fourteenth District. "Fourteen-Thirty-One"—all he said was 1431—we knew it was an emergency; we knew something was happening. It turned out the car wasn't where we had assigned him. He's calling for an assist and we don't know where he is. Everybody got still. Everybody in the Room is still. All the cars out there are still. Everything got real cold and still. I'm thinking, Oh God, what do we do? Cars began to come in on the air—they're panicking. "We got an emergency. Squad, did you hear that? Where are they? Where is he?"

The dispatcher who was handling this, Billy Bob, is in the middle of all this. Everybody in the Room's looking at him; the cars are all calling in—he's got to come up with something. He looks up at the screen where we track all the cars citywide. He picks out two streets. This dispatcher knew that these beat guys like to go to this one particular hot dog stand.

And that's where they were, at this one particular hot dog stand Billy Bob knew they liked, getting everything knocked out of them—four teens high on drugs were beating them up. The one that had the radio was a recruit—he radioed right before they knocked him to the ground—they couldn't get to the radio or get to their billy clubs or guns or anything and the guys were pulling the recruit from the radio. Once we figured out where they were, we sent cars out and rescued them.

Other coppers always think Dispatch is remote from them, like we're sitting around drinking coffee in the Room, but it's like being on the street—you feel like you're right in the cars with them. You feel like you're right out there with them in the car, on the street, in the alley, in the abandoned building, and whatever you do or say can make the difference between their living and dying.

They're attached to us. Whenever there's radio silence, no one's talking, I don't have any jobs to give them, nothing's going on—radio silence can last from two seconds to two minutes—someone out there will key his radio, press to see if it's working. Otherwise, he feels cut off. The radio is his umbilical cord to life. He'll say, "Is everything all right on the zone? Is something wrong with my radio? Radio check—" What he's really saying is, "Am I still alive?"

Anything can happen at any moment on the street. That's the rule out there.

The situations that seem the most unlikely to be dangerous are the ones that erupt into the most violent. The most tragic incidents have always come from the smallest incidents, usually traffic. The most innocuous stop that you'll make during the course of your duty is a traffic stop. But you don't know what you're stopping. When you're going to a dope flat, you know what to expect: resistance, probably having weapons, and things like that. When you walk up to a car with a little old lady sitting in it and she pulls a sawed-off shotgun on you, you're completely surprised. Who you're stopping is always the joker in the deck.

I once stopped two guys in a Cadillac—it was the only other car on the street at the time; we just wanted to check it out. It turned out they were driving around with a body in the backseat. They were on their way to dump it.

My partner and I were on the midnights, driving around, and we see a white Cadillac. It's the only other car on the road. So we pull up next to it, and the driver cuts me off; he runs the squad off the road. That's when I got hot. So I put on the siren, a chase ensued, the car crashed, they bail out, and now we're chasing these two guys on foot. I chase one, and my partner goes after the other.

I chase this guy for four blocks. Finally, he couldn't run anymore, I couldn't run anymore. I throw the cuffs on him and wait for the backup.

Meantime, the cars have pulled up to the scene of the crash. Somebody comes up to me and says, "Hey, a man was shot at the scene." I thought my partner had killed the other guy. We get back to the scene, and I say to my partner, "Hey, Jimmy, did you shoot this guy?" He hadn't. I couldn't figure out who got shot; there were only the four of us on the street.

It turns out there was a guy laying shot in the back of the Cadillac. He'd been shot five times and was in the process of dying. There were two guns in the car; one had five cartridges expended; the other was fully loaded.

They took the guy to the hospital and asked him who did this. He told them to go fuck themselves, and died.

I was with two other tac officers, and we were on our way to meet an informant that was going to set up a drug buy with Willie "the Wimp" Stokes. I was in the backseat, and my two partners were in front. I'm looking out the back window, and there's a car speeding up behind us, the driver's flashing his lights at us, blowing the horn. It's a male black driver and he's got a little kid with him. Should we stop? We don't want to stop, we're on the way to a drug buy. We're in an undercover car, but it's got identifiable plates, so if we don't stop, we'll be in trouble.

I exited the car and approached the car behind us. Now this guy had done the perfect police stop, it's what they teach you in the Academy: half of his car, the passenger's half, was lined up with the center of our car. His right headlight was dead center with the back of our car. A perfect police stop. They teach you never to pull directly behind the car you're stopping, but to park your car halfway on the car you're stopping so you give yourself some cover.

As I approached the car, I could see this guy, and he's holding a gun. Now, everything starts going through my mind: He's got the gun because this kid tried to rob him, or the kid's a burglar he caught in his house, or it's his kid and he found him with a gun—everything runs through my mind except what actually happened.

I go up to the man and tell him to put the gun on the dashboard. I see it's a .22 Magnum. The guy says nothing. He starts firing at my partners, who are coming out of the car; the way he had parked his car, my partners were in an awkward situation, they were coming out of the car with their backs to the guy. I returned fire as I began to run toward cover, toward this telephone pole. I hit the guy in the chest, so I thought, I got him. That's it. But he's not dead. He turns and shoots me twice; my partners are pinned in the car; they're half in and half out. He hit me in the groin; if he'd gotten me an inch lower, I'd be speaking a few octaves higher. It felt like someone punched me real hard. I flipped in the air and landed on my back. When I was on the ground, I felt the blood running down, trickling down between my legs on the right side of my body, but the pain was all on the left side, that's where the bullet hit bone. I could feel where one bullet came through and hit my pelvis, it slid right around and almost came out the upper thigh of my left leg. I kept shooting, I never went unconscious, I continued returning fire and eventually killed him.

One of my partners was on the radio screaming "Ten-One, Ten-One!" He's all excited. I could hear the dispatcher asking him, "Where are you?" He looks at the light pole on the corner and tells dispatch, "I don't know. Someone stole the street sign." So I called on my own radio—"I know where I'm at and I'm bleeding and I want to go to the hospital." I was pretty calm. I remember thinking, I haven't done enough in my life to have it end right here.

It seemed like it took fifteen or twenty minutes from start to finish, but actually from the time the guy stopped us to the time I was thrown in the back of the wagon, and I mean they took me and threw me in there, it took all of three minutes.

The only time I felt really weird was in the wagon on the way to the hospital. I started hyperventilating. One of the police officers with me raised my legs up; he said it'd get more blood to my brain. He said, "Stop breathing so hard." It worked.

When we got to the hospital, I'm holding where I think I'm shot. It felt like a large knot. The doc said, "No, you're shot over here"—on the other side—"you see the holes right here?" It just didn't hurt where I was shot.

Later on, I talked to the youth officer that interviewed the little kid. The kid told him that his father was very upset that day. He'd been stopped by some police earlier. The kid said, "My dad was really mad, and he said he was going to kill some cops." The kid said that when his dad saw our car, he said, "Those are policemen. I'm gonna kill them." The amazing thing was, the kid didn't get a scratch. There were twenty bullet holes in that car, the glass was all broken, and the kid is totally okay. I found out his dad was a security officer for the Board of Education.

This guy never would have spotted us for police if we had been in our regular car, a '68 green two-door Chevy, but it was being repaired. So we had to use a pool car, your basic police four-door '78 Dodge, with plates beginning with ZA—that's how all cop-car plates were then. Anybody at all the least street-smart could identify this as a squad—the other car nobody would recognize. Also, my two partners were both white. Usually, if people see a black guy driving around with one or more white guys, they assume you're police. This guy assumed right.

I've used it in training: If you're put in a situation of using deadly force, don't fire once and think that the person you're shooting at is gonna go down. At least let three rounds go.

One of the first things that's imbued upon you when you come on this job is never think this guy is gonna come peaceful. Always assume he's gonna fight like Satan. With anybody at all.

When I was working on the West Side, as a matter of fact, I was standing around the desk one night, a policeman came in with a little boy in handcuffs; I estimated the little boy to be about seven. I'd never seen handcuffs on a little kid. I said, "What are you—goofy? What do you got the cuffs on the kid for?" He said, "This son of a bitch just stabbed me." He turned around, and there's a slit in his pants leg where the kid had stuck a knife in his thigh.

You can never tell who's gonna fight you. It could be anybody. A lot of times, people see coppers subduing somebody and they think it's brutality. They don't know what precipitated it. They think we're just exercising for the day.

When you're a copper, a lot of people will kick your ass in a New York second. Civilians don't understand the danger of fights. They don't understand that your gun is yours only as long as you're at a considerable distance from people. The moment you close with somebody, the gun belongs to whoever gets it. Cops have gotten killed with their own guns in street fights.

A police officer struggling with an offender may seem brutal, but it's because you have to defeat the guy, you have to finish them off right away or you're dead.

I had an Iranian guy one time. I stopped this guy for going through a stop sign. He got out of his car, came back to the squad car, and knelt down on the street with his hands folded. He's going, "Please! Grant me amnesty! Grant me amnesty!" I finally said, I said, "Have some dignity about yourself. Go back to your car, would you please?" I says, "You are *not* going to jail." Kneeling on the street. People are looking around, what did the cop do to this poor guy, you know?

You gotta know when to turn it on and when not to turn it on. If you turn it on at the *wrong* time—and there are police officers who do that—it escalates things.

That's the problem with some women police; you know, they want to come on and be the hard-ass all the time, they're Jane Wayne, they're Dirty Harriet; they think they got something to prove, and it ends up just escalating things. It's not good.

There's certain times that you *have* to come on strong as a policeman. I'm not an aggressive person, but I think I know enough, when I'm in a situation and I know I have to take control of it and start screaming and motherfucking people, to do it. And I think I know when *not* to do it too. Sometimes you have to turn it on, because if you don't, you'll get yourself hurt.

* * *

I learned this when I was on the street. If you're gonna lock somebody up, there's no reason you gotta be an asshole. I mean, if the guy's an asshole, fine. If he's not—don't treat him like an asshole. I've had people when I was a patrolman tell me, "Officer, you just ruined my stereotype of police officers." Because they *expect* to get beat, they *expect* to get kicked around, and when you sit there and joke with them while you're doing the paperwork, they can't understand it. They actually say, "Hey, I don't mind going to jail. You can lock me up anytime." Some of these habitual people, they get locked up three times a month or so; they'd rather get locked up by a guy that's gonna have some fun with them than somebody who's gonna kick them in their cojones.

Ever notice two policemen talking to each other on the street? They never look at each other. One is always looking behind the other. They very seldom look each other in the eye. It's a survival mechanism. They want to know what's coming up at them.

We see things that you would never see. And if you did see it, you wouldn't know what you were seeing.

For instance, I took a course at DePaul University once in deviant psychology. And as an experiment in the course, we had to walk around downtown for an hour and come back and tell the prof and the class what we'd seen.

So here we are, a gaggle of maybe twenty-three people walking around the Loop. We get back, the girls were saying, Did you see the dresses in the windows of Saks? The guys were saying, Did you notice how congested the traffic was? And then it came my turn. And I said, "Well, did anybody see the guy that was fighting with his girlfriend and he was gonna jump off the bridge into the river?" And the prof says, "I didn't see that." I said, "My gosh, they were no further than five feet from you." And I said, "Did you see that one guy that was trying to get his hand in the woman's purse?" He said, "I didn't see that!" He thought I was making it up. I said, "No. That's what *I* saw. I'm sure that's not what you saw."

Nobody saw it. Not a soul. And here was this guy, we walked right past him, standing on one of the stanchions of the Wacker Avenue Bridge, and he was telling this girl he was gonna jump in the river and kill himself. And she was telling him not to. A few seconds later, he got down off the stanchion and they walked off. And you couldn't have missed it, I didn't think. Apparently, you could—twenty-two of them didn't see it.

Seeing what's really going on—that's what they used to call "street eyes."

It's your first day with your FTO (Field Training Officer). He drives the squad. You're too nervous to drive. You don't know where you're going anyway. And all this stuff is coming at you. I remember looking down at my new blue pants and my gun and thinking, Okay, I'm the police. Now what?

Anyway, it's your first day. The police radio's on; you can't make sense out of it; your FTO's talking to you constantly; you're hearing all these sounds from the street, languages you've never heard. You're seeing things you've never seen before. And you're confused as hell.

Suddenly, your FTO stops the squad and says, "Okay, let's get out, kid." He jumps out and flings somebody against the wall and takes a gun off of him. You're looking at him in total disbelief. How'd he know that? This guy must be the Great Carnac.

Ten years later you've got a kid driving with you and you see something, and *you* fling somebody against a wall. And the kid's looking at you like, How did he know? And you know it's not magic.

The biggest thing you learn out of the Police Academy, if you're lucky enough to have guys with a lot of experience teaching you, is, is what they call "reading the street."

Say you're responding to a burglary-in-progress or stickup call, reading the street means *not* just pulling up in front of the place, but being very much aware of people leaving or cars leaving the area, or coming towards you—grab a couple license numbers—be aware of who's around.

You have to learn to read the street. It's the whole thing out there.

Some coppers never learn. I don't know why; they might just be lazy. I was on the street a couple years, and I thought I was getting pretty good at it when I happened to be assigned to work with a guy who was—dynamite. He and I had been driving in the car for maybe an hour and a half, and I was just talking and he's talking to me, as partners do driving in a squad car. And he says, "Tell me something. The car that just passed us going the other way. What did the driver look like?" I says, "I don't know." "That's my point," he says. "Wake up!" Then he says, "From now on, all night long, I want you to tell me what the driver of the car that just passed us *looks like.*"

This was a hell of a learning experience. Ironically, he and I came on at the same time, but he worked for two years in a very fast district, and I worked in the Thirty-ninth, where there was nothing but a rest home.

You always want to know what's going on around you. Always. When you're walking or driving, you're constantly scanning, right sidewalk to the left sidewalk, left sidewalk to the right sidewalk. You just look for something out of the ordinary. Something that doesn't look right. And the best way to do it is—if it catches your eye, if it makes you take a second look, look at it a third time. Satisfy your curiosity.

A big thing is seeing if people fit the area. It's like you look at the street like one of those "What's wrong with this picture?" drawings. You constantly look—Does he fit the area? You always ask yourself that. And if the guy doesn't fit the area *and* he's carrying a gym bag, you stop him.

It would be really beautiful if you could just look at people and tell what their potential for crime was. But it doesn't work like that. People who have criminal looks turn out to be bankers or stockbrokers. And those persons who look like bankers and stockbrokers turn out to be con men, burglars, and killers.

Ever see on TV where the police car pulls up to the scene of the crime with the siren going? The cops jump out? Now that's completely absurd. If you want to *catch* the fellow, you're gonna turn your siren off a couple of blocks away.

But there's a lot of policemen who will have their sirens going on all the way up to the front of the place because they *want* the guy to get away. They don't want the paperwork. They don't want to go to court.

I can remember when I first came on, I worked with a fellow—first thing he told me when I got in the car with him—"Hey, listen. We make a pinch, we're going to court. I haven't been to court in fifteen years. I'm not about to make it number one." In other words, he hadn't made an arrest in fifteen years. It's disheartening.

Something we never do—and you see them doing it all the time on police shows—if you're coming up to a call during the dark hours of night, you never, never close the door on the squad car. Because the guy inside hears the door slam—all of a sudden, hey, doors are slamming out front—he doesn't need to know who it is coming up.

If you're going down a dark alley, and you want to walk back to something that you just saw and you don't want the people that you just passed to know that you're coming back, what you do is, very softly step on the emergency brake to halt the car, very softly, because what happens when you hit the emergency brake, the brake lights don't light up. And the guy you want to get doesn't see you make the obvious stop.

* * *

You turn the lights off if you're going down alleys, or side streets, or if you're looking for someone—a call has just gone out, and you're looking for someone. You're cruising like a submarine, and you're geared for the sound of silent running.

And every Joe Citizen in the world has to flash their lights at you and tell you your lights are off. Or honk their horns. "Officer, do you know your lights are off?" "Yes, we know."

We have fun chasing the whores. They're street-wise; if they see a squad coming down the street, they run and hide in the gangways.

So we act like we're going to an in-progress call. The whores can see the silhouette of the Mars light even a few blocks away, so they just stand there and watch. We'll whiz past them, circle the block real quick, and grab them. Or we'll just come to a screeching halt right next to them.

Streetwalkers organize their lives around cops' schedules. They keep close watch on the vice cops and the district tac teams. They know the guys they can outrun and outfox. They know when we're out there and when the watch changes. Their peak times are shift changes. They can do a lotta, lotta stuff in half an hour. Sometimes we switch shift times to confuse them. They get real perturbed at us—"What you doing out here? You're not supposed to be here *now*. You're not playing by the rules."

Most whores are junkies. That's why they're out there. More of the white whores than the blacks are junkies, though. A black whore will drink, a lot of times, and use the money to support her family. A white whore is almost always a junkie.

Ninety percent of the sexual activity on the street is oral copulation. It's easier for the whores. They don't want to invest time in you. You're nothing more than a quick meal ticket.

You're a nickel bag of coke. So the less time I can spend with you, the more time it gives me to walk the street and make more money. If I have to spend time with you with frivolities, then I miss two extra tricks.

A whore who is into narcotics knows more about what's going on in the street than anybody—more than the police, more than her pimp, more than the people who own the dope houses, more than the average gangbangers in the street—she knows more than *anybody*. She's standing there watching everything that's going on. She is a book of knowledge.

This one whore I talked to was a farm girl from Iowa. She told me she got the idea of being a prostitute from watching Angie Dickinson on *Police Woman*—she just thought it looked like a real glamorous big-city life. The last time I saw her, she had abscesses all over her arms, teeth missing, she looked like hell.

I knew another whore who'd leave work and go in the drugstore and buy things like *Family Circle* magazine. She had a little kid. I remember her with armloads of all these homey magazines.

Sometimes, you'll see a little pile of clothes in a gangway, or next to a garbage can, or under a parked car. Whores like to keep a change of clothes on the street with them in case they're gonna be out a couple days or in case they get arrested and have to appear in court the next day. A lot of times, when we arrest them, they'll say, "Would you mind just driving me over there for a minute? I gotta get my clothes." They're afraid, especially if they put their clothes next to a garbage can, that another whore will steal them.

I used to work as a decoy prostitute. I'd be standing on a corner while some guy drove around the block ten times, checking me out, sticking out his tongue, getting up his nerve to solicit me.

And I'd think, *What* am I doing here? What am I doing? I've got a son at home. We go to Little League. We go to church on Sundays. We're real normal. And I'm standing here waiting for some guy to ask me to blow him.

We arrested one guy one time for soliciting. He told us he told his wife he was going out to buy formula for the baby. Another guy told us he did this while he waited to pick his wife up from novena.

What the fuck is a recreational drug? There's no such thing. We see it out there, people turned into vegetables. Beautiful girls selling themselves on the street for drugs.

I once knew this whore, Saline. A *beautiful* girl. She got involved with a kid—a barber, a pimp, and a burglar. He was on heroin. He turned her on to it.

I could see her gradually deteriorating. She'd bring guys to shitbag hotels on North Clark. I'd ask her, "How do you know you're safe?" She'd say, "Once that door closes, I don't know *what's* gonna happen." All she knew was she had to get money for her pimp and herself for heroin.

One day, the pimp called. "They just took her away. She jumped." She didn't jump. She was thrown from a window at Oak and Clark.

If you see a woman rubberneck, she's usually a pickpocket or a whore. Whores rubberneck. They know what's going on. As a rule, whores know more about what's going on in the street than anybody.

The *guy* whose head is on a swivel, the rubberneck, that's the guy who's probably looking to commit a crime. When you see a guy looking all around him, the trick is to not be seen by him, just to kind of lay back and let him look around, follow him to where he's going.

For spotting burglars, the old one used to be, "Look for the guy carrying a pillowcase that looks full." Now it's, "Look for the guy carrying a gym bag." We stop them most of the time.

Mostly, they're legit. But you'd be surprised how many times the guy drops it and runs.

You can tell if somebody's just out of prison just by looking at them. They've got what we call a "joint body." They do the prison strut when they walk down the street.

Say you're a young fellow, you're five-ten, weigh only 160 pounds. You go into prison. You're fresh meat, baby. You're gonna be breakfast for these cons.

The first thing you do—you start pumping iron to have strength to survive in the joint. You get a big chest, huge arm muscles. It's an attitude you want to give off to people; it says, Get outta my way, don't mess with me.

These guys get out of the joint, they come at you down the street, they look like gorillas. They swing their torsos when they walk; they look menacing. You see somebody like that walking toward you, you get out of his way, right? He's got the joint body, the prison strut. You can spot an ex-con in a second that way.

I've sat on so many places, I can tell—a lot of times, if I know that's a dope house across the street, I can tell by somebody coming down the block, by the way he's walking, he's gonna go to that dope house. My partner never believed that. I've done it with him. I see a guy coming a block away, I says, "He's going to the dope house." Sure enough, that's where he went.

It's just a different walk and a different look to people heading for the dope house. They're *strolling* like they got a place to go—and they're heading for it. And then you can tell if they copped or not. If they ain't, they come out, it's like they're scratching their head, thinking, Okay, where do I go next? If they copped, they're striding out of there—now they got something to *do.*

One of the hardest things to come up on is the gang fights. Pulling up on the scene, and seeing a fourteen-, fifteen-, or sixteen-year-old kid laying on the ground, dead. Shot to death.

I always get the same feeling, because I have my own kids.

It's a bad feeling, just looking down and seeing . . . it's a kid laying on the ground. It's not an adult. And for whatever reason—because somebody flipped a gang sign or they were in the wrong neighborhood—and now they're dead.

We handled a drive-by street-gang shooting where a fifteen-year-old girl that was riding in a car with five other people was shot right in the neck. She was sitting in the middle of the front seat, between the driver and another passenger. The guys, members of the Cobras, pick the girl up on one corner, she's the girlfriend of one of the Cobras; they pick up another friend of theirs on another corner, and they ride north. These guys from the Latin Kings had been riding around behind them all night and happened to see this car pick up this guy. They follow this car. They were aiming for this kid who was picked up last, see, who happened to be sitting on the door, passenger side. The first car comes to a stop sign. This car pulls up next to them, this one guy aims at the guy that's sitting on the passenger side, he sees it coming down, he ducks, the girl gets it right in the neck. This is in retaliation for a shooting that happened the previous week where one of their guys got killed. The girl goes into a coma, she dies a week later.

Street gangs do a thing called false flagging to flush out members of a rival gang. That's giving the rival gang's hand sign or slogan, like "All is Well"—and if the guy responds, they kill him.

There was a third-year marine home visiting his mother in one of the projects. He had his back to a building some gang-bangers were hanging in front of; they didn't recognize him. So they give the opposition slogan. They call out, "All Is Well" to him; he said, "All Is Well" back to them. They shot him six times.

People always ask—"What if my kid sees a gang member who represents?" Tell the kid, *Don't respond* in any way.

Basically, there's two types of street-gang murders. There's street-gang rivalry murders and there's dope-related murders.

The retaliation murders, those happen among the Pee-Wees, they're kids eight years old to thirteen, fifteen, and the Juniors, thirteen to twenty years old. The Pee-Wees run errands and guns, are lookouts. The Juniors are the most active in street murders. Narcotics murders, that's with the Seniors. Those guys are killing people to run the narcotics amongst the street gangs.

A lot of your gang-related murders are THC and PCP-promoted. THC, that's a marijuana extract, almost like hashish, and PCP, that's the animal tranquilizer. And there's happy stick—a marijuana cigarette laced with PCP. Terrible stuff. They get fired up on it, and then they talk about doing a hit, and then they go out and do it. You know how they do a hit? It's like us three are pissed off, we're talking about ain't it a shame so-and-so got killed yesterday or last week or last year, and us three would say, Well, let's go do a hit. That's how they do it. Simple as that. I got a car, you got a gun, let's go.

We recovered a custom-made T-shirt of a big shooter; he was the chief enforcer for one of the gangs. The T-shirt reads, in these big letters: CHEIF ENFROCER. This guy must have intimidated the guy who ran the T-shirt place so much that he printed the T-shirt exactly as he spelled it.

They don't fight over turf so much anymore. They fight over the distribution of narcotics. They're fighting over dope and dope profits. Narcotics is turf now.

Street gangs are the main narcotics dealers at the street level. Since Day One, street gangs have always been involved in narcotics. For the past seven, eight years, it's been their main criminal activity. They're the ones that get the dope out on the street and sell it on the street.

* * *

Most of the money they get from dope goes to their attorneys. A lot goes on cars; they got some nice rides. You see BMWs, Mercedes Benzes, Cadillacs, with the occasional bullet hole. Some invest in property.

They own buildings. They buy property out-of-state. Automobiles, guns, and all that. But they're smart. They won't put anything in their own names. Nothing goes in their own names.

Believe it or not, gangs have values. They have rules. When some guy's saying, "Man, they came over here and they made a hit and I was walking with my mother"—that's low-down, they call it, that ain't right. "This guy has no respect at all"— that's what they say.

In other words, it's all right for you and me to shoot each other and kill each other when we're by ourselves, because we're gangbangers. These guys know what gangbanging's all about. But it's just like the old-time chivalry thing. If I see another gangbanger with his mama or his little kids, and I'm an old-time gangbanger, I'll give him the respect. I'll say something *to* him, like "You ain't shit," you know, but I'm not gonna shoot him.

It's unbelievable. These guys are constantly offenders and they're constantly victims and they're constantly witnesses. One week, you have a guy as a witness. The next week, he's a victim. The following week, he's an offender.

You gotta know how to talk to these guys. It's a finesse game; it's not a physical game. The cornerstone is being able to approach somebody and say, "Listen, something happened here. What did you hear about it?" You don't just get out of the car and go over and kick this guy's ass or tell a guy to get off the corner for no reason.

You know, that macho act with these gangbangers doesn't work. I've seen gangbangers laugh at cops. They just stand there and laugh.

* * *

We're working undercover one time, and we're trying to make a buy off this black gangbanger. This black dude's talking in jive. He goes, "Hey, bro, where you from, man?" This guy I'm with goes, "I'm from Sheboygan." You know, Wisconsin. And the black dude is like—"Whoa. Where's Sheboygan at? What you doing in Sheboygan, man?" The cop is wired, too, so the whole time he's saying this, the guys in the car are listening. They're like "Sheboygan!? What the?—he didn't have to say *Sheboygan.*" Needless to say, the black dude didn't sell to us.

The gang is everything to them. Street gangs don't have to recruit; they're not running around looking under mattresses for recruits; kids *want* to join. A lot are born into it. I've been at christenings where the baby being baptized is wearing gang colors. You go to a gangbanger funeral, the casket is draped in the gang's colors.

In dealing with people on the street today, if you instill in their minds you are crazier than they are, nobody will ever mess with you. Nobody fools with crazy people. Nobody wants to mess with somebody who's nutty, unstable, whatever. That's the same all over. I know a guy who's cultivated a twitch, just for the street.

Only two kinds of people stare at other people: nuts and police. If you want to be safe on the street, make eye contact—stare at them directly. They're gonna think you're a nut or a copper. They won't mess with you.

Usually, the criminal has a tremendous instinct of who to pick on. Street guys are expert at singling out the weak.

When offenders pick victims on the street, like when robbers are looking for targets, they look for people who walk with their heads down, people who look kind of sheepish. Most women walk that way; my wife walks like that; I tell her she's a crime statistic waiting to happen. What would spook anybody looking to commit a crime is somebody who looks right at them.

We had a rash of purse snatchings one time, and we set one of our women up as a decoy. What we had to instill in her was, "Don't walk like the police. Walk like a mope. Don't keep turning around."

She wore a police radio in an ear plug. She starts walking down the street. We're watching. "Okay, he's coming up behind you. Get ready, because he may whack you. But *don't turn around.* We'll let you know when he comes." She keeps walking.

As soon as he comes up behind her to grab her purse, we say, "Let it go." She let it go. As soon as he snatched it, she took off after him, and the rest of us converged and got him.

Women have limitations, I'd be the first to admit it. We're not as strong as the men. But—as a woman you can do things. I remember we were driving through Lincoln Park one night, and I was sitting on the lap of one of the guys I work with. We were laughing, but we were working. We sat there like a couple, watching someone break into a car. And he knew we were right there; didn't pay any attention to us. I'm sitting in my partner's lap, I have my arm around him, and I'm talking into the police radio I'm holding behind his head: "Okay, he's down. Someone get over here to the other side. Hold on a minute—Wait—wait. Oop! There goes the window." And they moved on the guy. He just thought we were a couple sitting there, necking.

Nobody wants to work four to midnight or midnight to eight on Christmas Eve or New Year's Eve. That's when all the families get together, they start drinking, and they kill each other.

Faithfully, every holiday season, I warn my people to be very cautious because, especially Christmas and New Year's, people who are not too stable to begin with might decide to suicide themselves. This is a common police problem during the holidays.

So one Easter Sunday, I had just delivered that lecture. We were working days. And within an hour, I got a call from one of my cars that had gotten waved down on the street. The fellow said, "There's something wrong here. Will you come with me?" So the beat officer did, into a tavern down the street.

What he saw when he entered was a man lying face-down, who had had one of these stand-up microphones, the old-fashioned ones with the big mike, he had had that stuck up his rectum to the point where only a foot of the shaft—and the stand—was visible to us. We had to take the bolt cutters and cut it off. Believe it or not, the guy was still alive, but just barely.

What had happened, we found out after the investigation, he and his partner—they were gay—anyhow, these two fellows owned this particular tavern. And in order to cut corners, they were in the habit of cleaning the place up every night themselves. They took turns—Monday, Wednesday, Friday for you; Tuesday, Thursday, Sunday for me; that kind of thing.

They had a lovers' quarrel. And the one fellow waited till he knew his friend was in there cleaning the place up, and he snuck back into the joint and hit his friend over the head with something, I don't remember what it was, knocked him out, and then he inserted that microphone. The guy died shortly afterward in Illinois Masonic Hospital.

The beat officer who handled the case said to me, "How did you know that was going to happen on Easter?" He says, "You just told us to be careful at roll call." I said, "This is the season, pal. Holidays. Some people can't handle the holidays."

I've been on the force for twenty years. It seems there's more women kill themselves on Mother's Day than any other day of the year.

The worst call in the police department is a domestic disturbance. The emotional level is just so high; it's a very volatile situation. And you walk in on the middle of it. What happens a *lot* is, you come in, they start siding against *you.*

I've had a vase broken over my head in a domestic. Another time, we ended up fighting with an entire family: a husband and wife, a son, a daughter, and a grandmother. It can get real hairy.

We had a domestic where it ended up with a woman with a gun on me. She was sitting on the gun the whole time we were in there; I didn't realize it.

The landlord of the building told me as we went up, "Those people have a gun in there. Be careful." So when we walked in, this woman was yelling; she's going off on us and she's getting up and down and stuff. All of a sudden, she sat down real fast on this couch. She has her hand down by her crotch, so I grab her arm. My partner grabs the guy. I turn to see her and she's a big woman—she pulls out this big six-inch-barrel revolver, a .22, and it's staring me right in the puss.

The only thing I could think of to do was to grab it by the cylinder. See, if you can grab the cylinder, as long as the gun doesn't screw up, if they try to pull the trigger on you, the cylinder won't turn. That's with a good gun. But with some of these bullshit guns these people have, they can turn the cylinder by hand. Or if the cylinder is broken, it can go off.

Okay, so I grab it—she's trying to pull that trigger, right?—I got it by the cylinder. I give her a whack in the puss with my other hand and pull the gun away.

I was lucky she didn't have a bad gun. If you get one of those and grab the cylinder, you're out. You lost. You're dead.

I answered a domestic one time; by the time I got there, this woman was kneeling next to her husband, holding his throat together with both hands. She had slashed his throat from ear to ear. Then she had a change of heart, I guess.

* * *

I'll tell you where a lot of brutality beefs come from: You get a domestic, you get to the house—there's the wife, sitting on the couch, all bloodied, there's the mother-in-law, sitting on the couch, all bloodied; the husband's drunk—he's in the bedroom. You go in there. He's got a bayonet on the headboard of the bed. You take the bayonet and put it in a dresser drawer. He wants his knife. He lunges for the drawer. You pull your gun, he grabs at it and says, "Okay, kill me." Now the wife and the mother-in-law who called you to arrest the husband are climbing all over you and your partner because you have to subdue the husband to make the arrest that *they* wanted. Two or three days later, a complaint is registered that you beat up the husband.

We answered a domestic, a homicide, one time where the offender was arrested. This was two gays. What happened was, one gay cut the other across the upper abdomen and then cut straight down. Then what he did, he cut the guy's penis off and stuck it in his mouth and then he jumped on this guy—and all his bowels and crap like that are hanging out.

We walk in and it's like "Yo-oh-oh!" This guy's just sitting on the couch. We said, "Did you call the police?" He says, "No, *I* didn't. This is my roommate. And he was cheating on me." Just as calm and as cold as could be.

People like that are scary. Because they can look at you; it's like they're looking right through you.

My old partner and I got a call one night, right out of roll call. We're on the beat car. "Go transport a homicide suspect." We were in a good mood, him and I. We go over to Erie, it's all Yuppie rehab now, but then it was all fleabag hotels, and we go to the homicide scene. There was a guy stabbed four or five times. And then there's this Mexican guy. The Mexican is the prime suspect, but they don't have anything on him other than he met the police in the hallway when they showed. That's it. That's all they have to go on.

So the dicks handle it, and the sarge, who I knew from Homicide, says, "Do us a favor. Take this guy back to the station." So I put my arm around this guy, and I say, "Come on. What's your name, Ricky Riccardo or something?" I was just kidding around. We put him in; we didn't handcuff him; we just put him in the car and—we wanted to stop for coffee. So I say, "You want a coffee, Ricky?"

We get back to the station, I put him in the interrogation room, and I say, "Let me ask you something. Give me your name," and I get all the preliminary information from him. I'm just baby-sitting him till the dicks get there. The guy says to me, "You know, he shouldn't have messed with my cat."

So I dummied up. You gotta dummy up. You play dumb. Never let anybody know what you're thinking. If people want to think you're stupid, let them think you're stupid.

I said, "What are you talking about?"

"He shouldn't have kicked my cat."

Now, I *know* what's going on. Now, I *know* this is the offender; ain't no doubt in my mind.

I said, "What are you trying to tell me?"

"If he wouldn't have kicked my cat, I wouldn't have stabbed him." Now, we got him lock, stock, and barrel. I didn't Mirandize him before this because I didn't have to—I didn't ask him anything pertinent to the investigation. Now remember that. The only time you have to give somebody the Miranda warning is if you're going to interrogate him regarding a criminal investigation or a criminal charge. So *now* I advise him of his rights; I got another guy in—bingo, he's gonna 'fess up. And all because we were nice to him.

A lot of people confess to me. I've taken statements from offenders who weren't even my prisoners. One time, there was a rape suspect in the station house, he asked me for a match. This guy was under arrest for rape, but they were real thin on what they had. So I give him a light; I ask him a couple of questions, and he starts telling me this whole story—I don't believe it, this guy's telling me everything.

People want to talk. It's like with child molesters. You tell

them, "You have a problem. We want to help you," and really
you want to beat the piss out of them, but you can't. If you
come on with that approach, you're not gonna get to square
one.

My old partner used to sit and talk about his brothers with
whoever we brought in. I'd hear him saying to a burglar, "Well,
you know, I can understand your problem. I have a brother
who's a burglar." Then he'd be talking to a child molester—my
brother the child molester; a rapist—my brother the rapist.
This guy had more brothers!—and he's talking about his
brother the car thief one night to this guy we caught with a
slim-jim, and the guy confesses to two murders.

Ninety-nine percent of this job is jawbone. You've got to know
how to talk to people, from the high-line lawyer to the gangbanger on the street.

Who else deals with every faction of life? We deal with every
faction of life, everybody—from the big shots on Lake Shore
Drive to the scumbags who run the dope houses.
We see it all. And you know what? We are the last to judge.
Believe us. We are the *last* to judge.

The alleged cynicism of the police. You see what we see, it's
gonna affect you. Police are the biggest bunch of softies in the
world. They're the biggest patsies for a hard-luck story. They're
the last to judge.

I've had the same dream for years. In my dream, an offender
is shooting at me, and I'm shooting back, but the bullet never
gets to the person I'm shooting at—it gets to within a foot and
then it just drops. The bullet never gets there. I've been having
this dream since I've been on the police force; it started *right*
when I came on. Over the years, I've talked with other officers

about it, and they've told me they have the same dream. I'm glad to hear that.

We had a call once of a man with a shotgun. He was holding his ex-girlfriend with the gun right at her neck. We're talking to him—"Come on, cool it, you know. We're your friends." While we're talking to the girl, he kills her. Here's the girl he supposedly loves—what's he gonna do to us?

He pleaded guilty on insanity, and he beat it. He killed in cold blood and he got off.

You have real bizarre things happen all the time. It doesn't bother you till you get home and go to bed. Then you can't sleep. You can't sleep. Your heart is pounding. You keep thinking, What if . . .? What if . . .?

I'll tell you how paranoid cops are about AIDS. One time, we're working the projects, and we get a call of a domestic about two blocks away, in Yuppieville. We're the fifth squad car to pull in. It was a frame two-flat with an illegal staircase going up one side.

My partner and I start running up the stairs to get to the call, and suddenly at least eight cops come running out of the apartment. They're almost throwing themselves down the stairs. They're falling all over themselves running *away* from the apartment we got the call on.

"What's the matter?" We figure it's gotta be a bomb, at least. "There's blood! There's blood!" They're all yelling and falling all over each other down the stairs.

It turned out a couple of white lesbians got in a fight, and one woman cut her hand open. The hand was gushing all over. No cop wanted to go near her.

It was like one of those old silent movies—the exact opposite of what cops are supposed to do—these coppers are all running the wrong way.

I'd sure hate to be a guy bleeding to death on the street today.

* * *

An old lieutenant once told me this is how you should do CPR on the guy lying in the gutter when there's a crowd around: You bend over the guy, and you keep saying: "Die, you s.o.b. Die."

A lot of cops are afraid to work the projects. They're afraid to go in there. They say, "Why do you want to go in there?" The only thing I'm afraid of is sniper fire, but you can't think about that. You can't think about the danger.

If you work the projects, you have to be on your toes. You have to constantly, constantly be on your guard. Constantly. I don't care if things look rosy, you have to be careful. Because the one time you let your guard down, that's when things will happen.

Any time you go in the buildings in the projects, when you get out of the car, you always look up—to see if anybody's in the windows, so you don't get bottles dropped—if they fire a salt-shaker at you, and they're up ten floors, if it hits you in the head, it will kill you.

If there's two of you, when you get out of the squad, one guy will always watch the windows; the other guy will eyeball the lobby. You eyeball the lobby first, to make sure nobody's about to open fire on you. If the lobby looks clear, then you look in the hallways to see who's in it or what's in it. You run up and down the stairways—we call working in the projects "running up and down stairs"—because you never want to take the elevator. They're stuck, mostly, and they get stuck real quick if the police are in them.

You'll find that a copper's prejudice is always directed at the poorest segment of the society where he serves.

New York cops think Puerto Ricans are the scum of the earth. Out West, Southwest, the coppers know nothing about Puerto Ricans, blacks, Appalachian whites. *They* hate American Indians. In the Northwest, there are cops who hate *Eskimos.* And when you get coppers together, each one says to the cops from other parts of the country, "Listen, you think Puerto Ricans are bad . . ."

I hate Yuppies. I can't stand them. You arrest them; they always say, "You can't do this to me. You don't know who I know," and all this shit.

You ask me why I work in the projects. We did a raid one time, knocked the door down—and these were steel doors and steel frames, so it takes a big battering ram and it takes a few whacks and it's a sound you can hear in the next building. I mean, it's big bangs.

We knock the door down. I run to the back of the apartment, to the washroom. And some guy's just standing there taking a leak. And he turns around and looks at me, just like—he's used to white guys knocking his door down and running in with guns. Now *that's* cool.

Now *this* scared me. I was riding down the street one day, and some kid walked up and stopped me. He told me, he says, "I think the woman that lives next door got murdered last night." "What makes you think that?" "I think I heard her get murdered." So I said, "Oh, okay."

So I walk up to the door, knock on the door awhile, no answer. I try the door; it opens up. I go in, I'm going all through the house. Nobody in it. I'm yelling, "Police! Police!" Nobody answers.

I get up to the second floor. The windows are all blocked off with paper and blankets and stuff. It's an overcast day; it's real dark. There's no light bulbs in any of the lights. All I got is a flashlight.

And I looked in this bedroom, stood in the doorway and looked for a good . . . you know, you knew something was there, but you didn't know what.

I looked for a good minute and a half, two minutes. Couldn't see anything. Then I saw a little doll laying in the corner. It turned out to be the woman. She was a real small, very thin woman. And when I went right up to her and looked at her with the flashlight, it still didn't . . . she didn't look real.

Her sweater was pulled up around her neck. She'd been stabbed in the chest. And she was dead. And her head was tilted way back in such a way that it didn't look like it had a head. I didn't know what I was looking at. To see this thing in the corner, but I didn't know what I was looking at. It's hard to describe; it's really hard to describe. You couldn't see the head; you couldn't see the face. All you could see was this real small form, back in the corner.

After you go to the morgue and you see a few autopsies, you think you've seen everything. You see dead bodies; they've got the lungs out, they cut out the heart. You leave the morgue and eat. You get a pizza twenty minutes after. It means nothing. Nothing. I worked the wagon for nine months; we'd have a suicide victim or a homicide victim. We'd drop the body off—at that time, you had to strip the bodies yourself—and go eat.

The first shooting I went to, I thought it was nothing, but I couldn't eat that afternoon. This guy robbed a tire store, he pulled out his gun, he didn't know how to operate it, and the guy from the tire store pulled out *his* gun and shot this guy in the head.

Two hours later, I got called to the hospital. The s.o.b. was there who was shot in the head. I had gotten sick over this guy; two hours later, I'm guarding him—the bullet had curved around his skull and came out the back. They gave him some aspirin, a Band-Aid in front, and a Band-Aid in back. And he was asking me for a cigarette two hours after I was sick over him because I thought he was dead. That was the last time I felt sick about anybody getting shot.

When you're a dispatcher, the other side of working the radio is handling emergency calls. 911.

I was at a very low time in my life when this happened. I was so low that just the night before this happened, I prayed to know why am I living. I'd always tried to help people, but at that point it seemed like everybody I was trying to help was betraying me in some way. So I prayed—If I'm on the wrong track, God, let me know. Please tell me what my purpose is.

I'm sitting there on the zone, it's a Sunday, with my head almost on the console, I'm so depressed. This lady called. I answered—"Chicago Emergency." Before I could finish, she's screaming—"My baby's not breathing—you've gotta call an ambulance—he's not breathing—" "Hold on"—I got the fire department. I remained calm. I'm still detached, I'm withdrawn anyway because of all my problems. The fire department comes on, I give them the information, they verify the address, we disconnect.

And then what I call my innermost, my inner voice said to me, "What would you do if she calls back?" I thought, I'd ask her if she knows mouth-to-mouth resuscitation. Then I handled several other calls, and, lo and behold, she calls back. You have to know, it's a rarity for the same call-taker to get the same person. A rarity. It happens maybe once out of every hundred calls. It just doesn't happen. I got her again—"My baby's still not breathing! Oh my God!" She was gone, she's just hollering and screaming. "Miss, do you know mouth-to-mouth resuscitation?" I said to myself, "What have I done? Oh my God—I can see the lawsuits. This is going against departmental regulations, you're gonna get yourself in trouble." But I'd already asked her. She said, "No, I don't. Can you *help* me?"

Believe me, when she said can you help me, I forgot everything else. I forgot my problems. I didn't have any problems. She told me the child was completely out, no sounds, no anything. I asked her to open the baby's mouth and look in it. "There's a lot of foam in the baby's mouth." Now, she's not holding the baby, a neighbor's holding the baby and the mother's relaying all this information to the neighbor lady.— "Open his mouth and look in. What is in there?" "She says there's a lotta foam, a lotta stuff." "Suck it out." "She says suck it out." "Now. Have her put her mouth over the baby's mouth and nose and suck it out. Turn the baby over." She repeats it—"Turn the baby over. Pat the baby on the back." I could hear the lady—boom boom boom. "Look in the baby's mouth"—she repeats it—"Now breathe in the baby's mouth and nose with your mouth," and they did that. "Did you see the baby's chest raise up?" "No, no, nothing happened." We went through this several times—"Turn him over, pat him on the back." Oh my God, what else can I tell her? "Now, turn the baby back over. Press the baby on the stomach right underneath his chest bone."—She repeated it—"Don't press too hard"—she repeated that. "Is anything going on?" First she says the baby gurgled a little bit, and then she gets hysterical all over again. "Calm down, Miss. Miss—" "Oh, my baby's dead!" "Miss. Miss. *Do* this!" That brought her back. "Turn the baby over again"—I say this with sternness in my voice to bring her out of her hysteria. She was gone, but every time I gave her a command, she'd snap back and repeat it. We got into a rhythm: "Turn him over. Pat him on the back. Breathe." I switched over to the fire department. The ambulance still wasn't there.

"I'm gonna stay on the phone with you. Breathe into the baby's mouth and nose. Turn him over. Pat him on the back." Nothing happened. Now the baby's been out a long time. If the baby's heart stops, it's all over.

I asked her again, "Is the baby breathing?" "Let me check— No, no, he isn't breathing." She's hysterical. We got into the rhythm a couple more times. "What's the baby doing now?" "Let me see—Yes! The baby's breathing! Yes, yes, he's breathing, oh he's breathing!" "He *is* breathing"—I was saying that for the other dispatchers; they were all listening. Everybody's going, Yayyyy! "Is the fire department there now?" "Yes, yes. They're just coming in." I asked the lady, "Are you okay? Because now that the fire department is there and the baby's okay, the most important thing is, are you okay?" "Yes. I'm okay." She hung up.

That was it. I had gotten an answer to my prayer. Regardless of personal thoughts and feelings, I had a purpose. You do have a purpose for living. You get out and you begin to live again. That was the answer to my prayer. I was in a position where I could help that lady and her baby, but I tell you, that baby helped me.

I came to a scene once, a woman had chopped her baby to pieces, her newborn. She was absolutely crazy. She hadn't slept in three days, her family knew it, and they gave her no support. I read her profile when they finished up doing the interview and everything else—that all she wanted was to have another baby.

This was a perfectly formed baby girl. She just hacked this baby; she took the head and the torso, in two pieces, and legs and arms, and she put all the parts on top of each other on the bed in the bedroom, and she took like a ceremonial sword that had been hanging on the wall of the bedroom, a long ceremonial sword, and she had put it through this pile all the way to the hilt, and it went all the way down to the floor.

When we came in, she was stark naked, spitting at us. And the baby's father was pissed at us because he wanted to get in the room to get his money off the dresser. He thought the police were gonna steal his money.

Dealing with adult deaths never bothers me as much as dealing with a child's death. You figure the poor kid never got a chance in life, you know. The adult—they had something—forty, fifty, sixty years. You don't feel so bad about that.

You've gotta keep your emotions under control when you deal with child cases. You get so angry at people for being so stupid or uncaring.

I handled a case once, this baby died. There was no man in the family; this woman had maybe four, five kids; this woman had the grandmother living there with her. The grandmother and her had gone out drinking and left the kids at home. And the baby was on a bed next to a radiator, one of those old-fashioned stand-up radiators. The bed was right up against this—and the thing was on. The baby got over against this thing and got its head against it, and it burned into the head of this baby. A horrible wound on its head. The baby was six months old. That's one that didn't make it.

The ignorance or the unconcern. You wouldn't leave a baby that small. How the hell could you do it? You'd have to be the dumbest person in the world or the most uncaring person in the world. The upshot of that one was, it was ruled an accidental death.

You see all kinds of things. And you have to develop certain defense mechanisms to keep yourself from . . . you can't carry that stuff home. Maybe you give your kid an extra hug when you get home.

The kids really get to us. There's just so much abuse, physical abuse, sexual abuse. That's one thing you can't separate yourself from. It's much easier—say, a dope dealer gets killed because he ripped off another dope dealer. Maybe you've seen the guy that got killed a few times; you locked him up a few times. Then he's dead. Who cares? That makes sense. That's how they live. But the kids really get to us.

The better cops—they don't necessarily have more intelligence. But they have adaptability. So I can turn around, and at four-thirty, handle a homicide. At six-thirty, I can handle a lost child where I have to take a little boy and take his hand and walk him up to the fifteenth floor where he lives, get him in there; then I might have to coldcock some woman's husband, and lock him up, and then be able to go home without hitting the booze or snorting ten lines of cocaine in order to calm down.

The three big things in the police department are alcoholism, an unbelievably high divorce rate, and drug abuse. Any big-city police department, you're gonna have officers fooling around with narcotics, anywhere from Valium to cocaine to heroin. The divorce rate is unbelievable. A lot of police officers after a while just can't relate to their wives for whatever reason— there's a million of them. Shift work is one cause. You don't see each other anymore. You have a hard time relating. You go in a shell, like.

One of the real hazards of police work is that your whole life gets so focused on catching the bad guy. There's a great deal of pleasure in outwitting the bad guy. I imagine with some guys it's even better than sex. You hear guys gloating, "I really got this son of a bitch." Some guys get so uptight over it.

Getting the bad guy can be like gambling—it takes over everything; it's addictive. Guys have lost their wives and their kids and their families as much as a gambler, just by virtue of being *too much* of a police officer. A lot of cops live for that rush. Nothing else means anything to them. They eat, breathe, and live for the chase.

We run the complete spectrum of police officers. Guys who are like *that,* to the guy who gets on the job, puts on the uniform, and doesn't do one thing more for twenty years.

You become warped. You get a warped sense of reality. You have to. The biggest defense coppers have is gallows humor. They've got to have it or they go nuts.

See, you have ghoulish policemen. I tell you, though. It kind of goes with the territory. See, we have a sense of humor that to somebody who doesn't know cops would seem terribly gruesome. To us, it's extremely funny.

Back in '72, we had a plane crash. A plane caught the telephone wires, went down, took down a couple of houses, killed a bunch of people on the plane. The pilot looked so natural sitting in the seat that they thought he was still alive, and he was dead. One of the victims was decapitated. And what happened was, the ambulance crew got there, they had a young female on it—and a wagon man told me this and swears it is true: He holds the head up and says to her, "Want to take this one?" She screamed and ran off. This brought howls, peals of laughter from the cops. This was the funniest thing they'd ever seen. Now this is sick, but that's how it is with cops.

We had a guy in one of the projects—lived on the first floor—and every time the police would come to his house, he'd go right through the window, hit the ground running, and he'd be gone. We could be standing outside the apartment windows, he'd be out so fast, and running so fast, he'd be gone. He'd just come right out through the window, and as he hit the ground, he was already running. He's in motion, and he's moving, and he's running, and he's gone.

One time, police come to an apartment on the eighth floor. They were after somebody else. When they come to the door, he—he forgot he wasn't at home, and he jumped out the eighth-floor window. And the policeman who was standing on the ground—we always have somebody stand under the window when we're after drugs or guns so when they throw it out, you got it—the policeman said as this guy comes out the window, he was running. And it was like it dawned on him all of a sudden where he was, and he started like trying to *climb.* It was almost like Wile E. Coyote in the Road Runner cartoon. He never ran from the police again.

We delivered a singing search warrant once. This was for a guy who had illegal guns, he ran a fish restaurant and takeout place, fish and chips and shit like that, in Area Six, and he lived above the store.

We were told by the informant that he was gonna be real dangerous, and he'll go for his gun—he always keeps a gun in the store with him, and he's got a bunch of guns upstairs. So we got the warrant, and we figured we'd serve it on him at the store. We're sitting around trying to think how we'd do it, and one of the guys says, "We gotta do this one with style." And another guy says, "Let's do a singing search warrant, like they do a singing telegram." I said, "That's it." So this girl that was working with us that was very creative sat down and wrote a little poem to a song, the *William Tell Overture.*

Four of us went in the fish place. We had two guys go in earlier; they're sitting there eating. Her and I walked in together, walked up to the counter, the guy's behind the counter, we asked him his name, he says, "Yes, that's me." So I say, "We have something to say to you." We both had the words with us; I had a pitch pipe with me; I blew on it—hmmmmmm—and we started singing:

> *"Because we're great and we're the best*
> *We got a warrant for your arrest*
> *And just because you're such a louse*
> *We're e-ven gonna search your house."*

And he was, like, startled. I tried to hand him a copy of the search warrant, but he wouldn't take it. He backed away, and he starts running back toward the kitchen. The informant had told us he kept the gun back there. So with that, myself and one of the police officers climbed over this fish cooler and then jumped over it, and one of the other officers went through where there was a door to the back, and we trapped him. He was going for the gun. Actually going for the gun. So we ended up wrassling him and getting him handcuffed and that. He ended up beating it in court, Gun Court.

When I worked the street, we always kept a bag of fireworks in the front seat of the squad. You'd see a group of gangbangers on the corner, toss out a couple firecrackers, watch all the gangbangers bite the dust.

We had to use firecrackers because with the new cars, you couldn't backfire them anymore. That was great, when you could backfire the old Chevys. Then the gangbangers would be crawling in each other's pockets. Some people say, "Well, that's mean." But . . .

So we had this bag of fireworks in the squad. We carried it on the floor on the front passenger's side. There was a big Silver Salute in there, cherry bombs, plus all kinds of other stuff, some really heavy-duty fireworks.

One day, I'm driving, and the two guys I'm with are in the backseat throwing little-bitty ladyfingers in the front seat at me—they're going pop!-pop!-pop! I'm saying, "Come on. Knock it off."

So as they're throwing these little ladyfingers at me, one lands on the bag and starts a fire. We're in front of the Conrad Hilton. So they say, "Put it out!" "Bullshit, put it out. I'm getting outta this car."

I stop the squad in front of the Conrad Hilton, open the door, and I run into Grant Park. So *they* open *their* doors, and they run into Grant Park. So here's these three police opening their doors and running across the street into Grant Park, and here's all these tourists in front of the Hilton—looking.

All of a sudden, the squad goes *boom! boom!,* and it's shaking and rolling, and smoke comes pouring out of it. We look around; we're behind trees. We cross the street back over to the car, wave some of the smoke out, get in the car, drive away.

And all these people are looking and pointing, you know, like "This is Chicago. This is a rough place."

I was new on the force, and I had my first death notification. I had to tell a woman her husband had just been killed. I just dreaded doing this. I remember sitting in the squad in front of this woman's house, trying to get what I had to say exactly right. I sat there for about half an hour, mentally composing what I had to say. I went over it and over it. It was one of the hardest things I've ever had to do. "It is my sad duty . . ." No. "It is my unfortunate duty to inform you that your husband has been killed." I got it.

So I go up to the front door; I'm so nervous; a woman answers it, and I start. "It is my unfortunate duty to inform you that your husband has been killed." She looks at me and says, "What did you just say?" Oh no. I start it again. "It is my unfortunate duty . . ." "Wait. Wait. You wait right here. I gotta wake up my kids."

I'm standing there feeling just miserable. I hear her yelling through the house—"Kids! Get up! Come in here!" They all come in. "Now, you tell them what you told me." I do, and they start hugging each other and dancing around. "Officer, you just gave us the *best news*. Kids, that rotten s.o.b. is dead at last!"

Being a police officer is basically an experience-based career. You've gotta have a lot of experience to be good at it. Unfortunately, by the time you get enough experience, your career is about over.

You can put people in a classroom and you can say, "Okay, guys. You are now police officers. And these are the kind of things you're gonna face." But you haven't earned your street degree. Until you're there and you feel it—you know, being in some cold flat where some poor teenage girl is having a baby; there's nothing in the place; they're heating the place by turning the burners on, on the stove, and seeing a baby born in those kind of conditions. Or seeing a person dying on the floor from being stabbed in the throat in the same kind of surroundings. You see so much of that. Talk about the survival of the fittest— there are areas of Chicago where that's the absolute rule.

You never stop learning. You never get your street degree. The person who says that they have their street degree or they've learned it all is the person that's going to wind up either dead or in a very compromising position. They've closed their minds. They're gonna wind up having a problem.

There is nothing more unrealistic than TV cops. A real cop show would be the dullest thing in the world. It'd have to show how most police work is boring. It'd have to show all the bull- shit calls: A man reports a scratching noise—it's a cat scratch- ing on the wall.

It would have to show an eight-hour day with seven minutes of stark terror—eight hours of normal heart rate with a few seconds of terror, where you don't know what's coming at you, what's gonna happen next, every hour or two.

You never know what's going to happen. The whole world can come to an end in your last few minutes of duty, right before you leave your watch. Or—right before you retire from the force. We've had cases of police officers working their last tour before going on pension. And they've run into a situation where they're killed. The guard is down.

You never know what can happen to you. This one took me a long time to get over.

It's toward the end of shift. You start to wind down. Some- times the job can be very boring, especially if you work in a place like . . . I was working the First District. The First District: the Loop, State Street, LaSalle Street—busiest times are during the day, when all of that one million people come in to work.

But at five o'clock, between then and about eight when those one million people go home, there ain't *nothing* happening.

I'm doing the end of the four-to-twelve, and there's nothing going on. It's wintertime, it wasn't real cold; it's getting there, though.

And I'm cruising up and down the side streets, you know, just to have something to do. A call comes out—"Two suspicious men at the drugstore between South Water and Wacker Drive on the west side of Michigan Avenue." One of those, where you go in and you buy a lot of cut-rate stuff—soap and toothpaste. "Two suspicious men at the door, trying to get into the drugstore after closing." And I'm within view. I look up, at the end of the block, no cars are parked at the end of the street, there's nobody on the street. Two guys come around the corner the same time the squad's coming up. They look at me and I look at them and they cross the street and I make a U-turn and they cross the street again, so now we're passing and crossing each other on the street. Now, I'm saying, "I'm gonna stop these guys."

So I'm doing three things at one time: I'm stopping the car, I'm picking up the microphone on the radio—I tell them, "This is One-Twenty. Stopping two suspicious men, South Water, between Michigan and Wabash"—and I'm taking my gun out of the holster. Now the stainless-steel revolvers had just come out, and I had just bought one. Stainless steel is almost like nickel, real easy to see. Four-inch barrel.

One of the guys I'm about to stop says, "Officer! Officer!" They're calling me before I can do anything. I'm rolling the window down, and this guy is coming across the street toward me. The gun's next to me on the seat, the car's in Park, the microphone is out, but somebody else is transmitting. Comes up to the car and he looks at me first. He's got to bend down to look in at me. He sees the gun, and his eyes go wide. He says, "Where is the Lake Street el?" I say, "The Lake Street el is back that way. Where are you coming—" I'm still sitting in the car. Nobody knows where I am.

I say, "Step back from the car." I get out of the car. Meanwhile, his buddy's still across the street. I say, "You stand over there." These are both black kids, neatly dressed, wearing caps, and they're wearing canvas construction-type gloves, those thick gloves. One's wearing the right glove, and the other one's wearing the left glove. I don't think about it. It's cold; they're sharing a pair of gloves. "You. Get on the hood of the car." "You come here. Come *here.*" Finally, you know, he comes over, "You get on the hood, too." "We ain't *done* nothing"—they're starting that—"Whaddid *we* do? *Why* are you messing with us?" I searched them. Finally, a tac team comes in and gets there just a hairs-breadth before the wagon assigned to the call. One of the wagon guys, a real smart-ass, I don't like him to this day, he comes up to search, and one of the guys says, "He already searched us." And he said, "Well, I don't know this guy. I'm gonna search you too," which I didn't like.

So he turns around, I say, "Okay. Let's start all over again." We find out they were trying to get into the drugstore, the manager wouldn't let them in because it's after closing, he's by himself. Smart move. The reason they wanted to get in is, they bought a bar of Dial soap—no joke—they had the bag, the receipt, and everything. They opened it up, and you could see that the soap was cracked in two. The bar is cracked. It has not been used. I said, "Well, but the problem is, when I asked you, why didn't you just tell me that? Why did you give me all this about the Lake Street el?" "Well, we had just . . ."

Now, I notice that the smaller kid—this kid is going through a nervous breakdown. "What's the matter with you?" I'm non-threatening, I'm talking to them, nobody's hurt them or anything. He says, "Man, it's just cold out here." It ain't that *cold;* I mean, this is winter—it's not that cold.

I looked at his fingers. The glove. "Give me your hand." I reached over and grabbed his index finger, the index finger of the glove, and I grabbed the barrel of a gun. There were four of us standing there. And I took the glove off—he's got a .32-caliber revolver, loaded, in his hand, with the finger around the trigger. And the other one—I look at the other one—he lifts his hand up—he's got a .38. He's the one that walked over to the car to talk to me. All he had to do was raise his hand, and he would've shot me right in the face. "Okay, you're under arrest."

I realized later—the five of us were standing there—the gun goes into the holster, the strap goes over the gun—we're standing there, and no one has got a gun except these two kids. They're standing against the squad car, and there's tac man, tac man, wagon man, wagon man, beat man—they could have shot off five of us before we could have reacted. None of us thought to search their gloves. You look in all the manuals: They tell you to search ankles, search the crotch, everywhere—but I've never seen "Search gloves" anywhere.

Later on, I'm talking to the watch commander, and things are starting to go—it's like I'm sitting here talking to you and all of a sudden I can't hear you anymore. He says, "What happened?" And I say, "Well, I . . . Listen, I gotta go back and talk to this guy. I gotta talk to him." He says, "Hey. Hey. Listen, don't hurt him." "I'm not gonna touch him."

I go back. I say, "Kid, come out here." I take him out of the tac office, take him down the hall. I said, "Did you ever consider . . . shooting me?" "No, no, never, I would never shoot a police officer." "But you came over to the car. Why did you do that?" "Ohhh, I wasn't gonna do that." "You go back in the room. Little one, come out here. What happened?" So he stands there. He says, "Bubba was gonna kill you. And I told him not to"—he wouldn't look at me, he said, "He was gonna kill you. I told him not to do it. He said that we had these guns. . . . And he said when he saw you, 'I'm gonna stop him. I'm gonna off this pig.' " "Go back and sit down."

I go back. . . . It's like, "I gotta go talk to him again. I gotta." I go to Bubba. I said, "Why did—" I says—"You were gonna kill me." "No-no-no-no-no, you know, I don't, I only . . ." I said, "So what stopped you? Was it the gun?" He said, "Man, I saw the gun, but I wasn't gonna do nothing, I wasn't, you know, I—" I said, "That's why you called me across the street."

He saw I was alone, and he was coming across the street to kill me. That's what he told his little buddy—"I'm gonna off this pig." He walked over, and I'm sitting in the squad. So you figure—the last thing I would have seen was the glove coming up. And I'd have been sitting there with a hole in my face and my gun laying next to me on the seat.

The Street:
Contributing Police Officers

OFFICER ELMER ATKINSON, CPD Headquarters. Atkinson joined the CPD as a cadet in 1967, where he worked with the Sixth District tac team in making narcotics buys and infiltrating a street gang. In 1970, Atkinson became a patrol officer and was reassigned to Sixth District Patrol till 1972, when he was assigned to the Traffic Division. Atkinson attended the Northwestern University Traffic Institute in 1972. Atkinson stayed with Traffic, working the expressways, till 1976, when he was assigned to the Englewood District, where he worked patrol and tac till April 1981. Atkinson went back to the Sixth District, tac, and served as a field training officer from 1982–87. Atkinson became the administrative aide to the commander of personnel in 1988.

YOUTH OFFICER AL AUGUSTINE, Area Five. Augustine is a twenty-year veteran of the CPD. Augustine worked the wagon in the Fourteenth District for two years, then was assigned to the Area Six Task Force, Special Operations, till 1980. He then worked patrol and tac in Sixteen, Eleven, and Twenty-three. Augustine became a youth officer in 1989.

OFFICER ANTHONY BERTUCA, Twenty-third District tactical unit. Bertuca, a former linebacker with the Baltimore Colts and the Miami Dolphins, joined the force in 1976. Bertuca has served in Twenty-three for the past fourteen years: two years on patrol and twelve years on the tac team.

SERGEANT JIM BIEBEL, Area Six Property Crimes. Biebel, who joined the CPD in 1967, worked patrol and tac in the Twentieth District till 1971, when he was promoted to detective and assigned to Area Five Burglary. In 1973, Biebel was assigned to Area Six Burglary, where he served as a detective for seven years before joining the prestigious CIU, a unit that tracked down career criminals. In 1982, Biebel was promoted to sergeant. Biebel worked in Area One Property Crimes from 1982–84. In 1984, he joined Area Six Property Crimes. Biebel also serves as a hostage negotiator; he's been with the CPD Hostage/Barricaded/Terrorist Unit from its inception in 1979.

OFFICER JIM DILLON, Eighteenth District, Rush Street Detail. Dillon spent eleven and a half of his seventeen years on the force working in the Vice Control Section, Prostitution Unit. Dillon worked patrol for six months and tac for four years in the Sixteenth District before being assigned to Vice, and has been assigned to the Eighteenth District since 1989.

SERGEANT JAMES DOLAN, Prostitution Unit. Dolan's thirty-two-year career in the CPD has included patrol in Morgan Park, serving in the Area Two Task Force (1961), and work in the old TUF Squad (the Tactical Undercover Function Squad, in which police acted as robbery decoys) from 1961 to 1963. Dolan was promoted to sergeant in 1962 and was placed in charge of the TUF Squad in 1963. After the TUF Squad was disbanded, Dolan returned to the Area Two Task Force, serving as a supervising sergeant till 1965. From 1965–68, Dolan worked in the Narcotics Unit. Dolan was assigned to the Area One Task Force from 1968–70, served six years in the Marine Unit, then served as supervising sergeant and watch commander, Special Operations, Area One, from 1976–88. In 1982, this unit became the Gang Crimes Unit, and Dolan worked Gang Crimes South from 1982–88, when he was assigned to the Prostitution Unit. Dolan was a containment officer for twenty-five years, first with Special Operations and then with the Hostage/Barricaded/Terrorist Unit.

SERGEANT ELLEN EGAN, Nineteenth District. Egan, who joined the force in 1980, worked the beat car for a year and a half and was in tac full time for six years in the Eighteenth District. Egan worked crime patterns, the projects, and Operation Angel (decoy prostitution) in Eighteen. In 1988, Egan was promoted to sergeant.

SERGEANT HIRAM GRAU, Gang Crimes North. Since joining the CPD in 1981, Grau worked patrol and tac for five years in the Nineteenth District and the tac side of Gang Crimes before being promoted to gang crimes specialist in Gang Crimes North. Grau made sergeant in 1988, was briefly assigned to the Thirteenth District, and returned to Gang Crimes North.

LIEUTENANT TED HEAD, field lieutenant, Seventeenth District. Head is a thirty-year veteran of the CPD. Head worked one year as a patrol officer before being assigned to the old Task Force, a mobile, city-wide crime unit that sent police as trouble-shooters into areas and situations deemed out of control. Head's five-year assignment with the Task Force included a stint in the TUF Squad. Head was a vice cop on Rush Street in 1966. In 1967, Head made detective, and worked in General Assignment in Area Four and Area Six. After his promotion to sergeant, Head worked on the street in the Nineteenth and Twen-

tieth Districts. Head made lieutenant in 1984 and has been field lieutenant in Seventeen since 1986. In 1970, Head represented Chicago
police as president of the original Chicago police union, the Confeder-
ation of Police (COP).

OFFICER DEIRDRE HILL, police communications dispatcher. Hill
joined the force in 1983, worked patrol in the Sixth District till 1986,
and has been a dispatcher for the past four years. Hill was awarded
the Chicago Crime Commission's "Law Enforcement Officer of the
Year" Award in 1989.

LIEUTENANT HUGH HOLTON, Commander, Personnel Division.
Holton joined the force in 1964 as a cadet, served in Vietnam from
1967–70, and became a patrolman in 1970, assigned to the Nineteenth
District. In 1971, Holton went to the Second District tac team. Holton
was promoted to youth officer in 1972, Area Four. Holton made sergeant in 1975, working the First District (the Loop) patrol till 1978. He
then studied at the Northwestern University Traffic Institute. In 1979,
Holton became administrative assistant to then–deputy chief Fred
Rice, who, while Holton was still administrative assistant, became
chief of the Patrol Division and then superintendent. In 1984, Holton
became administrative assistant to Robert A. Williams, deputy superintendent, Bureau of Investigative Services. Holton was promoted to
lieutenant in 1984, and appointed in 1985 as director of the Beat Rep
Program Division. In 1986, Holton became the commander of the
Sixth District. Holton has been commander of personnel since January 1988. Holton writes a monthly column on police procedure for
Mystery Scene Magazine.

DETECTIVE JOE LASKERO, Area Four Property Crimes. Laskero
worked on the tactical unit in the Town Hall District for twelve years.
He came on the force in 1970, served on the West Side, Fillmore District, on patrol for three-and-a-half years, and then was transferred to
Town Hall, where, before joining the tac team, he worked the prostitution car for a year and a half. Laskero was promoted to detective in
1987.

SUPERINTENDENT LEROY MARTIN. Martin is a thirty-year veteran of the force. Martin worked patrol from 1955–59 in the old Burn-
side Station, served in the Traffic Division from 1959–65, was
promoted to sergeant in 1965, and subsequently served in the Internal
Affairs Division, Organized Crime Division, Gambling Unit, and the
Youth Division. In 1975, Martin was promoted to lieutenant, and

served as field lieutenant in the Marquette Station. Martin was promoted to captain in 1981. Martin served as commander of Narcotics from 1980–81, as director of Public and Internal Information from 1981–82, as commander of Area Two, Detective Division from 1982–84, and as deputy chief, Patrol, Area Four. Martin became superintendent of police in November 1987. Martin has a master's degree in public administration.

SERGEANT ED MINGEY, Area Five Violent Crimes. Mingey has been with the CPD for twenty-four years, working four years on patrol, three years as a youth officer, and sixteen years in Gang Crimes North, both as a gang crimes specialist, from 1973 to 1977, and as a gang crimes supervising sergeant, from 1977 to 1989, when Mingey was promoted to sergeant and assigned to Violent Crimes.

GANG CRIMES SPECIALIST AUBREY O'QUINN, Gang Crimes North. O'Quinn has been with Gang Crimes North for fifteen years of his twenty-five-year police career. O'Quinn spent a year on patrol in the Fourteenth District and eight years in the Area Four Special Operations Group before coming to Gang Crimes.

OFFICER EDMUND PYRCIOCH, Eighteenth District. Pyrcioch has worked tac for a total of fourteen years out of his twenty-three with the CPD, a career that's included work with Gang Crimes North for four years and work as a homicide investigator for a year and a half in Area Four, called "the Murder Factory" by Chicago cops for its usual number-one ranking in homicide statistics. Pyrcioch has worked tac in Eighteen for the past ten years.

YOUTH OFFICER LINDA REITER, Area Five. Reiter came on the force in 1982, worked patrol in the Eighteenth District for seven years, including assignments in decoy prostitution work and female search in Cabrini-Green, until her promotion to youth officer in 1989.

GANG CRIMES SPECIALIST JOE RODRIGUEZ, Gang Crimes North. Rodriguez joined the force in 1972, spent a year and a half in the Town Hall District on patrol, and has been with Gang Crimes North since 1974.

CAPTAIN BOB SHEEHAN, watch commander, Eighteenth District. Sheehan, in his thirty-six years on the force, has served as patrol officer, homicide detective in Area Four, sergeant on the North Side, lieutenant at Patrol Headquarters, deputy chief of the Organized

Crime Division (1980–88), and assistant deputy superintendent. Shee-han's law-enforcement training has included the "long course" at Northwestern University's Traffic Institute and the program offered police by the FBI National Academy.

YOUTH OFFICER ROBERT J. SIMANDL, Area Four. Simandl is a national expert on street gangs, founder and chairman of the Midwest Gang Investigators Association, and a member of the California Gang Investigation Association. Simandl is also a nationally recognized expert on ritualistic crime. Before becoming a youth officer in 1989, Simandl served fifteen of his twenty-two years on the force as a gang crimes specialist.

OFFICER EDWARD TANSEY, SR., wagonman. Tansey, a police-man from 1951 until his retirement in 1986, worked patrol for twenty-one years and then the wagon, always in Area Six.

DETECTIVE EDWARD TANSEY, JR., Inspector General's Office. The elder Tansey's son worked patrol for eleven years after joining the CPD in 1966 and served as a detective in Area Six Property Crimes from 1977–90.

OFFICER ROSE TORRES, Vice Control. Torres joined the CPD in 1982, worked patrol and tac in the Twenty-third District for three years, including work as a prostitution decoy in Operation Angel, was detailed for one year to Women's Lock-up, and was then assigned to the Vice Control Section, Prostitution Unit.

OFFICER T. WARD, Eighteenth District. Ward joined the CPD in 1973 and spent the next seven years working patrol and tac in Four-teen and Nineteen. In 1980, Ward requested transfer to Cabrini-Green. Ward and his partner work "Special Investigations" in Narcotics and Gang Activity, centering on Cabrini-Green.

OFFICER JUDY ZYDOWSKY, Vice Control. Zydowsky joined the CPD in 1983, worked in the Twentieth District for four years as a tac officer, including work as a prostitution decoy in Operation Angel. Zydowsky has been in Vice Control since 1987.

VIOLENT CRIMES

There always comes some quiet moment when you're standing there with the dead person. And you know that if that murder is going to be avenged, it's up to you to avenge it.

It might be some old lady in her seventies—she's lived in the neighborhood all her life, the neighborhood's changed around her, she's been at death's door for the past twenty years—one night they come in and kill her for her few pitiful possessions.

And that's the one where you look at her and you say, "This is it. We're gonna get them."

–Detective Ted O'Connor

———

"I still see my first homicide victim," says a Chicago homicide detective of twenty-five years. "I can still see his face. He was a homosexual who picked up a guy in a tavern in Area Six. The savageness of the way he was killed—his throat was slit, his penis was cut off, he was disemboweled. We caught the guy who did it.

"I never forgot the victim. I still remember his name and address. I think about him every day."

Violent crimes cops say they're haunted by their cases—the homicides and suicides, the rapes, the robberies, the sexual abuse and exploitation of children. The evil they see stays with them, changing them, setting them apart.

"You can't work Homicide without changing," says a former homicide detective who now investigates the Mob. "Once you've walked into a room and had something fall on your head, and it's a piece of . . . brain matter . . . that dropped from the ceiling, you just don't go out to dinner that night and chat with your pals.

"I take a drive with my wife through the city," he continues. "I'll say, 'See this building? We had a guy with his throat cut here.' or 'See that building? We found a woman stabbed to death there.' My wife will say, 'Listen, I don't want to hear any more of this. Do you realize this isn't how most people see the city?' "

One homicide cop was literally haunted by his cases. "I knew a homicide dick once who quit; he couldn't take it anymore," says Lieutenant Jim Nemec, commanding officer of the Crime Scene Processing Unit in the Chicago Crime Lab. "He said he'd wake up in the middle of the night and see the murder victim sitting at the foot of his bed."

The traditional defense for all this horror is humor. Homicide detectives are famous for cracking jokes over anyone's dead body. They'll tell you they have to. Again and again, cops describe the role of gallows humor in these words: "If you didn't laugh, you'd cry."

Homicide may have more humorous touches than other divisions. The entrance to the Chicago Crime Lab, for instance, contains a display of the pasty-white death masks of John Dillinger and Baby Face Nelson. Until recently, the death mask of the building janitor was propped up beside the serenely smiling Baby Face. Another Crime Lab oddity is the pink plastic squid that bobbles in the waters at the bottom of the ballistics firing tank.

It used to be that homicide detectives worked Homicide almost exclusively. Then, in 1981, CPD caseloads were split into Property Crimes (burglary, boosting, con games, professional theft) and Violent Crimes (homicide, assault and battery, robbery, rape, sex crimes against children).

"The old Homicide Unit—it wasn't the Violent Crimes bullshit they have today," says one ex-homicide cop. "We handled serious assault and sex crimes too. But the way it broke down, if you weren't dead, we didn't have much time for you."

The way it breaks down now, there are still homicide specialists within Violent Crimes: detectives who love nothing better than a good homicide, detectives who talk about "entering the scene" of a homicide as if they were remembering entering Notre Dame Cathedral; detectives, commanding officers, and Crime Lab technicians whose expertise is sought on homicide stumpers.

Twenty-three specialists in homicide and its close cousin, robbery, talk in this chapter about what they've learned about crime, human nature, and themselves from encountering violent death and its attendant motives. Not all the specialists here are homicide detectives: one, Lieutenant Jim Nemec, heads Crime Scene Processing in the Crime Lab; another, Captain Tom Cronin, was selected by the CPD to be trained by the FBI in the psychological profiling of violent offenders; Detective Charlie Ford is a violent crimes detective who specializes in luring robbers as a stand-up robbery decoy; two are ex-wagon men, and several are street cops who are the first to come upon the scene of just-enacted violent death.

Most of them have worked in Area Six, Death's own cross-section, where homicide detectives move from the projects to the Gold Coast, processing corpses in crime scenes crawling with cockroaches or lousy with Lladros. Area Six Violent Crimes is dubbed the "Hollywood Division" by other cops, because ever since the splashy St. Valentine's Day Massacre and Dillinger's doomed trip to the movies, this particular CPD territory has had more garish, ingenious, and bizarre murders than any other part of Chicago. "Area Six doesn't have the *most* homicides in Chicago," says Nemec of the Crime Lab. "But you always find that the nuttiest murders, the really bizarre ones, are in Area Six." Cops in this chapter talk about murders and robberies they've investigated throughout the city, but most of the blood shed here pools in Area Six.

Some of the cops who speak in this chapter have retired, like Captain Frank J. Flanagan, first on the scene at the townhouse containing eight student nurses murdered by Richard Speck and first on the scene at John Wayne Gacy's crawl space filled with the bodies of young men— "I've been in worse situations," says Flanagan. Flanagan headed Homicide longer than any man in the history of the Chicago Police Department. Some have left Area Six, or have left Homicide altogether. One thing hasn't left them—the victims they've encountered.

"How could anyone ever forget working on a homicide?" asks one homicide detective. "You never forget. There are some cases cops carry with them to retirement. Some cases you carry with you in your head. You think about them every day. You never forget. . . ."

There is a torso that is found over in the Eighteenth District, in like a truck park. That's all it is—no arms, no legs, no head— just a torso. It has a shirt tucked around it.

The beat officers see this thing, and they don't know what it is. They come up and look at it, but if you've never seen a torso, it looks a little strange. All they can see is the pink skin and stuff.

So they call the homicide detectives and everything. The detective gets over there, and the beat officer goes, "Listen, I don't know what I got here. I'm not sure what it is. It *could* be a pig."

The homicide dick looks at the torso, and he sees that it's got a tie on, around the neck of the shirt. He looks at the beat officer and says, "Kid, pigs don't wear neckties."

They find the victim's business card in the shirt pocket with the offender's phone number on the back. Here the murderer went to all the trouble, cutting off the guy's arms and legs and stuff—we found out the guy had an appendectomy scar—the murderer cut off above the scar—this guy went to great pains. And he leaves the victim's card in his shirt.

It took a while—it goes back and forth. The deal was that the offender in this case had made a business deal with the victim to sell him machinery, some machine tools. They had made an agreement, and the victim had sent him like sixty thousand dollars, and the machine tools never came. So the victim called him up a bunch of times. Finally, the offender said, I need another thirty thousand dollars. So the victim came to Chicago for the sole purpose of talking to the guy about the machine tools. And the guy murdered him.

We finally arrested the guy five or six days after the murder. When they bring him in, some good detective asks him to pull down his pants. And there are bloodstains *all over* his shorts. And it turns out it was the victim's blood. The guy never changed his shorts since the murder. That's how this guy got to be known as "Dirty Bob."

Dirty Bob gets charged with the murder, and he's held in jail for a while and he gets out on bond. Ten days after he gets out on bond, we get a call from a local police department in Michigan. These guys went out to their shooting range, and they found all these body parts. So we found the rest of the victim's body. But this guy had wrapped him up in Chicago newspapers with some . . . gear parts and a handful of receipts with his company name on it.

I don't think this was psychological, unless stupidity is psychological. Is stupidity psychological?

I tell you what. If offenders ever got bright, we'd be in a world of trouble.

Most murderers are stupid. So many of the murders we see are dumb in the sense that it's so obvious who the murderer is. And in fact there is not even an attempt to cover up the fact that the killing was committed.

Murder has one of the highest clearance rates of any crime that occurs just for that reason. You're standing there covered with blood—now what do you do? Or you did it in front of thirty witnesses in a tavern. It's very simple.

They do things like—people keep evidence. "Take not, leave not" would be a good motto for any criminal.

There was a cop involved in an off-duty shooting. It was a traffic confrontation. He got out and wound up shooting the guy. And he left. Fled the scene.

He kept the gun; it was his own gun. Kept the car. He was arrested five years later because he got in a domestic beef with his girlfriend he was living with. She went to the police and said, "You know, I've had it with this guy. He killed a guy four, five years ago."

They went over and arrested him. He still had the same car that was used at the time, and they took his off-duty revolver and matched it up, and it matched the slug that killed the guy.

The intelligent, Bundy-type killer is the exception. Mostly, we get crimes of opportunity and passion. The victim and the offender are known to each other—if not intimately, at least there's some acquaintance that they can find. It's seldom the kind of premeditated, involved, complicated thing like you read in Agatha Christie.

Most murders are about absolutely stupid things. When you have to put down the motive for these killings—you're almost ashamed to put it down on paper, they're so ridiculous. Typical is the murder growing out of whether the angel or the star went on top of the Christmas tree. That was an actual motive.

Over on the West Side, back in '72, I remember one brother stabbed his brother to death over a turkey leg. It was a senseless killing. He grabbed the butcher knife, plunged it into his brother's heart, and killed him over a turkey leg.

* * *

I had a girl shot in a tavern because she didn't lower her radio. She came in the tavern, was having a drink, had her radio on, some guy asked her to turn down her radio, she said, "Fuck you," he pulled out a gun, shot her in the chest with a .22. The call came out. I picked her up, she was choking and gagging, she died in my arms. I checked her ID. She was fifteen years old.

We had two guys murdered over an ice-cream cone. A guy comes over to see his brother-in-law. Mr. Softee Ice Cream comes by, so the brother-in-law sends out his kid and gives him thirty cents to get an ice-cream cone for him and his guest. So the kid comes back with one ice-cream cone. "How come you didn't get one for the brother-in-law?" "Mr. Softee told me I only had enough for one."

So the father gets his pistol; the brother-in-law gets his pistol that he brought over to the house. And they decide they're going to go out and talk to Mr. Softee.

Mr. Softee sees them coming, so Mr. Softee gets out his gun, shoots the brother-in-law, and then shoots the father, as the father's going after Mr. Softee. We get to the hospital. Two guys are dead, another's in critical condition. Mr. Softee and the brother-in-law died. All over a fifteen-cent ice-cream cone.

A lot of the murders we get are crimes of passion—but you hate to use the word "passion," because the idea of a crime of passion is the guy coming home and finding his wife in bed with another guy. In most of our murders, the passion is over who gets the last drag on a marijuana cigarette or who gets the last swig of Richard's Wild Irish Rose wine.

Literally, if you took Richard's Wild Irish Rose wine off the market, you'd probably prevent half of all homicides. Invariably, there's a bottle of it somewhere in the crime scene. It's the murderers' national drink or something.

It's the most heinous crime you can commit. And the penalty for committing it is capital punishment. So, therefore, murder has an aura of importance.

But after you've been working Homicide for a while, sure it's important, but it doesn't seem so serious anymore.

A woman was shot in the leg. She bled to death. Four guys were sitting around, drinking around a table, in the same room as the victim. We got there, and one guy told us, "It was an accident. I tried to save her. She was a sweet lady. She was my landlady. I tried to save her."

I could see what he did. He tied a tourniquet on her leg *below* the wound. He was pretty proud of it—"I was a medic in the army," he said. He probably killed her, but I didn't want to tell him that. It was hard for me to keep a straight face.

You don't call the cases by the victims' names, usually. You have to find some way to relieve the horror of what you're working on. So we make up names for them. Like "Stubs and Tubs"—You come in; the sarge says, "You're working on Stubs and Tubs tonight"; that was for the double murder of two female drug dealers—one was an amputee, the other was obese. Or "Bum in a Drum"—"How's it going with Bum in a Drum?"—this was an unidentified male we were working on, found stuck headfirst in a garbage can.

We had a call one time of a man stabbed. This was a domestic disturbance. We're walking up the stairs, and we were met by a black woman. "Is there somebody stabbed here?" "Yeah, my husband's stabbed. He's up in the kitchen." So we walk into the apartment down a long hall into the kitchen, and he's sitting there—his back up against the wall—and he's eating greens and neck bones—I remember this distinctly—a big plate of greens and neck bones, and he's eating them. So I say, "Hey, man. What's the problem?" "Ain't no problem here."

So I look on the floor, and I see a big puddle of blood—it was three feet by three feet, a big, huge pile of blood. "Are you stabbed?" He says, "Uh-huh." I said, "Where are you stabbed?" I'm looking at him, and he's eating neck bones. He says, "Right here." So I look, and I jump back. He has a butcher knife going through his back and coming out his stomach at an angle, like a skewer. So I say, "How do you feel?" And he says, "I'm *hungry.*" He was about six-four and about 400 pounds. About six of us had to carry him over to the hospital.

Eighty percent of murders are domestics: husband-wife, girl-friend-boyfriend, boyfriend-boyfriend.

It's mostly a spontaneous act, not premeditated. A lot of times, murder is a mistake. The majority of homicides are done when somebody knows their victim and, in a time of anger, reaches out and does something totally irrational.

Most people are remorseful after murder. They keep saying, "I didn't mean to. I didn't want to. But I plunged a butcher knife into him twice."

Murder weapons—they use whatever's handy. Murder is, in most cases, a spontaneous act, and whatever is the first thing they can pick up is what they're going to use. Bricks and rocks and bottles, electric fans, frying pans, gasoline, table legs. We get a lot of barbecue-fork murders in the summertime.

Most killers are men. We don't normally see women who kill. Women are just more masochistic than men. They commit suicide rather than homicide.

When we *do* see women who kill, they kill their own children. A woman is far more likely to kill her own children than a man is. Here, we're talking about paranoid schizophrenics. They have delusions, hallucinations. They act out on their kids. They feel they're saving their children from this horrible world. They consider it a mercy killing. They look at everything through fractured glass.

Many times, it's a gentle killing, smothering, suffocation, drowning. Mothers stay away from violent murders of their own kids; it's the men who do that. After the killing, the mother bathes the child, gets it all clean and perfect. Then they put the

body in nice clothing, its best clothes, put the child in bed, and
fold its arms in the death pose.

If you're gonna be killed, you'll probably be killed by someone
you know. The most brutal homicides take place in the closest
relationships. The most dangerous place to be is in your own
home between Saturday night at six and Sunday night at six.
That's *still* the most dangerous place to be.

The most savage stabbings occur between husband and wife,
boyfriend and girlfriend, boyfriend and boyfriend. Stabbings
indicate far more anger than killing someone with a gun. Especially with repeated wounds. When you get forty, fifty, a hundred stab wounds, you're talking about somebody that's really
mad at you.

There was a family-disturbance call, a neighbor called in,
heard screaming and yelling. Went there, I was working a one-
man car. Knocked on the door, guy come up to the door, he
opened up the door . . . his pants were like half-open, he had
glazed eyes, he had blood on him, and he was eating a sandwich, a bologna sandwich. And he says, "I think my mother's
sick. She's in the basement." And I'm like . . . he's covered in
blood; he's got blood all over him. And he's eating the sandwich.
    Being of sane and sound mind, I was like, "Let me call some-
body to come over here." At that time, our radios were in the
car. I went outside, and I called for a backup. And I went back
inside, and I waited. And this guy's sitting on the couch. He had
the sandwich, and he's sitting there eating the sandwich. He
had a deranged look. Looking at him, he just didn't look like
he was there with everybody else.
    So the backup comes in. The guy says, "My mother's in the
basement." The one fellow stays with him, and the other officer
and I go down to the basement. We went looking around; I had
my flashlight.
    There was a storage shed. And he had chopped her up with
an ax. I got sick. I've seen some nasty things in my life, but

seeing this woman chopped up was not one of the most pleasant things in the world.

He did everything we told him to do. There was no fight. We told him to sit down on the couch, he sat down. We told him to come out to the wagon to go to the station, there was no fighting, there was no struggling. All the aggression he had had gone out of him. He used it all up on his mother.

Then, when the father came home from work—"Why did he do this to my wife, his mother?" And I told him, *"I* don't know why. He's *your* son."

We found out from the father that they had committed him to a mental hospital and he was like a walkaway from the place. The father said he was very perturbed about being committed.

After that, I never saw him again, because he really was a mental case. It never went to court. He just went back to the hospital.

And I was at the door, you know, talking to him. Eating his bologna sandwich and his mom in the basement, chopped up. I thought about that a long time.

As far as passionate crimes, jeez, the homosexuals are the ones that come to mind for really throwing themselves into their work, so to speak. You generally find the most ferocious crimes are homosexual. Now you're getting into what you think of as passion, romance, the emotional-type thing.

We had one years ago where two fruits were at the consummate stage of amorous adventure and one fruit bit a piece of the tongue off of the other fruit. And the second fruit, the bite-ee, was so incensed that he not only killed the biter, but—*disemboweled* him, looking for the piece of his tongue. We came up on this crime scene, and you know, you expect a little blood and guts, but this was *literally* blood and guts.

Homosexual murders are seldom just a quick gunshot or quick stabbing. They are always these complicated things. The crime scene, instead of being nice and neat and in the corner of the alley or something, it's always spread over a ten-room apartment.

* * *

Some homicides are very neat. Some are almost pleasant. Somebody who's been strangled isn't bad at all. A single gunshot wound is not as ugly as a throat that's been slashed. The worst is the gaping wounds you get from a shotgun murder.

The murder victim tells you a lot about the murderer. There are *reasons* for everything done to the body. You look at how the body is displayed. If the murderer covers the body, it may show some remorse; it may show a close relationship—"I'll cover it up. Maybe it will go away." If the body's uncovered, it indicates the murder was done by a total stranger. He doesn't care. If the body is flagrantly displayed, the murderer may be thinking of who's going to come through the door next—he wants to shock or hurt the person most likely to come in and find the body.

When you work the wagon, the most feared call is "Check suspicious odor." Fresh homicides you can handle all day. It's the ones that aren't discovered for a few days, or weeks, that are bad, the stinkers, the ones that eventually pop open. You'd rather do ten fresh homicides a day than one popper. Rotten meat is Chanel No. 5 compared to a popper.

There are different ways to handle the smell at a scene. Cigars, of course. Wagon men are famous for smoking cigars at scenes. A lot of homicide dicks stick cigarette filters up their nostrils. Or they take fresh coffee grounds into the scene, throw them in a frying pan or pot on the stove, and turn the gas or electricity on underneath. When I worked the wagon, I always used to carry a glass vial filled with my favorite shaving lotion and cotton balls and put the balls in my nostrils before we walked in.

* * *

A real warning sign to any homicide detective is when you see the wagon men standing around *outside* the scene. Then you know you've got a bad one.

You take the body home with you. It's the kind of smell that stays in your clothes and your nostrils.

We had a case, an uncertain homicide or suicide, and the detectives questioning witnesses. A woman had been fighting with her husband. The Crime Lab guys went in there and found the gun in a policeman's waistband. Supposedly, the weapon was found in the victim's hand, and the allegation was that the husband had killed his wife and put the gun in her hand. The evidence technician now proceeded to fingerprint the victim, and in fingerprinting her, he found a roll of prints on the card that showed the outline of a word. So he looked, and here—in the victim's hand—was impressed the marking from the gun. A rare occurrence when a person dies and they go into this spontaneous rigor mortis called cadaveric spasm; the grip is so tight. This mark had embedded itself on her hand, and that was proof that the victim had the gun in her hand when it was fired.

Suicides have what are called "hesitation marks" on their wrists. You see a few scratches and then the big slice. There are a lot of nerves right under the skin there, and when you start slashing your wrists, it really hurts. That's why you see a couple tentative marks and then the big one—they get it over with.

When you're at the murder scene, you look at what's been taken and you find out who it belonged to originally. Many, many times, the killer takes something back from the victim after the murder—"You bitch. I gave this to you and you deserved this once. Not anymore. I'm taking it back."

* * *

If a killer spends a lot of time with the body, he probably lives in the neighborhood.

If you want to establish time of death, you look at the associative events surrounding the death. Check to see if the mail's been brought in. See if the newspaper's still at the door. Check to see if anything's cooking on the stove.

You can also use this to see who was with the victim last. One of the suspects says, "I haven't seen him for two weeks": you check through the victim's mail or his datebook, and you see they went out together a few days ago.

We had one last Christmas Eve, an employee beaten to death with a hammer. His body wasn't discovered for three days. The employer said, "I haven't seen him since the last day he worked five days ago." This was something that could be corroborated by other employees.

So we worked backwards. We found out where the victim drank. We went to the bartender: "When was the last time you saw him?" "He was in here with his boss a few days before Christmas Eve. They had a vicious argument." That was the night before his death.

The first step in any murder investigation is always to contact the last person to see the victim alive. Or you key in on the one who discovers the body. Many times, the person who discovers the body is the killer.

This premise mostly holds true: In the case of a murder, the victim knew the assailant, the assailant knew the victim, or a combination of both.

Your first approach to a murder is, "Let's start looking at all the people that this fellow knew." So what you do, you grab the address book, letters, the date book. And you go, "Where were *you* on that day?" to all the victim's acquaintances.

* * *

I'd like to see Polaroid cameras air-dropped into the ghetto and given to everybody at birth. All the gangbangers and dope dealers we've ever seen love to take pictures of themselves and their buddies. They've got pictures of themselves cutting dope, pictures of themselves and their buddies with their guns, pictures of themselves sitting on their beds with piles of money.

We've solved more than one murder by going through the dead guy's belongings and finding Polaroid pictures of him and his killer with their arms around each other.

A lot of murder victims are dope dealers, prostitutes, gangbangers. Especially dope dealers now. The dog-ass of society. A lot of the guys we handle, we think, One day, the body we turn over is gonna have your face on it.

Crime snowballs. What starts as a burglary can turn into a home invasion. A street robbery or stickup turns into murder. Most robbers have a propensity for violence anyway.

Years ago, criminals specialized. People did robberies, and that's all they did. Burglars did burglaries, and car thieves were car thieves. Not anymore.

Today, we have . . . we call them—animals. They're just opportunists. They'll do anything. They go up and down apartment building halls knocking on doors; they get in one, if a woman's there, they'll rape her. It's just an afterthought. It's just, "Well, she's there, she's vulnerable, I might as well take her." With these animals, these opportunists, if somebody's home, then Violent Crimes gets it, because it's gonna become a robbery, an armed robbery, a rape, and a homicide.

A lot of murders start out as robberies. They're robberies that went bad. The victim panics, or the offender panics, and shoots. They compound it.

I remember one little girl, this was right before Christmas. Her parents managed the building they lived in, collected the rents for this large apartment building. Somebody came in to stick *them* up for the rents.

The father pushed the door closed on these four guys. They

had a shotgun. The shotgun went off and hit the little girl in the chest. She had a hole in her, six inches around, right in her chest. She landed underneath the Christmas tree on top of all the Christmas presents. That was a heartbreaker.

People fear robbery more than any other crime. Mr. Stranger Danger is gonna jump out and hurt me. That's what they fear, the physical injury. And they're right to fear it. There's been just a phenomenal increase in the past few years of the incidents where the victim is physically harmed. We get a lot of cases were the people hand over the money and then they're beaten, kicked, and turned on, really unnecessarily—they're not trying to grab the offender, they're not trying to prevent him from fleeing, they gave the guy their money, but the guy turns on them and beats them. And that's because there's a basic aggressiveness and savagery in robbers.

Most victims of street crime—if they were at home watching *Little House on the Prairie*—whatever happened never would have happened.

A lot of crimes happen to people who are in the wrong place at the wrong time, and they *want* to be in the wrong place. A lot of our crimes start with the so-called victimless crime. There's a prostitute involved, there's gambling involved, there's narcotics, something like that. We get an awful lot of robberies we investigate where it's people from the suburbs, they're downtown at two in the morning, get robbed. What are they doing there?

They're there for some sort of a reason. They're there to buy dope, they're there to buy a woman, something. They're off-color. They have little hobbies that they do maybe one or two nights a week, and in doing so they become victims of crimes.

They're out of their element. They're at the mercy of predatory people. Street people are like predators in the jungle. They have a tendency to weed out the weak.

These things are impossible to solve, because the victims lie to you. They don't give you all the facts, because they're covering for themselves. It's amazing. They think we have a block of wood between our ears. They really do.

A lot of guys try to be robbery decoys, but they never get robbed. They're not putting out the right vibes.

The key is to look like you're completely helpless. You don't want to act crazy, because street people don't attack crazy people—if you've ever arrested a crazy, you know they're unpredictable and have tremendous strength. So street people leave crazies alone. So you try to look helpless. I act drunk and I drool. If you look semi-alert, your chances of getting robbed are slim, and if you *do* get robbed, you'll probably get hurt. But if you look completely blind drunk, your chances of getting robbed are more, and your chances of getting hurt are less.

You have to pick your spots. *Semi*secluded—if you're completely in a public way, your chances are down, and if it's too secluded, they may want to kill you. Always standing up. If you're laying down, you don't get the right kind of characters— you get new guys, guys without records; they figure this is easy. But when you're a stand-up decoy, you never get a cherry. Over 95 percent of the characters who rob you when you're standing up have been in the pen before.

I don't wear my regular good clothes, because I'm slumping against walls and these cretins are crawling all over me.

You try to control the situation. You set up for it. If you do the drunk act, I'll compare it—it's like going duck hunting and using the duck call or not using the duck call. If you're not using the duck call, you might get a few birds hanging around the pond, but it sure helps if you've got a few decoys blowing.

Most robbers—it's unbelievable—these characters all do the same stuff. They all have the same body language. They all say the same thing.

I always know when somebody's going to rob me. They're like great white sharks with some meat dangled in front of them— they nose around, they prod you a little bit, see you if react, then they swim away, they come back. They might make a loud noise, see if you react.

When they come back the second time, they look up and down the street. They swim away again, they might recruit help, come back with two or three guys.

They almost always feel you out before they strike. It's very rare that they just jump you. They come up, ask me if I'm okay. They might grab hold of my arm—"Are you okay?" Then they get you under control. Sometimes one holds me and the other goes through my pockets.

Once they get to that point, the actual robbery—before that, they're looking for people, for police—but once they're into it, they're oblivious to everything going on. There could be a million cops right there, and they'd never notice. They're into it. I have to wear a watch with an expandable band, or else they'd try to saw my wrist off. One time, they ripped my bulletproof vest off; they thought it was a bandage. One guy's telling his pals, "Hey, this guy's got a bandage on."

The longest time is waiting for them to hit. Sometimes it takes half an hour of their going back and forth, sizing me up, checking me out, before they hit. But the actual robbery only takes a minute or two. My backup's down the street. I let them leave, give the signal, and point to the guy who's got the stuff. The backup comes in if they see me getting hurt. Before that, there's no communication between me and the backup. They're in a van or car, watching the sharks; the partners might say to each other, "That guy looks like a taker."

Most robbery victims are women. And you know how robbers verbally accost their victims? We know this from robbery victims. They don't say, "Your money or your life." They say, "Give it up, bitch."

We had a nine-cent armed robbery. The two people that did it are now doing life in Michigan for murder and armed robbery, and they would have killed our victim in Chicago. Over nine cents.

It was a Bonnie-and-Clyde type of situation. David Allen Harris and his girlfriend, Maria Trevino—David Allen Harris had just gotten out of the penitentiary in Michigan; he did time for armed robbery. Three months after that, he hooks up with Trevino, his girlfriend, and they start committing armed robberies.

They needed transportation. So they murdered a twenty-one-year-old woman in Grand Rapids, Michigan, just to get her car, for a getaway car. It was a brutal murder. If you want, I'll tell you what they did to her. If you don't mind.

They abducted her from outside a saloon where she worked, took her out to a rural area outside Grand Rapids. They stripped her naked. David Harris put the gun up her rectum, fired two shots. Then they put a bullet in her head.

The two of them left, they went to Toledo, Ohio; they're doing other stickups. They got rid of the Grand Rapids car in Toledo, they need a new car. So one night, they're waiting, and they see a sixty-year-old woman was stopped at a stop sign. David Harris walked up to her, and with the same gun he killed the girl in Grand Rapids with, fired six shots at this woman through the window, dragged her out, left her right on the street, they took her car and left.

They came to Chicago. We're getting information and leads. They come to Chicago; they stay at the Tropicana Motel. While they're there, they decide they need another car. David Allen Harris goes out to find another woman with a car. He finds a woman parking her car in the underground garage of an apartment building. She has a small baby in the backseat of her car. She's getting the baby out of the restraint seat in the back. Harris walks up to her at gunpoint, he says, "Give me your purse." With that, she's trying to get the baby out of the car, there's a timed alarm in the car, the alarm went off. Harris grabs her purse out of the car and took off. He probably would have killed her, the M.O. was exactly the same, and he already killed two women the same way, but the alarm saved her—it took him by surprise; he grabbed the purse, took off. There's nine cents in the purse.

Two days later, the woman's walking down the street—she spots him. She calls the police, me and my partner go out, she points him out, we stop him, we go through him, we find twenty .22-caliber bullets in his pockets. We tell him he's charged with armed robbery in the city of Chicago. He takes us back to the

Tropicana Motel. We encounter his girlfriend. We find a sawed-off shotgun with 179 rounds of ammunition and a .22-caliber pistol, which turns out was the weapon they used to stick up the woman and was the murder weapon in two states.

They were charged with armed robbery here; they were tried and convicted of murder in Michigan and Ohio. There's no death penalty in either state, so they're both serving life sentences in Jackson, Michigan. If the governor of Michigan ever pardons them, the state of Ohio will be waiting at the prison door for them. So they'll never get out.

There is no Sherlock Holmes. There is no Kojak. There is no Hunter. The good detective on the street is the one who knows all the weasels and one of the weasels will tell him who did it.

Crimes are solved, first, because the suspect told on himself or somebody told on him. I would say that accounts for 80 percent of crime solution. Somebody told somebody something. Twenty percent or less are crimes where circumstantial evidence is used to solve it.

Women drop dimes on guys all the time. Women are the best sources of information. What happens is, when men get a lot of money all of a sudden, one thing they do, they get new clothes, a new car. Many times, they get a better-looking girlfriend or the wife's left at home while they're out partying. So they drop a dime on the guy.

There's something we call the "Guilt Indicator." Over and over and over again we see it. I can't tell you how many scores of times I've seen it myself. This is it: We have three suspects for murder. You throw them all in the interrogation room, handcuff them to a wall. Come back later, one guy's asleep. That is an absolute indication of the person's guilt.

Why? If you're innocent and you're accused of killing somebody—think about it. Think about it. We come get you, slip the cuffs on you, drag you in, put you into the interrogation room, take that cuff off of one arm, cuff it to the ring on the wall, and leave you sitting there—would you be going nuts or what? You'd be going, "I just can't believe—they—I can't—what's going on?—what?" If you're staring at forty years in the joint, could you lay down on the floor of the police station, cuffed to the wall, and go to sleep?

But think about the offender. Ever since he killed, he's been petrified. He's sat up for three days, he's gotten no sleep. "What can I say? What can I do?" He's just waiting for that knock on the door.

When he's charged, it comes as a relief. He falls asleep. I don't know how many times we've all seen it. A guy is charged with two counts of murder. You'll open up the door into the interrogation room and the hand will be in the air, cuffed to the ring in the wall, and the guy will have his head on his arm hanging there, sound asleep.

It's nothing you're going to introduce in court or anything, but it's a pretty good indication. An innocent man will be going crazy. A guilty man goes to sleep.

We see murderers walk in and out of our offices constantly. It all depends on who is handling the case. With some cops, they just go through the motions, they question them, hold them, release them. Some coppers never get a confession.

The game is—can you con a con? They think they're the smartest things going; they think they can slick you.

But good coppers can con a con. You get his confidence going, you give him his out, you play the sympathy.

Even the most hardened killer falls victim to a sympathetic interrogation. Let's say a man who's suspected of killing his wife walks in, and he tells you what she did to provoke him. And you look at him and say, "Boy, I'll tell you one thing, pal. If anybody ever needed killing, she did." The guy will come right out and say, "That's why I did it."

A nine-months pregnant woman was found strangled to death; she hemorrhaged, there was blood all over. There was a dirty storm-door window outside the kitchen where she was killed. We found a fresh outline of a human head in a listening pose on the window. Sometime during the night, before she was killed, her killer had put his head to the window to listen.

The neighbors told us that a guy had been bothering this woman and her twin sister for some time. The dead girl's family suspected this guy too. We picked the guy up, he took a polygraph, and under the pressure, he confessed to the examiner.

I spent twelve hours with this man. He was a multiple personality. While I was alone in the room with him, he told me about this other person who was evil who he couldn't control. He said the other person was winning.

At one point, he did a Jekyll and Hyde on me—it was like watching Spencer Tracy transform himself. His head went down, he was trembling—he came up laughing. He told me what a chump the other guy was, and I wouldn't get shit out of him. He went back and forth—the first person was a timid, earnest simpleton. The second guy was strong, smart-alecky, evil.

We contacted the State's Attorney's Office. I explained that you have to get *both* these personalities to talk if you're gonna get a confession.

This young state's attorney marches in the room, draws himself up to his full height, and says, "I am the assistant state's attorney. I represent the people of the state of Illinois." This guy stood up, went in a corner, and curled into the fetal position. "Get this state's attorney jerk out of here!"

If you're interviewing a withdrawn guy and come on like gangbusters, he'll withdraw into his shell. With others, you *want* to induce stress. You want to keep that asshole puckered.

It's amazing how many people *will* talk. I've had guys that have been in the penitentiary two or three times. You'd think they *should* know better, that they'd know, if you confess, you go away to jail.

Almost nobody keeps their mouth shut. Everybody talks. A lot of them give you a lot of bullshit and lie to you and try to turn the story around to justify what they did. But very, very few people, when you advise them of their rights, just sit there and say, "Well, I don't want to talk to you." Very, very few. I'd say 95 percent will give you some kind of story. Maybe it's not the legitimate one, but they'll start talking.

It never ceases to amaze me in some of these grisly murders these guys are up for, you think, My God, if he'd just shut his mouth, there's nothing we can do about this. But they just—they just spill their guts.

It's very hard for people to understand why anybody would confess. Lawyers can't understand it. They think it must have been under duress.

But the killing of another human being is such an incredible experience—it's a very emotional experience to take the life of another human being. For most people, it's a haunting, frightening experience. Fortunately, the killer wants to tell somebody. If he doesn't go to the cops, he'll tell a friend, a relative, and maybe that friend or relative will go to the cops. If the murderer hasn't told anybody else, if he's kept it inside, once we get them, they're exploding inside. They don't know if ghosts will start appearing, if they'll get the chair, if they'll go to prison and get beaten on and raped by convicts. . . .

Nobody, unless they're a little psychotic or something, nobody's gonna give you the whole story right up-front. They give it to you in dribbles and half-truths and they twist it around. And what you do is, you go back and you check whatever in the story can be checked out, and then you confront them with inconsistencies in what they're telling you. Usually, after a while, the truth or at least the majority of the truth will come out. They'll usually always keep a little something back. Sometimes the silly stuff they'll keep back—they might say, "Okay, I ax-murdered this guy," but they're a little ashamed to say that they defecated on the floor. "Did you crap on the floor?" "No, no. I didn't do that." The guy's not ashamed to tell you he racked this guy's head off with an ax; he's ashamed to tell you he pooped on the floor. Stuff like that. Little quirks.

Most murders are spontaneous. The ones that are premeditated, who knows? Those we might not only not solve, we might never even find out that they're murders. If the guy is clever enough, he can make it look like a suicide or an accident or even a natural death.

We knew a woman who would have committed the perfect murder. She had a perfectly planned murder. Her only mistake was she picked one of us to commit it.

The way we got it, a black kid goes into the Eighteenth District station and tells the cops there that a woman just approached him in the subway and asked him to kill her husband. They call us. He tells us he's waiting for the subway at Chicago and State and an Oriental woman came up and said, "I'll give you two hundred dollars to kill my husband." "So what did you tell her?" He tells us he told her, "Yes. Give me your phone number, and I'll contact you."

So we took him back to the Violent Crimes office and had him call her. We told him to tell the woman he couldn't do it, but he has a friend who's just released from prison, and this friend would call the following day. Then we got a court order for a wire and eavesdropping equipment. I call the woman up, I say I'm the guy's friend, and we arrange a meeting for the next day.

This is at the el terminal, out at Jefferson Park. She comes up, we make small talk. She says she's a housekeeper for a woman whose husband beats her, and they both want to have this guy killed. She tries to get the price down; she's offering me $150 to do it. I say it's gotta be $200.

Twenty-four hours later, I call her. Here's her plan: "We've gotta wait till the old man's asleep. I'll call you then. You go to the apartment. I'll let you in through the back door. I'll give you a pillow and a coat with long sleeves so he won't scratch your arms while you're smothering him. It'll look like natural causes."

Now it starts getting hilarious. I'm trying to get her to talk as much as possible, but she says, "We can't talk. The phone could be tapped." My partner and I are looking at each other like—I guess! She starts referring to the old man as the dog. "The dog was bad. We have to put the dog to sleep."

So, a couple days later, I get the call—"Come on over." I come in through the back door, she gives me an overcoat and a pillow. The pillow has plastic around it so that if he vomits during the murder, she can throw the plastic away. It turns out, *she's* the wife. There is no housekeeper.

I say to her, "Give me the money before I do it." There was a bit of a discussion about how much she was going to pay me; she wanted to get the price down and pay me after the murder. I said you've got to give me half before, half after. She hands me a hundred dollars. I pull out the star. "You're under arrest."

She dashes over to a chest of drawers. She's rummaging around and pulling out knives from this drawer. My backup hasn't come up the stairs yet. So now I'm *shouting,* "You're under arrest," and my backup's *still* not coming—the radio went bad. So now she's got this knife. I grab both her hands, I'm fighting with her, trying to get the cuffs on, she's a little woman, she's only about five-foot-four, but she's fighting hard. I've got both her wrists, the money, and my star in my hands. We're wrestling around. I keep shouting, "You're under arrest!" Finally, my backup comes up the back stairs.

My backup and I go in to her husband—this guy she's been trying to murder is sleeping in bed; he's in his seventies. Grandpa. We wake him up. We tell him what his wife was planning on doing. He falls out of bed and has a heart attack.

He didn't die right then, thank God. They take him off to the hospital. We talked to him again after he got home from the hospital. It turns out, she was a Filipino immigrant. He was a lonely widower. He went to a dance, she latched onto him. A week later, they got married. It was three months later that she tried to kill him. He was sick anyway; he had some kind of terminal illness. He died pretty soon after that.

You know what her defense was when this went to trial? Her defense attorney said the old man was a sexual acrobat, he was driving her crazy with his sexual needs. Now, we saw this guy, he was laid up in bed, just about breathing his last—sex was the *last* thing on this guy's mind.

She served two years. Shortly after that, the U.S. attorney asks me to testify at a deportation hearing. Her time in the U.S. was about up, and there was the criminal incident. I go to the hearing—she's got an old guy with her. She had latched onto another poor old guy, another widower, and married him. Here's this lonely old guy, he said he knew the whole story, and he was ready to stand behind her 100 percent—"She'd been framed; this was a wonderful woman." There's a lot of lonely people out there who'll do anything for love.

They never told me what the outcome of the deportation hearing was. I don't know what happened with her and the second old man. But the first guy—she would've gotten away with it. It was nearly the perfect crime. It just would have been an old duffer who died in his sleep.

Ever since this incident, the guys in the office call me "Pillows."

There's a parlance we use. "Smoking gun"—that's for the guy standing there, with the gun smoking over the body when the police arrive. Or the "known but flown"—that's when you know who did it, you got an eyeball, an actual witness, or an earball—somebody who knows who did it, but he wasn't on the scene. And then there's the third category, the mystery—"We got a mystery." We don't know anything. We also call this a "luncher"—we may end up eating this one.

Only about 5 to 10 percent of homicides are true mysteries. These are the senseless killings, the stranger-to-stranger killings, murders for no apparent reason. No confessions. No eyewitnesses. Only the crime scene to go on.

The crime scene tells you what happened. It doesn't lie. People lie. Crime scenes don't.

* * *

Policemen are notorious for screwing up crime scenes. The first thing they do is pick up the gun—in order to prevent the victim from killing anyone else, I guess. It's inherent in the policeman. I wish I could tell every cop who ever gets called to a scene, "The best place for your hands at a scene is in your pockets."

Any crime scene now, check refrigerators for bottles that might contain blood. Check for hypodermic needles that might be used for drawing blood. Check the freezer for body parts, animal and human.

Satanic cult murders are out there. It's not to say that it's everywhere. But people certainly are doing these things.

In a satanic murder, the right arm of the victim may be tied behind the body. The right testicle may be missing. The body may be drained of blood; the heart may be removed. Human or animal feces may be smeared on the body or found in the body cavities. There may be missing body parts: the heart, genitals, index finger, the tongue—that's for telling secrets.

When I teach classes about satanic crimes, I always watch the heads of the coppers in class. After a while, you see guys nodding; they start bumping each other. They've seen this stuff.

In any homicide, your best piece of evidence is lying on the floor.

The crime scene itself tells you a great deal about the killer. What the criminal profiler does is look at the action—look at what occurred and try to backtrack and come up with the type of personality that would have done that.

The scene shows what kind of person the killer is—whether he's what they call in profiling, "an organized personality": the clever killer who plots the perfect murder, or the serial killer— he's the John Wayne Gacy, he's the Edmund Kemper, the Ted

Bundy, the Green River killer. This guy is smart. Very well planned. Leaves very little clues. He's in charge. He's only going to give you what he wants to. Very difficult person to catch. Very difficult.

Or the killer could be—the second category they use in profiling is the "disorganized personality": that's the inadequate person, the loner, the guy who feels wronged, for whatever reason—he lacks planning and cunning; he commits his crime in a frenzy and leaves all kinds of clues—this guy may kill someone he knows, he may kill a stranger that he *thinks* he has some relationship with—or this guy can be a mass murderer.

When a murderer commits his murder, it's probably the most significant thing he'll do in his life. So you examine the crime scene carefully: what the murderer does to the body, whether the body was dead or unconscious when he did those things, what kind of weapon he used, what time this occurred, all these things can point to the personality of the murderer.

The crime scene reflects the personality of the murderer. You walk into a person's home, you can tell what kind of person lives there. Well, you can also see the personality of offenders at crime scenes. For every *what* at the scene there's a *why.*

For example, a facial assault. When you see a facial assault on a victim, the vast majority of the time—it's personal. The murderer is somebody who knows the victim and is mad as hell at them.

Many times when you see a female killed for no apparent reason and you see a lot of force used on the face, you start looking for someone who knows her. When all the likely suspects are eliminated, then you look for the inadequate personality this woman might have known, however slightly. The inadequate guy—say the murder victim is in a service profession, she's a waitress—the inadequate personality is the guy who comes in the store, has a cup of coffee, the girl smiles and says thank you—he thinks, She likes me!—this guy misinterprets kindness for sexual interest. He may continue this secret fantasy in his mind that he and the girl are having a torrid affair. He loves her; she has no idea who he is.

This guy is out one night and he sees "his lover" with *her* lover, she's kissing the boyfriend good night. This guy goes into a rage, he waits for her to get inside her house, he walks up to the house, walks in, does a blitz attack. He kills her for cheating on him.

The inadequate personality premeditates murder in fantasy, but he commits it on the spur of the moment. His crimes are committed in a frenzy—with his victims, you'll find multiple stab wounds, groups of wounds. Many times, he doesn't set out to go to kill. It's not really planned. Usually, the weapon used is a weapon of opportunity rather than a weapon of choice. The murder might be triggered by environmental cues—this guy sees a terribly violent movie, say, with violent sexual scenes done to a woman. He comes out of the movie or comes out of his house after seeing the movie and sees a woman. He tries to perform the violent sex he's just seen on this woman; she may be a stranger; she may be someone he knows.

With this guy, death is quick. But lots of stuff happens after death. More than likely, he won't move or conceal the body. He never moves the body after death.

This guy is rarely a serial killer. He does poor planning and leaves lots of evidence.

You study the crime scene, and you start building the blocks. You look at how the offender attacked. The type of attack tells you the type of killer. Was it a con? Was this a guy who could talk the clothes off a woman? Or was it a blitz attack? This is the attack style of the inadequate personality; when this kind of personality kills, he is going to make that victim unconscious or dead immediately.

What the murderer does to the body and what time he does it to the body is very important. It tells you what kind of person he is. If all the activity, or a great majority of the activity, is done postmortem: cutting or slashing or the insertion of foreign objects into the orifices—if that's done postmortem, that tells you that this is a very inadequate person.

Here is a person who probably has spent most of his life—most of his sexual life has probably been masturbation fueled by pornography. Now, all of a sudden, he has got a real, live person. Here is a real, live body, but I want it to be a doll that I can play with. I can't play with someone who's alive. So I have to either make it unconscious or kill it first. Now, he's got the body. For years, he's seen photos. And now he's looking at—and there are orifices that he's seen photos of. Very seldom will you see penile penetration from an inadequate person. He's not sure what's up there. He may stick his finger up there—usually not even that, a pen, stick something else up there. Exploring. Almost like a child. That's why lots of times you'll see mutilation of the breasts. What is that thing? I've seen every single woman has one, but I've never felt one and I don't know what it is. Exploratory.

If you see clothes that are ripped, torn, or still partially on—that shows an inadequate personality. Why is that? First of all, these guys can't talk a woman into taking her clothes off. And it's very difficult to take clothes off a dead person. Ask a nurse or the attendants at a morgue—it's dead weight.

Now the guy who's a con, the guy who's got the gift of gab, he's going to get the clothes off. Ted Bundy could charm the clothes off his victims. He could literally charm their clothes off of them.

The Ted Bundy–type killer doesn't do all the exploratory stuff to bodies afterwards that inadequate personalities do. He doesn't need to. He's into power and control. Now what's the biggest power and control? Over life and death. I am God. *I* decide whether you are going to live past this day or not. And *that* is a sexual trip for these people.

Power and control. The big motivators of murder with both inadequate and serial killers. This is what most criminals seek for—power and control. A lot of people say, Well, hey, you can say that, but now somebody like a stickup man, he wants money. How many stickup men take their money and invest it? They don't. What do they do? They go out and squander it. It's power and control. With both organized and disorganized killers, it's power and control.

Serial killers are extremely personable, likeable people. It's hard not to like them. Mass murderers are not personable. They have some mental disorder, and one day, they blow. Whereas with serial killers, it's not something they have. It's something they *are.*

Mass murders—the kind where the guy comes home, picks up his rifle, and says to his wife, "I'm going to McDonald's to hunt people," are usually triggered by some loss. A significant event. The guy may have just lost his job. That was just the straw that broke the camel's back. And stress. You look for those precipitating stress factors. How much does that straw weigh that breaks the camel's back? A lot of times, it may be very insignificant.

There was a series of murders in the New Town area. Women were found strangled, in their bathtubs, placed in their bathtubs, with something put on top of them to hold them underwater, a television set or something like that.

We eventually found the killer. Tommy Lee Jackson. He told us he'd prowl apartments, and if he came across one with a lone female inside, he'd rape and kill her.

He was a serial killer. He was in the navy for a long time. He told us he'd be on a ship that was stationed out of Boston or something, and he'd be committing murders up here when he should have been on his ship. The navy is hesitant to broadcast that sailors are off their ships, or else they don't know about it. So this guy always had the perfect alibi—"Hey, I was on a ship a thousand miles away."

He told us about one. He met a woman at a bar, she took him home. After they had sex, she was asleep, he was up and stealing. He said he was going to leave and take her stereo and stuff with him, but she woke up. He killed her. He strangled her in the bathtub. It's a lot easier to strangle somebody when they're underwater. Strangling somebody when they're fighting with you—if they're underwater when they're gasping, it's a lot easier.

He told us that after he killed the women, he knew he did something dirty, so he cleaned them up in the bathtub.

Killers don't just start out at twenty-five, saying, "God, I think I'll sexually assault some woman and burn her breast." It's a thing that started many, many years ago. And it grows into a cycle.

There's something they call the "homicidal triangle"— they've found that most serial killers have this in their past: animal abuse or animal torture in the teenage years, bed-wetting in the teenage years, and fire-setting in the teenage years. These are real strong indicators of future trouble.

When you talk about the sadistic killer, it's the kid that has had this fantasy for years. This kid has a power-control fantasy, a sadistic fantasy. The sadistic killer not only likes to inflict pain, but he gets a sexual gratification from the reaction he obtains when he inflicts pain. Power and control.

He may start out when he's ten, eleven years old, ripping apart his sister's dolls, tearing an arm off a doll, twisting the head off. The kid might stop there. He gets out of it. But then there's the kid who stays with it, and realizes that he's not getting any reaction from the doll. He wants that reaction. The next thing will be maybe an animal. Maybe a little kitten. Stick it with pins. Kittens sound a lot like the high-pitched scream of a woman. So now, this is a very good sexual stimulation for this kid. He goes out looking for animals to torture. And maybe he'll grow out of it. Maybe he won't. And maybe animals aren't enough anymore.

Someone with a mental disorder, if they blow on just one homicide, you'll see by what they do to the body.

But when you see good, solid killings, the killer doing things like cutting off the heads and hands of the victim to prevent identification, you've probably got a serial killer. You can tell a serial killer by the crime scene. Nobody's that good the first time out.

Serial killers all have certain traits in common. They're almost like fingerprints.

In the early eighties, the FBI and some homicide detectives started interviewing serial killers who had been in prison for a while. They came up with common traits they all have. They came up with the kind of information you're not going to get from a psychiatrist.

For example, serial killers love to talk. When they talk about their murders, they talk about themselves in the third person. They feel no guilt. None at all. They rationalize. They blame others. If their M.O. is to pick up female hitchhikers and then murder them, they blame the victim—"She should have known better than to hitchhike."

And the thing is, they get a *kick* out of the fact that the victim did most of the activity: "Hey, I invited them, they didn't have to come. Hey, listen: I was just driving down the road, minding my own business, and this girl was hitchhiking. Well, hey, she shouldn't be hitchhiking. A lot of bad things can happen to her. I'm just gonna show her. It wasn't my fault."

David Berkowitz, New York's Son of Sam. He told us something about taking an item like a pen or some insignificant thing from the crime scene—insignificant to anyone but him. When David Berkowitz went back out looking for another victim, he had a fantasy to fill. He had what he wanted in his mind. And when he was unable to fit a victim to that fantasy, he went back to a previous crime scene, he took his significant item along, and sat there and fantasized about the crime he committed there maybe a month before. He told us he had the same sexual stimulation that he had on the night he did the crime. Berkowitz isn't the only one who told us that.

Now this is an extremely important piece of information to give a policeman: that maybe if you have a serial killer working in an area, you might want to look at those previous crime scenes. He may come back.

What killers like to do is, at a later time, relive the crime. The fantasy started and was fulfilled, and now I have it again. You know, we look back on our fond memories and say, Hey, that was great. Killers take trophies from the scene. That's my conquest. I dominated that person. I controlled. I was God.

The serial killer takes a trophy. The inadequate personality takes a souvenir.

Offenders have told us that they will take a piece of jewelry from the female victim, take it home, and give it to their wives or girlfriends. And when they were going to make love to them, they would have the wife or girlfriend wear that piece of jewelry so they could fantasize about the killing while they were having sexual intercourse.

Serial killers love to drive. Every single one of them says it. They'll just get in that car and drive for hours, days. They'll put eighty thousand miles on a car in a year. They always say, "I just feel free when I'm driving." And they cruise, looking for the right victim. Serial killers always look for a specific type of victim.

They drive around with bodies in their cars. Think how you would feel if you were driving around with a dead body in your car. Most people would be nervous—What if a cop stops me? But with serial killers, it's not a dead body. It's a piece of paper. They're taking out the garbage.

Many times, with serial killers, we find the abduction site and we find the dump site. We may never find the kill site. The person who dumps the body after he's killed in some other place is a very difficult person to track down.

We all like comfort. A killer feels this way. He wants to be in an area where he's comfortable. So if the body is from point A and is taken to point B and you can tell from the crime scene that he spent a significant amount of time at point B, that's telling you he's comfortable there. He may live, work, or frequent the area of point B, so when you start developing suspects, you start looking *here* rather than point A, because this guy is going to be comfortable here.

If you're a killer, you're not going to take the victim or the body someplace that you're unfamiliar with. It's that comfort zone. We all want it. Killers want even more of it.

There's a new trend around the country. Real estate saleswomen are getting murdered. A guy sees the real estate ads in the paper with the little pictures of all the firm's salespeople. One of them fits his type. "Hmmmm, I think I'll see Sally." He calls the firm and asks for Sally. "Hi, Sally, I just moved here. I've got a high-stress job, and I need to get away. I'm looking for an old farmhouse way out in the country. How about if I meet you tonight at six?"

Where's she going? To a deserted farmhouse. Who's she going with? No one. Is she going to go? *Yes.* More and more of them are turning up dead.

We know what serial killers look like at the time of the killing. All the survivors and eyewitnesses to these murders say the same thing: "His face was emotionless. It had no expression. It was as though he was in a trance. His voice had absolutely no expression."

There was one couple out West that survived a serial killer. They knew this man; he had worked for the wife for years and had murdered others—this time, he decided to pick on them. The wife later said, "I looked right at him. I *knew* this man. But he looked different. He had no expression on his face. He kept talking in a monotone, over and over. He'd say things like, 'I've got to close the blinds. Now I've got to turn the lights off.' " It was like he was reading from a script, going over a mental checklist that he'd already gone over time and time again.

The typical face of this kind of killer is rigid and set at the time of the killing. They'll stare right through you. That's the scariest part.

The serial killer will read *everything* he can about his crimes. He may return to the scene, contact the family, the media—he loves it. When police talk to the media, they should know that the serial killer's watching. You never want to say you've exhausted all leads. You want to keep this guy nervous.

Be very skeptical of people who want to volunteer for the search party. The killer will often join up. He'll offer his help. It's a thrill for him. He's pushing that edge. He's thinking, Look at those stupid coppers. *I'm* the one who did it, and they don't even know.

Everybody says serial killers *want* to get caught. Bullshit. They don't want to get caught—they just want to push it a little closer to the edge each time. The more fearful something is, the better they like it. It's like a psychic oxygen for them.

They don't just suddenly stop killing. They don't say, "Okay, now I've got twenty-two dead girls. I reached my limit." They keep going till they're arrested or they die.

With serial murders, before the killer is caught, what people always say is, "What bizarre person did this? This guy's got to have one eye, he's got to be covered in green slime and have a hump on his back." And what do they look like? They look like Ted Bundy.

Most of your bizarre killers, when they're discovered, it's always interesting. You can go back through old newspapers, and the reporters always go around and see what the next-door neighbors say. And what do the next-door neighbors say? "He was the nicest, finest person. Great kid. I don't believe it. He was so nice. Real quiet."

That's what we want from neighbors. We want a very quiet neighbor. And if he's a quiet neighbor, he's the greatest neighbor in the world, even though he's killed thirty-three boys and buried them underneath the crawl space in his house.

And the funny thing about the newspapers is, *always,* under the picture of the killer, there's always the quote from a neighbor: "Nicest guy in the world."

There are always signs with these bizarre killers. There are *lots* of signs. But you know what? We're way too busy with our own lives to notice. We feel, As long as my neighbor doesn't bother me, I don't really care what he does. We don't care about signs.

Take for example, the Vampire Killer, this guy out in Sacramento in the mid-seventies. He had eviscerated, cut women, taken their blood out, drank their blood, bathed in the blood— real, real bizarre behavior. One of the things the neighbors said: "But he was a real nice, quiet individual. He was a nice kid. He had a real knack for animals. See, we gave him the little stray kittens and dogs from the neighborhood, and he must have trained them very well, because we never heard them after that." And they never heard the little kittens and puppies after he took them in because he killed them.

I have almost no faith in the ability of the psychiatric profession to tell me if somebody is safe. I don't know if psychiatrists for the defense are incompetent or if they're attempting to maintain a facade to collect their check—they're just terrible; they're constantly releasing *maniacs* into society. They have the worst track record of any profession.

With forensic psychiatrists, guilt gets lost in a maze. They always seem to forget what the victim looked like after the murder. You know why? Because they don't *want* to see what the victim looked like. Go to a crime scene? They never go to a crime scene. They don't even want to see the pictures.

But they testify on behalf of the accused—"Poor guy, he's been deprived since he was a kid, victim of child abuse—all kinds of problems." I can understand that.

But there's another side. There's the victim. You know, this guy, disadvantaged youth that he is, is still *breathing*. The victim isn't. They seem to forget that.

Everybody worries about the rat's rights. You see two old people in court, victims of a robbery. The lawyers are ready to send the old people home and make them come back a dozen or more times to satisfy the rat's rights. Victims have no rights.

Murder trials. The defense attorneys always ask about the interview room: "Do you have a bed in there? Did you bring him food? Did you offer him cigarettes? How many times did you take him to the bathroom?" You might as well be a hotel bellboy.

This is common. The lawyer for the defense pleads Not Guilty. He attacks the arrest, the lineup, et cetera. If he loses these, he pleads Guilty.

This is outright chicanery. What is the lawyer saying? He's saying, "This is a game. This guy is guilty as hell, and now that you didn't buy the Not Guilty ploy, I'll change the plea." The guy gets twenty, and he's out in three.

I handled a murder where a guy took his pregnant wife and their two-year-old kid to the lakefront and shot and killed them.

He shoots his wife and baby. They fall into the lake. He grabs his baby he had just shot in the head out of the lake, runs up the beach, flags down a squad car—"Oh my God! My baby's shot! Help me! Help me!"

He came up with a horseshit story that some guys were stalking him. He says as he was coming out of the house, he sees them in a van. Any normal person would go back home or go to a busy area. What does he do? He goes to an isolated area, the Foster Avenue Beach. He pretended he was shot too. He was shot right in his jacket where he had a picture of his wife and kid with a paperweight right underneath. You know how you carry your kids' pictures around with a paperweight attached.

He confesses. A year later, he's sitting there in court—he

looks better than the lawyer—he's got all his stories ready, because they've had the police reports for a year. They get our reports for a year before trial—it's like the Bears giving their game plan to the Vikings ahead of time.

His lawyer brings in a motion—"He had wet clothes on. He was cold. You never allowed him to change." They're making us the bad guys when this scum killed his baby. The lawyer puts it before the jury: "It was Christmas Eve. His wife and baby are dead. They put him in a room. His clothes all wet and cold." And the jury's going for it. Yeah, yeah, the poor guy.

There was no bullet in *his* head. He was a convicted thief, a robber, a sometimes con artist. Now, he's got a *new* role, that of attorney. At the trial, he's neat, he's dressed, he's looking around, taking notes, jumping up—he should be sitting with his head bent; if he's innocent, he'd be in grief. It's all a game.

There *are* evil people in the world. People tell you they're sick, they need help. I hear that all the time. The ones who tell you that—*they're* sick to think it. People say killers need help. They don't need help. They need to be locked up.

We've seen parents kill kids because they wouldn't stop crying.

Within two days, on the twenty-second and twenty-third of December, I saw two murders of children. One mother shot the four-year-old because she wouldn't stop crying. The next day, we got another call. A mother threw her baby against the wall because the baby wouldn't stop crying. The baby burst like a ripe melon. I couldn't believe it. Merry Christmas.

Any cop would be a liar if he tells you, "I never care." There's got to be some escape, even if it's sitting in a bar till 4:00 A.M. telling war stories. I've handled cases where I cried with the families of the victims. The day that I can't feel is the day I know I've got to quit.

I once handled a case where a woman lost her husband and her son in the same morning. At 5:00 A.M., she was in bed and

heard some noise upstairs. She woke up her husband—"Go upstairs and look." The husband went up and confronted a burglar. The burglar stabbed him to death. The wife hears the
struggle and runs across the hall to get her son—"Jimmy,
Jimmy, help Dad." The son goes upstairs, and *he* gets stabbed.
I spent a lot of time crying with that lady. Those are the cases
you walk through walls for.

I had a recruit with me one time, she cried like a baby at this.
We had a guy, he was watching his girlfriend's baby. And the
baby was crying. He couldn't stand the noise and he kept telling
the baby to be quiet, and the baby wasn't and he drowned it—
this was a six-month-old baby—in a bucket of water. Aside
from the mother crying, I had a female partner that was crying.
My partner at the time. I told her, "If you carry on like this at
every scene that you come up to, you better go get another job
because you're definitely gonna end up seeing a psychiatrist for
yourself because you just can't take it personal like this all the
time." She was relatively new on the job and it was probably
her first homicide that she had seen.

I guess I'm cold. I had no feelings whatsoever. It's not nice to
look at . . . I *did* have some feelings—it's not nice to look at, but
I'm not gonna let it bother me.

You can't take it personally, because then it's gonna affect
you. And that's the hardest thing to differentiate—it's somebody else; it's not me. One time I had two friends killed on the
job. That *was* personal, and I did cry. But if it's somebody else,
you have to keep that away.

Near the end of February 1974, a call came in. Two men shot
in a tavern near Foster and Ravenswood. Went in there. There
were two policemen that I worked with lying in a pool of blood
on the floor. I had had dinner with them half an hour before.
They were both killed, and they were guys I worked with. I
cried like a baby.

Up until that time, my first four years on the job, it was a big
game, party time, and I thought this was the world, you know.

And February the twenty-seventh, 1974, reality came in. It wasn't a game anymore.

They used to have cops working Homicide exclusively. No right-thinking manager in industry would ever allow an individual to be faced with that kind of trauma. Old Irish Catholic cops would go to Communion every day. Others would climb into the bottle. Anybody that's spent time exclusively on murders becomes almost paranoid.

When I worked Homicide, I was living in a nice neighborhood. But I wouldn't take out the garbage without my gun. I'd be at home, reading a book, and I kept my pistol next to me. Because they were never going to get *me*.

I think the absolute hardest thing that we have to do is notify somebody that their child is dead. You go to the house and, you know, "Why are you here, Officers?"; it looks like they're waiting for this person to be home. That's really rough when you go there and you're thinking, How the hell do I tell these people? How am I going to do this? You know, you're walking up the steps, and you see it's a regular house like you live in. And then they answer the door, and they're not expecting anything; you know, it's just, "Hi, what are you guys—can I help you? Come on in." How do you start? That's the hardest part of the job.

We had a death notification years ago in a very affluent neighborhood to a mother that her child had died at school. He just suddenly collapsed in the gym and died of God knows what. They called us out to the school just to kind of check it out. And he was dead, and we went and we told the mother.

That mother—she didn't say anything. She went into the other room and picked up her baby, a young baby, and just started walking back and forth across the apartment. She wouldn't acknowledge us or anything else. She simply walked back and forth across the apartment. And we, we didn't know what to do. We ultimately got some of the neighbors and family to come over. Someone fainted; someone started crying. But she just picked up the baby and paced back and forth. That was it.

It was like she blocked out every other thing and every other person. She blocked everything else out. You could have walked in that apartment and taken everything out of there, and she wouldn't have known.

We found the body of a girl along the tracks. Her face was just a pulp. Who is she? We put the story on the news, asking for information. A guy calls, saying the description of the dress matches a dress worn by his niece. We get her address from the uncle and talk to the mother. She hasn't seen her for a week, not since she went with her boyfriend.

We talk to the boyfriend. He knows nothing. Finally, he tells us what happened. He's with her, they go out, they go back to his place, he has sexual relations with her. That's all fine. Then his buddy comes in, and he says, "Take care of my buddy too." She won't. He grabs a pitchfork and pitchforks her in her face and all over her body.

Then he and his buddy take her out and dump her. To make sure she won't be identified, they take a block of cement and bash her face in. So there we were, with this pulp.

He felt perfectly justified. "She should have had sex with my buddy."

My first homicide case, a death investigation, a baby. I was called to the hospital. "Where's the baby at?" They point me to a room. I walk in the room and here's this little baby, a little two-year-old, laying naked on a gurney. Its eyes were open. It was stiff and dead.

I'm looking at this little body—there are marks and marks and marks all over it. It was hard to find any spots on the body that *didn't* have scars or welts. There were burn marks from cigarettes. Marks from a belt—you could see scars left from the horseshoe mark on the belt and from the tongue of the belt buckle. Welts—we later learned they were from a cord on an electric coffee maker.

The baby's eyes were wide open. And every time I'd walk around and look at it from different angles, it looked like it was staring right at me. I walk around the room, around the gurney, examining the body, looking at him, and it looked like his eyes were following me. It was eerie. I tell you, it brings you back to reality. You relate it back to your own kids—how could somebody do this? How could *anybody* do this?

Then I go to talk to the doctor. I ask him, "Can you tell me what was the major injury here? What was the cause of death?" The doctor looks at me and says, "This little guy just gave up. He just said, I quit."

Then we started the homicide investigation. We go out to the house. This was a HUD bi-level, about ten years old, fairly new. And when you got to the front door, the stench was enough to knock you down.

We go in. There's no electricity; we're in there with our flashlights. We find a room that has a toilet completely ripped out. You figure, this is a violent home, it's nothing for them to rip out a toilet bowl with all the other stuff going on.

We go upstairs. One of the rooms—the stench was unbelievable—I've investigated stinkers, bodies that aren't discovered for five days, a week, and they blow up and bust; the smell from them leaves you gagging—this was worse. This room with the stench was the room where they defecated. They'd go and shit on the floor and shovel the shit into a corner.

We go in another room. Here are plastic milk bottles, gallon milk bottles. Hundreds of them in the room. And they're all filled with urine.

The family was downstairs. We got everybody together, the mother, the father, and two other kids. The father told us what happened. He said the baby knocked over one of the urine bottles, and he chastised the baby by beating it with a cord. They told us that after the beating, the baby crawled under the Hide-a-bed. He didn't come out for a long time. They finally looked under there—the baby was under there, dead, so they brought him to the hospital.

The father's explaining this to us. He didn't see anything wrong with the corporal punishment he'd inflicted on this baby. He told us, "You got to discipline them."

You stand there and you listen to stuff like this, and you just want to beat the living dogshit out of the guy. They're always talking about police brutality, but you see these things, and you want to beat the shit out of the guy. But you have to use restraint. I worked Homicide for five years. I finally had to get out, I couldn't take it, I had so many hatreds building up. Boy, does it get to you.

We never close a case. We just solved two homicides from 1976. There are cases you carry with you to the grave; you're always thinking about them.

The last thing you ever want any killer to know is that you're at a dead end. You want to keep that sphincter muscle tight. You want to keep him looking over his shoulder, you want to keep him thinking that when that knock comes, they're coming for me. Because if you let them get comfortable, he's gonna figure—"I got away with murder."

My thought when I came on this job was that nobody should get away with murder. I still believe that. I just believe—there's a lot of crime that happens, and people get away with crime daily. Nobody should get away with murder.

Violent Crimes:
Contributing Police Officers

SERGEANT ED ADORJAN, Area Six Violent Crimes. Adorjan has worked Homicide for twenty-three years, as a supervising sergeant in Area Six for the past eleven, and before that, as a homicide detective in the old Homicide Unit. Adorjan joined the CPD in 1959, worked Vice and Gambling in Eighteen, was assigned to the CPD's first tactical unit in 1963, and became a homicide detective in 1967.

YOUTH OFFICER AL AUGUSTINE, Area Five. Augustine is a twenty-year veteran of the CPD. His first two years on the force were spent working the wagon in the Fourteenth District. He then joined the Area Six Task Force, Special Operations, till 1980, and worked patrol and tac in Sixteen, Eleven, and Twenty-three. Augustine was promoted to youth officer in 1989.

CAPTAIN THOMAS J. CRONIN, Fifteeth District. Cronin was selected by the CPD in 1985 to be trained in criminal assessment and profiling by the FBI's National Center for the Analysis of Violent Crime. Cronin joined the force in 1969, worked patrol in the Thirteenth District until 1971, when he became a crime analyst. In 1973, Cronin was promoted to detective and worked Robbery in Area Two for two years and Robbery in Area Five for two years. In 1977, Cronin made sergeant, and in 1985, became a lieutenant. Cronin, who has a master's degree in social justice, is one of only twenty police investigative profilers in the United States.

DETECTIVE BOB ELMORE, Area Six Violent Crimes. Elmore joined the CPD in 1977, worked patrol in Fourteen and Twenty-three for one-and-a-half years, made detective in 1979, and was assigned to Area Six Robbery. Elmore has been a violent crimes detective since 1981.

COMMANDER FRANK J. FLANAGAN, retired. Commander of Homicide, 1961–70, director of Chicago Crime Lab, 1970–77, chief investigator, Medical Examiner's Office, 1977–85. Captain Flanagan headed Homicide longer than any commanding officer in the history of the CPD. His thirty-year career encompassed investigative work in the old Hit-and-Run Unit from 1947 to 1951, training in the Army Criminal Investigations Division, and working as a homicide detective from 1951 through 1961.

DETECTIVE CHARLIE FORD, Area Six Violent Crimes. Ford specializes in robbery decoy work and has been with Area Six Violent Crimes since 1981. He worked as a robbery detective in Area Four from 1977–81, in the Mass Transit Unit as a robbery decoy from 1974–77, and in the Area Six Task Force from 1971–74. Ford joined the force in 1968 and spent three years in patrol.

DETECTIVE JIM GILDEA, Area Six Violent Crimes. Gildea has been a robbery and homicide detective for the past twelve years. Before that, Gildea spent eight-and-a-half years working Special Operations and a year and a half on patrol. Gildea joined the police in 1966 as a cadet and went on patrol in 1969.

DETECTIVE PAUL HAGEN, Area Six Violent Crimes. Hagen joined the police in 1971, was on patrol for eight years in the Eighteenth District, became a detective in 1979, and was assigned to Burglary on the West Side. Two months later, Hagen went on to Sex Crimes North and worked in the Sex Crimes Unit till it was disbanded in 1981. Hagen has been in Area Six Violent Crimes for nine years.

LIEUTENANT TED HEAD, field lieutenant, Seventeenth District. Head is a thirty-year veteran of the CPD, working patrol, TUF Squad (robbery decoy detail), Vice, General Assignment Unit detective, and as supervising sergeant in the Nineteenth and Twentieth Districts. Head was promoted to Lieutenant in 1984 and has been field lieutenant in Seventeen since 1986.

DETECTIVE TOM JOHNSON, Area Six Violent Crimes. Johnson became a police officer in 1976, and worked patrol and tac for five years before becoming a detective assigned to Violent Crimes.

DETECTIVE SCOTT KEENAN, Area Six Violent Crimes. Keenan became a police officer in 1971, worked eight years on patrol in Twenty-three, spent one year in the Preventive Programs Divisions, became a detective in 1978, and was assigned to Area Five Burglary. In 1980, Keenan joined the Sex Crimes Unit. Keenan has worked Area Six Violent Crimes since 1981.

LIEUTENANT JIM NEMEC, commanding officer, Crime Scene Processing Unit, Chicago Crime Lab. Nemec, who joined the CPD in 1965, has been with the Crime Lab since 1968, where he was an evidence technician for two years, worked with the Mobile Unit for eight years, and served as Crime Lab watch commander till 1985. Nemec has headed the Crime Scene Processing Unit since 1985.

DETECTIVE TED O'CONNOR, FBI/CPD Organized Crime Task Force. O'Connor was promoted to detective and was assigned to Homicide three years after joining the force in 1967. O'Connor and Adorjan were partners in the old Homicide Unit, under Captain Flanagan, from 1973 to 1978. In 1978, O'Connor went undercover in an operation targeting Outfit-controlled businesses, then into the DEA Narcotics Task Force for five years. O'Connor then served as the sex crimes analyst for the CPD and as administrative aide to the deputy chief of detectives. Since 1988, O'Connor has been part of the Joint FBI/CPD Task Force investigating unsolved Mob hits.

DETECTIVE CAREY ORR, Area Six Violent Crimes. Orr came on the CPD in 1978, was a patrol officer in Fifteen until 1980, when he was promoted to detective and assigned to Area Six Violent Crimes.

DETECTIVE BILL PEDERSEN, Organized Crime Division. Pedersen worked for six years as an Area Two violent crimes detective before joining the Organized Crime Division, Asset Forfeiture Unit, in 1989. Pedersen, who joined the CPD in 1968, has worked in Auto Theft, the Special Investigations Unit, and for ten years (from 1973–83) as a narcotics detective.

LIEUTENANT CINDY PONTORIERO, field lieutenant, Twenty-first District. Pontoriero, the first woman detective in the CPD, was assigned to Area Five Homicide in 1972, to Sex Crimes North in 1980, and to Area Five Violent Crimes in 1981. Pontoriero has twenty-three years on the force and seventeen years' experience as a violent crimes detective. After being promoted to sergeant, Pontoriero served as Area Six sex crimes coordinator from 1985 through 1988. In January 1989, she was assigned to Detective Division Headquarters, and she was promoted to lieutenant in 1990. Pontoriero joined the force as a policewoman in 1967.

SERGEANT TOM REYNOLDS, Major Accident Investigations Unit. Reynolds, who joined the force in 1965, spent nine years as a robbery and burglary detective in Areas Four, Five, and Six before being promoted to sergeant and assigned to Major Accident.

YOUTH OFFICER ROBERT J. SIMANDL, Area Four. Simandl is a nationally recognized expert on satanic cults and satanic crimes who has lectured extensively to police officers across the country concerning the detection of ritualistic crime. Simandl has been a police officer for twenty-three years. Simandl served as a youth officer and in the

Task Force before working as a gang crimes specialist for the past seventeen years. Simandl became a youth officer in 1989.

DETECTIVE JAMES SPENCER,   Area Six Violent Crimes. Spencer has been on the force since 1971; he worked as a patrol officer in the Fifteenth District till 1973 and then was assigned to Special Operations in Areas Five and Six for seven years. Spencer has been in Area Six Violent Crimes since 1980.

OFFICER EDWARD TANSEY, SR.,   retired. Tansey, a police officer from 1951 until his retirement in 1986, worked both patrol and the wagon.

DETECTIVE LAWRENCE THEZAN,   Area Six Violent Crimes. Thezan joined the force in 1973, worked patrol and tac in Twenty till 1975, then worked tac in Twenty-three and Twenty until he was promoted to detective and assigned to Violent Crimes in 1981.

DETECTIVE TONY VILLARDITA,   Area Six Violent Crimes. Villardita came on the force in 1978, worked in patrol in Twenty-three till he was promoted to robbery detective in 1980, and has been with Area Six Violent Crimes since 1981.

SERGEANT JEFFREY WILSON,   Twentieth District. Wilson joined the force in 1980 and was assigned to patrol in Twenty-four. In 1981, Wilson went to Twenty-three, where he worked tac for six years. In 1988, following his promotion to sergeant, he was assigned to the Eleventh District. Wilson came to Twenty in 1990. He will receive his law degree in 1991.

SEX CRIMES

A good portion of rapists actually hope that halfway through the rape, the woman is going to look up and say, "You are the greatest, and we're going to run off into the sunset and live happily ever after." Now that's just not your normal way to go out and try to impress a woman. That's just not going to happen. But since it didn't happen this time, the fantasy has got to continue. And the cycle continues. Maybe the next one, and the next one, and the next one. Where do you end? Where do you end?

Captain Tom Cronin,
CPD criminal profiler

Everybody knows a pedophile. They just don't know that he is one. *You've* come in contact with a pedophile. I guarantee it. There is nobody that doesn't have somebody in their life, that they've dealt with, that *is* a pedophile. There is no profession it doesn't touch. People don't like to believe this, but the level of involvement is so much higher than people think. Let me put it this way: Within any single square mile in any city in America, there's someone looking to have sex with a child.

–Sergeant Sam Christian,
Special Investigations Unit

Sex crimes may be the least straightforward of all crimes. Murder usually carries a clear motive, as do armed robbery, arson, bombing, sex-for-hire, drug buys. But the motives behind aggravated criminal sexual assault of adults are usually embedded in a tortured psyche. What passes as motive behind the sexual exploitation of children, encompassing child molestation, prostitution, and pornography, pales beside the garish horror of adults using children for sexual pleasure and profit.

Sex crimes are difficult to fathom. So are the offenders, the rapists who jump from behind bushes or appear at women's bedsides or con victims into accompanying them into a situation that could lead to rape/murder, or the child molesters and pimps and pornographers who find countless ways of trading on trust. They're difficult to fathom because the horror of the offense leads people to suspect some kind of monster as the rapist or molester. Sometimes, it *is* a monster, the proverbial "Mr. Stranger Danger." As one sex crimes investigator defines it: "Mr. Stranger Danger—Mr. Unknown, Mr. Abductor or Invader of some type, the guy who drags you off the street into the car or drags you off the street into the gangway, the guy who climbs into your bedroom window. Somebody you have no previous experience with, and it kind of indicates a random selection. . . ." But many more times, with both those who rape adults and molest children, especially with child molesters, the offender is someone you would never suspect.

Three segments of the CPD are involved in ferreting out sex offenders: the Youth Division, Violent Crimes, whose detectives are responsible for handling homicide, robbery, rape, and child abuse and molestation cases, and the Special Investigations Unit, formed expressly to target the sexual abuse and exploitation of children through "proactive" investigations—the SIU officers conduct undercover operations on child molesters, those who arrange child prostitution, and child pornographers. Proactive is the only way to go in uncovering this most secretive, virulent crime, says one SIU investigator: "Our opinion is that you should go out and find the crime. What better way to prove the crime than to get it in-progress or to follow somebody home and have him go to bed with a kid? My opinion is it's the only way to do it."

All these cops face what most people, and many cops, can't face. "It's the nature of the crime that people don't want to know about it," says a violent crimes detective. "When you work sex crimes, that's about the only specialty that nobody, including other coppers, wants to hear about. They think it's too revolting."

The sexual victimization of children appalls everyone—civilians, cops, criminals. "There's a respect among criminals for a good stickup man, a good burglar, a good bank robber," says a homicide detective. "But even among the worst offenders, child molesters are taboo. The short eyes do very poorly in prison. Because even your stickup man has a family."

Another cop, who's been a homicide detective for the past fifteen years, talks about his reaction to a CPD sex seminar: "They had taped interviews with child molesters. I've seen some of the most brutal things human beings can do to each other. This is worse. It got to the point where I thought, I don't want to see any more of this shit. They showed us two hours of slides, victimized children—it was like, Enough. This is too much. This is worse than homicide. At least with homicide, there's some passion, some reason, and then it's over. This goes beyond—it's evil. They told us one out of ten fathers abuses his children. I look around at my neighbors now—which one? They showed one child molester, this was out in California, they asked him when he started abusing his little girl. 'The day she came home from the hospital,' he said. It's too much."

Those who work sex crimes call it a "tough crime." Tough to figure, tough to prove, and endlessly tough on the victims. . . .

My partner and I investigated a case one time involving a rapist who was just drop-dead good-looking. He looked like Mark Harmon, only taller.

This guy was from Michigan. He grabbed a woman on the street—she was waiting in her car like at two, three in the morning for her boyfriend—he grabbed her on the street in her car, he raped her, he vaginally and orally assaulted, and left her in the car. He beat her so badly she was put in the hospital.

One of the people in the neighborhood saw the guy and wrote down the license number of his car. Turned out to be an out-of-state license number. My partner ran the license plate, got the name, called up the town, and found out that this guy had just been arrested for rape in Michigan, a date-rape kind of situation.

Now this guy was a graduate in engineering from a Big Ten school, he had been captain of the swim team and now had a job with a major auto company as an engineer. This guy was drop-dead good-looking. Not the kind of guy you'd think would have to grab a girl off the street and rape her.

And that's the trial tactic he used. He came to court, and he had a beautiful girlfriend. And she sat behind him throughout the trial. Our victim was a stewardess who was articulate and intelligent and came across that way.

But the jury got so confused on this, the verdict was Not Guilty on the rape, Not Guilty on the deviate sexual assault, Not Guilty on the aggravated battery—but Guilty on unlawful restraint. That verdict was the result of people's inability to think that this all-American, captain of the swim team, good-looking kind of guy is capable of that.

The popular misconception is that adult rape is about sex. It isn't. It's about power. So the handsome rapist's subliminal defense was, to the jury, "Look at this. I don't need rape." But once you understand rape is about power, then you understand this person obviously doesn't need to do it for sex; he needs to do it for power.

Rape is about anger, power, control, the need to humiliate somebody. It's not sex-driven. Many times, the rapist is also having consensual sex while he's going out raping. Usually, it's not the sex that delights them; it's the sense of power they get over the victim. With some rapists, they're not there for sex. They're there to inflict pain.

* * *

We had one sadistic rapist who brought a script with him into his rapes—he had the woman's lines all written out ahead of time. He fantasized this entire thing down to the script.

This guy had it down; he had certain names he wanted the woman to call his private parts: "Big Henry" or "Big Jake" or some stupid macho thing. Then the woman had to very specifically state what she wanted to do—obviously, she didn't want to do these things, but he wrote things that she had to recite back to him, usually in very graphic and vulgar terms. He'd say things like "What are you gonna do?" and then he'd show her her line "I want to suck your cock," and then he'd say, "Why?" and then he'd show her "Because I love the great big thing," and things like that. It was all written out. And if they missed their lines, he'd give them a crack, cause them pain.

He knew what he wanted, and he knew the responses he wanted. He knew what the questions were, but his victims didn't know what the answers were—this was his fantasy, remember?—so he wrote it out for them.

Old women get raped. They're targets. Some rapists pick on old women because they're easy victims. Other rapists pick on old women because they're a symbolic victim. Say a guy's grandmother has just gone into the hospital—he lives with Granny, and he's angry at her for leaving him and maybe for dying. He might go and rape an old woman because he's mad at Granny.

There's different types of rapists. The anger/punish rapist. Eight to 10 percent of rapists. He's not there for the sex; he's there to punish women for his own inadequacies or for whatever—things gone wrong. Things are bad in his life because of women.

That's, many times, the rape that happens at ten in the morning, in broad daylight. Because within twenty-four to seventy-two hours prior to the rape, he's had some significant stressor. It could be somebody died, or somebody goes into the hospital and nobody's there to fix my cookies and milk after work or fix my Campbell's soup. He's frustrated. So he goes out, projects that anger on somebody else.

This guy does the blitz attack. This is the guy who coldcocks a woman with a brick, leaving her dead. And she's just at the wrong place at the wrong time.

The date rapist, the "power-assertive" rapist, that's the guy who goes out and *tonight's the night.* It's about 8 to 10 percent of rapists. He's a sly, slick, smooth-talking s.o.b. The woman may have dated him three or five times before, or it may just be the woman he's with that night. He figures, I spend thirty dollars on you, and guess what, baby, you're gonna give it up.

This guy has a definite personality. His profile is he's self-centered, smooth with women, a drinker, very jealous, very possessive—he'll never let a woman break off a relationship; if she does, he'll go to great lengths to get her back so *he* can break it off; he's athletic, has a macho occupation, but just at the entry level. Usually, he doesn't use a weapon in his assaults: his fist, his manhood, is his weapon. In his mind, assaulting women is good for him. It makes him feel good about himself.

This is the last guy you'd bring in. He's looking good, dressing well. His defense is always—"Hey, do I look like a rapist?"

Sadistic rapists are a very small percentage of rapists, about 2 percent of them. They con women into going with them a lot of times; they usually like to keep the victim for an extended time, because the sadistic rapist has all these things he's gonna do to them, the victim. And more than likely, he's gonna cause such severe injuries to the victim that she's probably going to die. Many times, this starts out as a rape and turns into a homicide because the sadist doesn't know when to stop. The fear that comes back to him from the victim carries him away.

We had a real scary one. It was an incredible story, and, initially, when the press called and stuff, *they* were skeptical—"What do you mean, she got grabbed off the street? What do you mean?"

There was a woman in her early twenties waiting for the bus at Chicago and Halsted, she was coming home from a friend's, about eleven at night. A car pulled up, three guys got out and grabbed her, brought her into the car—one sexually assaulted her in the car—then they brought her over to an abandoned apartment in one of the projects. And then she was gang-raped by about thirty-five people.

I mean, the way she described it, it was really humiliating. They had her on a couch and they were selling her like for a dollar and cigarettes and stuff. The weird part about it was there were real young boys participating; they were making comments about her vagina, that it looked like a cat or something, like they had never seen one before. And one guy would put his penis in her mouth and another one would be putting his hand in her vagina—and laughing it up at the same time. And there would be a constant—dozens of people in the apartment—in and out, in and out.

What was really strange about it, I mean, other than all the usual horror involved, was that there were so many participants. And it was a thing where the word was getting around the entire building—"Go down to Apartment 304"—and all the younger kids in the building were in there watching, and the older guys would throw them out, and they had to come up with money.

The kicker is they bring her outside and they slit her wrists. We found the blood. I don't know what that was supposed to do—scare her? kill her? The cuts on her wrist didn't turn out to be exceptionally deep.

Arrests were made on it, but we couldn't get all of them. She couldn't identify all of them.

Here's the real terror of it. It was some time later when we talked to her again. She said she couldn't walk down the street, because every time she'd see a black guy, she'd think that was one of the guys who raped her—because there were so many, because she couldn't ID them. She was sitting in the office one time; I didn't recognize her, because she had dyed her hair. So *they* wouldn't recognize her.

I don't even like to think about that one.

Most rapists, a good 80 percent of them, are what they used to call the "gentleman rapist." They now call them the "power-reassurance rapist." But when we say the "gentleman rapist," we don't mean we think they're gentlemen. It's how they think of *themselves,* it's what they're looking for—they're looking for love, appreciation—doing it all the wrong ways. This is the guy who rapes because he's got problems with masculinity and he looks to rape to reassure himself he's a man. But he's not out to hurt anyone. He uses little or no force, maybe mild slaps to intimidate, but not to hurt.

He doesn't think he's hurting anyone by what he does; he doesn't see what he does as hurtful.

A male nurse, in a city out East. There were a series of rapes in a particular neighborhood, three or four of them; same general description of the offender, but the police hadn't caught him.

One night, the local hospital, about twelve-thirty, change of shifts. The male nurse is leaving, and one of the female nurses is being accosted in the parking lot. She's really being beaten by this guy. The male nurse goes to her aid and thwarts this guy's attempt at raping her, and holds him for the police. There's a big ceremony honoring him because the other hospital employees are very proud he's one of these guys who really get involved.

Two days later, the male nurse was arrested for all those series of rapes. He was the other rapist. And what they asked him, they said, "My God, you know, here you are, you're a rapist, and you went to this woman's aid." And he said, "Well, I'd never want to hurt a woman."

He didn't perceive rape as hurting. They don't see themselves as really bad. They see themselves as misunderstood, and if only they could get to first base, so to speak, women would like them and appreciate them. Especially if they run into a woman who, for whatever reason, doesn't fight back and they don't have to use a lot of force. Then it's kind of a neat thing for him.

The gentleman rapist's M.O. is the surprise attack. He doesn't know how to talk to a woman; he doesn't know how to start a conversation. So he needs to jump out from behind the bushes or to surprise the woman at three o'clock in the morning when she's laying in bed.

The gentleman rapist, the power-reassurance rapist, says things that are polite to the woman during the rape—"You have beautiful breasts"; "You have lovely skin." And *he* wants compliments from the woman. "Tell me I'm better than your boyfriend"; "Tell me my penis is the biggest you've ever seen."

He wants the woman to get involved in the rape. He figures once she climaxes, hey, she'll realize he's *it.* He might perform cunnilingus, he'll try to cuddle, to fondle. He believes if he can get her to appreciate his act, she'll fall in love with him. Often, he'll say to her after the rape, "Gee, if we only could have met differently, we could have gotten along." And she's looking at him like, "Will you just get the hell out?"

Women often feel guilt after they're raped. And rapists know this. We have all kinds of victims' statements where the rapist, as he was leaving, tried to give the woman a little guilt: "You shouldn't live in this neighborhood"; "You shouldn't be alone in the laundry room"; "You shouldn't leave the back door open like that."

Most attempt rapes come from the power-reassurance rapist. On the same night, if he has one unsuccessful rape, he'll also go out and get one successful rape.

Many times, this kind of rapist returns to the same victim. You'll find women who have been raped twice in six months by the same guy. This rapist, if he's had a successful rape, and especially if he's had some dialog with the victim—on a night when he can't find a new victim, he'll come back to the previous victim.

We've asked rapists, "Why did you go back?" They say, "She was good, and, you know, when I was leaving the first time, she smiled at me." To him, that meant maybe there was a little

something there. When in reality, the victim was smiling because he was *leaving*—Thank God it's over; thank God this
creep's getting out of here.

Many times, if this guy has any friends at all, he brags about
the rape as if he had a date. He talks about all the sexual things
that he did—and he *did,* only it wasn't consensual sex.

In his mind, it *is* a date. Rape night is date night. He prepares
for his date. Usually, this guy is a crummy dresser, but on his
"date night," he does something different. He'll put on a nice
shirt. We'll talk to his mother; she'll say, "Oh, on that night, he
said he had a date." This guy doesn't bathe, but he throws on
a shirt, maybe throws on after-shave. Many times, his victims
report that the guy who raped them had a weird smell.

These are the guys who take souvenirs. If they take a photo-
graph, they'll *prove* they have a girlfriend to their friends—
"Here she is. Here she is. Here's my girlfriend. Put her in my
wallet."

The big hulk who tears his victim's clothes off and causes all
this damage and brutalizes her and things like that—that's the
perception of the rapist by the woman who has never been
raped. He's the guy who comes in with a knife and knocks her
down and beats her. That's what we see in movies, TV, and in
the literature. When, in fact, the majority of rapists are just the
opposite. They're really mostly very wimpy, geeky guys, very
inadequate Casper Milquetoast–type guys.

With rape, the first fear that a woman has is, "I'm going to
die." She fears that the guy who's just dragged her behind the
bushes is the guy who's gonna do all these really bad physical,
sexual things to her—and then he's gonna kill her.

That's one of the reasons, we think, that for years, many
rapes never got reported. Because when she was raped by a
power-reassurance rapist, who really wanted to hold her and
touch her and caress her and talk to her after it was over, that

it wasn't the guy who wanted to kill her and she's just *re-lieved*—and she just wants to forget it.

Women always fear that they're not going to be believed. Especially if they get raped by a power-reassurance rapist, who doesn't beat them up, who doesn't cause them physical injury. If they weren't beaten, or threatened with a gun or a knife, if the guy's mere presence did it, they feel nobody will believe them. And they almost wish that the guy *did* beat them up, because then people would believe her.

So the legitimate victim always exaggerates the force and minimizes the sex. Because they want to be believed. And they don't want people to know that the man made her perform fellatio or that he anally assaulted her or made her do one of those things she wouldn't ordinarily do. So she normally will try to minimize the sex and exaggerate the force.

We've had assault victims in automobiles that have enough presence of mind to touch everything that they can—they're touching the door handle, the seat, the bottom of the seat, the dash, the door surfaces, anything that's steel—leaving their fingerprints all over the inside of cars. We've had victims that've been in trunks that do the same thing.

We've had other people that just, "Hey, I couldn't tell you if the guy walked through the front door right now." We say, "Hey, this is the guy. He admitted it." "I don't know whether he did it or not." I don't know if they block it out.

Sometimes I'm surprised what some of the victims can remember, tell us what the people look like, and some just can't. And people think that just because somebody can't tell you too much about the person, hey, this has got to be bullshit. But it's not.

If somebody can remember *exactly* what they were doing, you kind of question it. I can't remember what *I* was doing three days ago, so you kind of question too *much* memory.

* * *

One of the most difficult cases we get is false allegation. We do get them. Maybe the man in the woman's life is leaving; maybe she wants to get attention. This makes it rough on all the legitimate victims.

If a woman *hasn't* been raped, if she's making a false allegation, how will she know what to say? She'll base it on what she's seen on TV and the movies. Rapes on TV and the movies are far more violent than real-life rapes. Force *is* used in real-life rapes, violent force, but many times just the presence of the man, just that threat, is enough to intimidate the woman.

She comes up with the accepted fantasy of the brutal rapist, but she has no injuries, no physical evidence to support her claim of this brutal attack.

Women will sometimes mutilate themselves in order to be believed. But they don't attack the really sensitive parts, their nipples or their vaginal area. Everything that they *do* attack is superficial and within a hand's reach. All the injuries will be on areas of the body that can be covered up—never on the face or hands.

Somebody should do some percentages on the number of sixteen-year-old girls that appear at about . . . noon . . . on Sunday—and state they were kidnapped off the street and held against their will all night and sexually assaulted. What percentage of them have been with their boyfriend or another person?

Let's just say that a lot of warning flags go up when the sixteen-year-old comes in with the girlfriend, who's supporting her.

There are certain things that after a while you learn are flags that will pop up. You don't want to eliminate these statements; you want to be very careful. But you'll want to ask them certain questions if A, they're a young girl, B, they're in there with their girlfriend, and C, they say they've been kidnapped off the street at some ridiculous place, like at State and Madison at noon.

"Didn't anyone happen to *see* this?" "Oh no! No. The intersection was clear!" They're not experienced enough to lie properly. "What did this guy look like?" "Oh—*big.*" Oh yeah, real big. And he abducted her and held her—"Where were you at?" "A house. Big house." "What color was the furniture?" "Didn't have any furniture." Can't describe anything that was in the house. "How'd you get there?" "In a car." "What did the car look like?" "*Big* car." "Old or new?" "Oh, *old.* Old, old. And *big.*" "Any damage on the car?" "I dunno."

We had one with a sixteen-year-old girl who had been out all night with her boyfriend. When she got home, her mother was very upset. She got it all out of her. So they came in and wanted to report the crime to the police. She was underage; her boyfriend was twenty-three.

It seemed like it was the mom's idea to prosecute. To establish this, I said to the victim, "Do you want to prosecute this guy and send him to jail?" She said, "No, but can you make him marry me?" Which is not like the typical response of the rape victim.

A true rapist is a serial rapist. It's not a onetime thing. And they don't change their act, fortunately for us.

When you look at serial offenders—serial rapists, serial killers—you have to look at both the M.O. and the ritual. The M.O. is done for safety; they get better as they go along. But the *ritual* is done for the offender's satisfaction. The M.O. might change, but the ritual stays the same.

You might get a rapist who has the wife tie up the husband so he's forced to watch the rape—that's the ritual, that's what he gets off on. But then he puts a teacup on the husband's back—that's the M.O., that's his safety. If the teacup rattles . . .

You always think of the rapist as operating under the cover of darkness. But there's a lot that just walk in there at eight o'clock in the morning and rape. So it's not like on Tuesday nights, when the moon is full. Your serial rapist has his own schedule. Maybe he works Mondays through Fridays, so he rapes everybody on his way home from work, because he's gotta be home in time for dinner.

With serial rapists, usually by the time we get them, you can look back through their rap sheets and you can see it coming. They usually start out with exposing themselves. That's the start of it. Some wienie waggers are harmless, but it goes both ways. With serial rapists, it starts with that and it progresses to peeping and then rape. You look at their sheets and you can just follow it down the line.

Most rapists start out as Peeping Toms. But that doesn't mean that all Peeping Toms end up as rapists. It works one way, but it doesn't work the other.

When they become rapists, the peeping part is more for intelligence-gathering than for sexual gratification; they'll get the sexual gratification later on. It graduates. At one point, the peeping is the gratification, where they can stand back and masturbate and that's it. Later on, when they go on to raping, their foreplay, if you want to call it that, is the peeping. It's good for intelligence—when does the husband leave, who does the woman live with, when is everybody else out. And it stimulates them.

The foreplay on a rape victim that's scouted out usually starts two weeks before the attack—the rapist sees the woman and spends a couple of weeks doing intelligence on her.

It becomes a second job with them. It's a serious occupation. They get very ritual about it; they get very precise about it. They've got it down to a science.

A lot of voyeurism goes on in the morning, not night, like most people think. Women are less conscious of the need to be wary in the morning—they'll walk around getting coffee while getting dressed and never think a guy might be outside their window watching them.

That's power for him—"I see you, and you don't know." They find that extremely stimulating.

We had a serial rapist, he was called the "Hooded Rapist" because his victims reported he wore a hooded sweatsuit, who used peeping inside high rises to select his victims. He's in jail now.

He was very sophisticated in casing and conducting surveillances on his victims prior to assaulting them.

The unusual aspect of this was, he used a mirror. What he had was a little piece of mirror. He would pick out apartment buildings that had some distance between the floor and the bottom of the door; in a lot of the newer buildings, the doors are flush with the floor, but in the older ones, a lot of times, they've been shaved, or they just weren't as cautious then, so there's a gap.

He'd be out in the hallway. And he'd stick this mirror under the door, and he could look in the apartment. He would see who was in there and what the deal was—he conducted extensive, long surveillances. He'd get into a lot of these apartments— women left their doors open an alarming number of times. You'd think these people were from Kansas, the way they acted.

He'd know something about these girls by his surveillances. He'd stay outside their doors, like for a couple of hours, listening to them talk on the phone; he'd know as much as someone who put a phone tap on them. He'd know when they were going on vacation, when they'd be coming back. He'd go in their apartment, look at their underwear and stuff.

He was in one girl's apartment twelve times before he decided to rape her. This was in the same building where he lived. He knew that when it was cold, her door would be locked, and when it was hot, her door would be open.

People are creatures of habit. She came home every night at six-thirty, and by seven o'clock she was in the shower. And he knew that. He would go downstairs, and he'd walk all through her bedroom and go through all the things that she just wore and were thrown in the hamper, in and out of her bedroom, and her drawers and her closet, while she was in the shower in the next room. One time, when she was in the shower, he watched her in the shower. He came back. He later told us, "I was in there twelve times. Each time, I thought, Aw, it's just not right this time."

This guy really showed criminal progression. In the very early rapes, he was using the cord from the venetian blinds to tie the victim up, to control her. One time, he used the cord from the electric blanket. Another one, he used one of the victim's scarves. After about the fourth or fifth one, he started bringing stuff. So he started maturing as a criminal; he started making sure—"I don't have to go into a house and worry about their not having any cords. I can bring my own. I have it." And he started bringing his own knife, and he started bringing his own cords. And when they caught him, he had his little rape kit. He had pre-cut lengths of rope, some masking tape, a knife, and his little sliver of mirror that he used for his peeping.

When they brought him in, he talked for hours. He wanted to talk about it. He started peeping when he was twelve; he was peeping when he was in the navy; almost lost his job because of peeping. He told us he took a lot of time and a lot of patience. He'd come back twenty times if he had to. He was persistent. He did it in his off-hours. Whenever regular people were off playing with their children, he'd be off playing with his mirror. Some people collect stamps, some people do ceramics, some people jog—this guy looks under doors with mirrors.

Serial rapists and serial killers like to take souvenirs from the scene with them. We had one offender, a serial rapist, who did several home invasions within a few months.

In each of these cases, he took something. We kind of had determined that this offender was either furnishing an apartment or he had a girlfriend. One time, he took a stuffed teddy bear. Another time, he took a VCR, then an answering machine. In one incident, the victim had some elegant clothing— he took that. So we knew that, if we ever found him, we were going to find these things.

He finally was apprehended. The detectives prepared a search warrant, listing all of the items taken from the victims. We went to the address he gave, which was his girlfriend's. And when we got to the apartment, as soon as you walked in, there was the teddy bear.

The girlfriend was there. We handed her the search warrant and explained why we were there, and she kept saying, "No, no. This can't be." I said, "Would you do me a favor? Look at this search warrant and tell me if he ever brought you any of these items." Then she went into "Oh my God."

Sadistic rapists are heavy into video, into recording their acts to replay later. There was a guy out West who was raping and killing women; they called me up and asked my thoughts on him. They obtained a search warrant for his house, and they found all these videotapes, but they were all commercial, store-bought videotapes, you know, *Bambi* and *The Longest Day.* There were over a hundred of them.

I strongly suggested that they have somebody who was working midnights, got nothing to do, sit down at a VCR, and fast-forward through all of them. And lo and behold, on about three of them, midway through the commercial movie was footage of rapes and murders this guy had committed—and videoed. What he'd do is flip the tape out of the machine, put a piece of Scotch tape over that tab stop, throw it back in there in his camcorder, and then record what he was doing. And then when he was finished, he'd pull the Scotch tape off the tab stop, and it would look like it was just a normal tape.

These were rapes and murders. The guy camcorded two homicides and a series of rapes he performed.

If somebody sees that one crime works—a guy is a little bit sick and he follows some girl because she strikes his fancy for one reason or another, and—it works—he hits her at the proper time, she either submits or he's very skillful in his overpowering of her—it works.

Then, all of a sudden, you've got a monster loose. Because he says, "Boy, this works. Hitting a girl in an elevator in a high-rise building at this time of day . . . boy, this works." And he gets more confident, he gets more calculating, he gets *better.*

Then you've got somebody who can sit back, wait a week or two, and hit again. Solving those cases are very difficult. You've got a monster on your hands.

Some are real conniving. We had a guy, he was a former high school teacher. He was a former navy guy, and he would go to Great Lakes Naval Base and hang around these areas where they had the recruits, kids from towns where they weren't familiar with the Chicago area. He'd go into bars, restaurants, this shopping mall around there where they'd hang out. He could spot these guys, and he'd get friendly with them, like a former navy guy. He would tell them, "Meet me at such-and-such a day over here, and I'm gonna drive you to Milwaukee, where I've got an apartment, and we'll have girls come over for a party."

So he'd get one of these guys to get into the car with him, they'd have no idea where they were going. He was a bigger guy, he was pretty strong. He'd get them in his apartment on the North Side, and he'd show them books, try to get them drunk, and then attack them, start making homosexual advances towards them. Most of the time, these guys would try to fight him off, but they were smaller guys.

Here's where the problem came in. Often, when he was done, he'd take them back on to the highway, out towards Great Lakes, and just let them off on the highway. They'd go back to the base and say that they were attacked by somebody in Milwaukee. These guys would have no idea, because this guy would drive them on the highway, so they thought they were in Milwaukee. Or else, you'd have a lot of the kids who would go back and they'd be so ashamed at what happened they'd never tell anybody. But there were a number who did.

On one of the last cases we had with this guy—we had like two or three a day several days in a row where he was picking guys up—one guy went up there and he was able to fight this guy off; he hit the guy with an ashtray or a bottle and he was able to run out of the apartment. He flagged a police car down, and he took the policeman back to the guy's apartment, but he was gone. I got a call from one of the hospitals of a sex-assault victim, and here's this guy in a sailor's uniform who tells me the story of what happened and gave information on the apartment and the car.

So we had an idea of who the guy was. So we staked out the apartment and arrested him. He told me that he had been doing this regularly for years. And he said, "Listen, they come to my apartment voluntarily."

Later on, we did a search warrant on his apartment. When we searched the apartment, we found sailor caps in there with serial numbers that the navy didn't have records of anymore. He had a closet with like ten or fifteen sailor caps in there like souvenirs.

We had a guy who was a part-time law-enforcement official, he was a process server on the weekends with the Cook County Sheriff's Office. He picked a woman up on the street, took her back to his apartment, and drugged her. And when she woke up, she was being assaulted.

This girl moved here from a southwestern state, not real familiar with Chicago, she was trying to do some acting and modeling here. She had a job at a restaurant. In the morning, she was on her way to work, she got out of her building, and a kid came along and snatched her purse. She went into a food store across the street, and she says, "Listen, I don't know what to do. I just had my purse taken. What do I do?"

Meanwhile, our offender, the part-time process server, pulls up, and he gets out of his car. And he's got the gun on him and handcuffs on him and stuff like that. The guy inside goes, "Well, there's a policeman," so she goes up to the car. And the guy listens to her story, and he doesn't tell her he's not a Chicago policeman. He says, "Why don't you get in the car and we'll drive around and we'll look for this guy."

She gets in the car, and she's giving the guy a description of the guy who took her purse. And she's hearing police calls in the car—he's got a police radio in there. That's the reason the guy in the store sent her out to him, because he saw the antenna on the car, and then he got out with the gun and everything, so he said, "That's a policeman right there. He must be an undercover policeman."

She's in the car. But by luck, her boss, just by coincidence, is driving by, and he sees her getting in this car. And he pulls up and says, "Aren't you coming to work today?" And she says, "Well, this guy's a policeman. I had my purse grabbed. And he's gonna take me around to look for him."

And her boss tells us later, "I got out of my car, and I even walked up to the car. And I looked in, and I could see the guy had a gun on him; I could see the handcuffs in there; I could hear the police calls." He said, "It wasn't a squad car, it was like an old Oldsmobile, but I figured it was an undercover car." But just for the heck of it, the boss writes down the license number.

So this guy drives the girl around, and after about an hour and a half he says he's got to go to his apartment and get some paperwork. So she goes up, and the guy offers her a Coke. Well, she says the next thing you know, she wakes up and the guy has apparently just finished up a sexual contact with her. And she's like, "What are you doing?" And he says something like, "Don't worry about it."

When we got this guy—the boss writing down the license number was the clue that solved the case—he signed a consent to search, and we found a variety of drugs, pills and stuff, cocaine, grinders. Plus we found this stuff called 222 Aspirin, which is aspirin used in Canada; I think it's got a lot of codeine in it, and if you used a number of these pills, it could cause someone to go to sleep.

He admitted he had sexual contact with her, but he said it was consensual. The old story. He said, "You know, she was a real wild girl. I was on my way, I was serving papers, she needed help, I drove her around. And then she wanted to come back to my apartment and have fun. She must have got mad because I haven't called her back."

But he pled guilty in court. He got five years' felony probation. He's not with the Sheriff's Department anymore.

There's only two defenses to a sexual assault: "It was consensual" or "Hey, you got the wrong guy completely." That's it.

A woman is kidnapped off the street. She's kidnapped by two individuals: One is driving the car, and the other gets in the backseat with her. He's wearing a security-guard uniform. He slaps her around, beats her, knocks out her tooth, he sexually assaults her. Then he has the other guy drop him off at his apartment. And the other guy drives the victim around for a while, says, "You did the other guy. How about me?" She says no. So the second offender says, "Okay, get out of the car." Throws her out of the car. Victim writes down the license plate number and immediately flags down a squad car. Police are called; she tells her story.

She takes the police back to the first offender's apartment; we find the offender. We trace the license number of the car, we find the car, it's exactly the car she described, and in the backseat of the car we find the tooth.

The second offender, the one who didn't do the assaulting, says, "Yeah, this happened, but I didn't do anything." The other guy doesn't say anything.

It goes to trial. Now, the victim was forced to have both vaginal and oral intercourse. So the offender's defense was—it was an identity defense—he said, "It couldn't possibly be me, because I have a chain in my penis. And she didn't describe me as having a chain in my penis."

So, as a way of proving this, he produced both the chain and the penis in open court.

The thing was, it worked. The jury found him Not Guilty.

Rapists never view themselves as rapists. They all have a rationalization.

There was one guy we arrested for rape; he was a serial rapist. And he had been arrested before. And we were talking about his prior, and he said he didn't do it. And he'd already been convicted and been in jail for this. I said, "Why?" He said, "I couldn't possibly be a rapist because she took her clothes off. And if a woman takes her clothes off, it's not rape." Well, in all the cases, he made the victims take their clothes off. But in his mind, even if you're pointing a knife or a gun at somebody and they take their clothes off, it's because they want to have sex with you.

* * *

I've never had a rapist who remained silent after I read him his rights. Most rapists think they can talk their way out of anything. They think they're clever, that they can outwit you.

This happened out in the suburbs. A guy knocks on the door, dressed in a suit. He says, "I'm from the local hospital and I'm part of a graduate program, and my internship, we're offering free exams to the residents in the community."

He's picking on thirty-to-forty-year-old women at home alone. He takes a thermometer out of this little briefcase. He has a blood-pressure thing that you can buy at any Walgreen's. He takes a little personal history: "How old are you? How tall are you? How much do you weigh?" You know, B.S.

And then he proceeds to give them pelvic exams and breast exams for lumps. He did it two to three times in one day. I should say this—it was *reported* two to three times; he must have done it six or seven times.

Are people that naive? Yeah, obviously. They let a perfect stranger in their house, who comes in, they don't know him from Adam, and they let him do breast exams and vaginal exams. So I guess you don't have to be that slick.

A lot of women get raped out of politeness. It's really true. They're waiting for an elevator; they don't like the looks of the guy waiting with them, but instead of walking away, they get on the elevator with the guy and get raped. Or they let some-body in their house. Politeness.

You should fight like hell if you get attacked on the street, or in your home. The old thinking was, especially with women, submit, give in, maybe the guy will give you a break and not kill you. Now, maybe you will get raped, but at least you'll have the satisfaction of knowing you didn't just lie down and take it.

You don't know how many home-invasion scenes we walk in on where the people are sitting there all tied up and all dead. There'll be four, five people, a family, maybe some guests: enough to put up a fight. And you know they let themselves get tied up. You just know the guys said, "We just want to tie you up. We won't hurt you." You'd think the people would realize—why do they want to tie us up if they don't want to hurt us? But they bought it. It always gives us a little chuckle.

A woman was jogging along the sidewalk near her house. This wimpy guy, dressed in jogging clothes but with a roll of fat, was waiting behind a tree. He grabbed her, pulled her into the bushes, and rapes her. The woman is totally traumatized by this; she goes into therapy.

Then he goes after two boys, they were about twelve, thirteen years old. It's about nine at night. He grabs them off the street—"Come with me and I'll show you something." He took them in a backyard, and he told them to close their eyes and pull their pants down. He told them, "I'm gonna bring you the most beautiful woman in the world, and she's going to give you both a blow job. But you have to keep your eyes closed." They laughed at him. One kid said, "Mister, there ain't no beautiful woman. *You* want to do that." And they ran away from him.

As they're running away, he's standing there yelling to them, "Ha ha. Just kidding. This was just a joke. I'm trying to get initiated into a club. Ha ha."

The next time, he had a gun. There were two girls, about fifteen or sixteen, walking down the street. He jumped out from behind the bushes, pulled a gun on them, told them to get into this bush area between houses. One of them ran immediately. He still had the one girl. The other one, as she ran, she got half a block away and she turned and she yelled back to her friend, "Mary, run. Run. It's a fake gun." And the other one ran too. And he stood there and said, "That's right. It's only a fake. Fake gun. Ha ha."

Here's a very, very inadequate guy. Out of the thirteen assaults he committed, he was successful in maybe three. One successful attack was on a sixty-four-year-old woman.

A year later, his first victim, the woman who was so traumatized, is out jogging again. She's just finished a year of therapy, and she's back to running. He jumps out from behind a tree *again* and attacks her *again*. She's been through a year of therapy; she's just gotten her life back together after the rape.

She's not gonna go through this again. She beats the shit out of him.

Rape is about power; it's not about sex. With child molesters, it's different. It *is* about sex.

Five years ago, we executed a search warrant on a locker inside a Chicago Fire Department firehouse. There was an album inside containing homemade child porn. We arrested a fireman for child pornography and abuse. Here's one of the most trusted people in our society. You know, the fireman is your friend.

A pedophile can target kids, and they do that. They'll get themselves in a position—they might use photography, or they'll use their work, say they're a teacher or a counselor, to target these kids. And they separate the one kid that they feel is having a problem—he becomes the target.

One pedophile who was a teacher went so far as to pass out a questionnaire about home life to find out which kids were having problems at home. Then he'd separate that kid to do a little one-on-one counseling with him and sexually abuse the child.

Another guy, an ex-priest, would do the same thing. He'd go around taking pictures of groups of kids, and then he'd talk to kids about the other kids—"Do you know, ah, Joe So-and-so? His Dad doesn't live at home, right?" "Oh. No. They've been divorced for years." "Does Joe like to drink and smoke?" "Oh yeah, he smokes reefer all the time."

So that's the kid he's gonna hit on. He's not gonna hit on the kid that has two solid parents and a home or the kid that he knows is gonna run home and tell on him.

We pretend to be pedophiles. It's just a role-play. You do a role-play. Some of these things get pretty sick. One time, we set up a meeting with this one guy, an ex-seminarian. My partner was going to meet with him; me and the postal inspector were doing backup in the side bedroom. This pedophile showed up late for the meeting, and we hear him tell my partner, "Hey, I'm sorry I'm late, but I was in the park and I saw this twelve-year-old boy that was jogging, and he stopped to get a drink of water and I had to put my hand under his armpit and taste his sweat." And you know you gotta sit there and listen to this.

I'm sitting there with the postal inspector, and he's hearing this, right? And John's going, *"That's* it," he's going for the gun; he's getting his gun out of his boot, and I'm saying, "No, John. Wait! Wait!" And he says, "No. That's it! I'm gonna *get* this motherfucker!" He says, "He's a *sick* bastard!" He was ready to jump out and arrest the guy right then and there, he thought he was so disgusting. Finally, the guy produced some child pornography, and we *could* jump out.

Whenever somebody says, "Gosh, did you hear about that schoolteacher, that priest, that camp counselor, who abused the kid?"—it doesn't surprise me. It doesn't surprise me a bit. I'd *expect* it.

You know why? These people learn at an early age, usually at the onset of puberty, that they like kids. Everybody else is getting excited by the girls, but they get excited by *little* boys or girls.

If they know then, they have a career choice to make. Now you could be a lumberjack or a schoolteacher. They put themselves in a position where they'll have contact with kids; if they're smart, they'll become a teacher, a priest, a youth counselor. If they're not smart, they might become the school janitor, the groundskeeper at a camp.

So it never surprises me when a teacher, a priest, a Boy Scout leader, is arrested and charged with abusing a child. They knew about it, and they picked the profession deliberately.

There's two different kinds of child molesters: There's the situational child molester, the guy who will molest a kid because the kid's around. He's what we call a "try-sexual"—he'll try anything; it could be the family dog. Then there's the prefer-

ential child molester, the true pedophile, whose sexual preference is for kids.

The vast majority—and I'm talking the *vast* majority—of
child molesters my partner and I arrest are people who have
gained legal access to the child and molest them through either
vocational, volunteer, or family contact. That's the problem.
People think if it's a teacher in a school or somebody who's with
an organization, he's okay. We arrested a Boy Scout leader who
was molesting kids in his own Scout troop.

Let's put it this way—we've investigated a cross-section of
society. We've had college professors. The clergy's not immune
to this. We've investigated a lot of Boy Scout leaders, child counselors, social workers, day-care-center owners and workers.
We've had a lot of teachers. I certainly don't want to imply that
all people in child-related fields are like this. But I've super-
vised and been involved in more than fifteen-hundred investigations. I think that qualifies me to give an opinion. Some of
these people aren't working with kids out of the goodness of
their hearts or out of compassion for other human beings;
they're there because they're pedophiles.

With offenders who molest kids, you pick up that they genuinely love kids. It may sound perverted to say this, but they
genuinely love kids. A lot of times, when I talk before groups,
they get real upset at that, that kind of notion. "How can somebody love a kid and go ahead and do this?"
   You can't hide that. And that's what people see, say, in somebody who operates a day-care center and sexually abuses kids—
they see this concern for children, they see somebody who
really likes kids. And they go, "Somebody who really likes kids
couldn't possibly do this." This nice day-care-center owner, this
nice coach. People get confused at that. But pedophiles genuinely love kids—*and* they have a sexual desire for kids.

* * *

Pedophiles take their time in the seduction process. It's just like a man dating a woman. They're not gonna go home that first night and jump in bed. He's gonna kind of feel the kid out and gain his trust before he makes a move on him. He might make a move and the kid rejects it and he'll back off for a couple months. Because they don't have just one kid going at a time.

And that's another thing police have to learn—a pedophile does not abuse one kid. If you get a bona fide pedophile, don't stop after you get one kid. Keep digging, because you're gonna come up with—I'd say the average we have is five to seven kids on a case with one pedophile. We've talked to pedophiles who've molested hundreds of kids in their lifetime. We've found computer listings of kids; they computerize the kids and rate them with different things the kids can do.

This is something I go insane trying to tell my children. For years it was that you would tell children about Mr. Stranger Danger, the outrageous, scary-looking stranger that you should stay away from.

But sex offenders, as a rule, are very, very normal-looking. Most of them have families, children, jobs. It's usually not the weird-looking guy lurking around the schoolyard; it's the nice-looking young counselor at the Y who's fondling the kids. Now, I tell my kids, "Look out for one you know already. Look out for the one you know."

That's the worst part—when a kid has trusted someone and he gets abused, and now he doesn't trust *anybody.* That's the horrible repercussion. He's now been shaken in any trust he had.

There *are* exceptions to the rule. Mr. Stranger Danger *is* out there. There *are* individuals who pick up children, torture them, and murder them. They do exist.

* * *

I had a case where a young boy, he was walking right in front of his parents; they were on their way to see a movie, and this kid was grabbed off the street. Boy, that was a nightmare.

He's walking in front of his parents, six o'clock at night. He's a little bit ahead; they're looking in windows and stuff—he's kidnapped. Twelve-year-old kid. They got up to the theater, and they couldn't find him. He was gone.

The offender put him in the trunk of a car, drove him around, takes him to some deserted spot, like railroad tracks somewhere, anally assaulted him, forced him to perform fellatio, and he fellates the kid, puts him back in the trunk, and drives him to a northern suburb where he assaults him again.

He takes him up to the suburbs, where he pulls off Highway 41 to a motel. There's a service road that runs right behind it; he pulls off into the service road, makes the kid get out of the trunk again, he sexually assaults the kid again, and then he hits the kid in the head and leaves him for dead. With a hammer.

And he leaves him for dead. He drives off. Well, the kid's only stunned. When he wakes up, he goes back to the motel and makes outcry there.

How this guy gets caught—we're looking all over for him; the suburban police are looking for this guy; they're using helicopters; the kid got the license number, but it's an out-of-state license; they run this number in every state in the Union, which is no easy trick.

What happens is the offender gets arrested on the South Side for the same thing. The offender's not a real aggressive guy—in the first offense, he picked a kid who was even less aggressive than he was; he said, "Come with me," and the kid did. But then he went to the South Side and tried it on one of the South Side kids, and the South Side kid told him to fuck himself. A neighbor runs out, an off-duty policeman, and he gets arrested.

Well, we don't make the connection. A police reporter finds out about it and puts it on WGN Radio. So the suburban police are listening to WGN; we're listening to some madman on the radio. They call us up and say, "Wait a minute! This is the same guy!" We're going, "Huh? The South Side? A jillion miles apart?" So they had to tell us. In the end, we got him to confess.

He was a nice guy who worked in a grocery store. An assistant manager. A nice, quiet kid. He was about nineteen or twenty. The kid was a nice kid; he wasn't a bad kid. No one ever suspected. You know, a good, neighborhood kid. Never been in any trouble. But he had these bizarre sexual fantasies—and he was a gay kid living on the Southwest Side of the city of Chicago; that's scary.

The moral of that story is—how does anyone get abducted walking down a crowded street at six o'clock in the evening? It can't happen, right? It *can* happen.

In the majority of cases, child molesters are pillars of the community. And what happens in mass-molestation cases, if you look at them throughout the country, what happens after one of these is discovered, there comes an immediate breakdown in the community. There comes strong support and strong condemnation. The people charged get strong letters of support immediately after the charges are filed.

That's the way these cases always break down. Because people trusted the person charged, and they need to do that because—if I put my kid in a day-care center where I think he could get abused, it would make me crazy, so you rationalize to yourself that the person charged couldn't possibly do it.

Believe the child. Believe the child. Let me just say this. If you listen closely to a child, there are some things that a child simply can't make up. Where does a child of three or four years old learn about sticking this in there or that in there, sucking this or doing that—where does a child learn this? It's not from *Sesame Street.* It's because it happened to the child.

The court system's tough on kids. It's tough on kids being interviewed. A kid won't talk when you've got two social workers, three detectives, and five uniforms in the room. Who would?

Then they drag a four-, five-, six-year-old kid into the courtroom—look at the courtroom, look at the judge. They're scared to death. Put them up on the stand. Put them in front of the grand jury. Some of them, they draw a blank. They can't remember their names, much less their stories.

Several years ago, I was working the midnights, my partner was off, and I got a call from the sergeant; he said, "Go to the hospital. A kid's been assaulted. It looks pretty bad."

So I get over to the hospital and there's a little white kid, he's about five or six years old at the time. And he has been sodomized and really beaten severely. He's all bloodied, and quite obviously he's suffered rectal trauma.

Over the next several days, I talked to the kid with some counselors, people that deal with child trauma. The story comes out that he had been on the street and he met a guy carrying a suitcase. The guy that was talking to him said he wanted to play and he was going to go away and he wanted the little boy to go with him. The little boy didn't know him from Adam. Just "I want to be your friend"; something to that effect.

The little boy went with him. He said the guy he was talking to seemed to be nice. The little boy kept referring to him as another boy, but he's giving me the size of an adult. So he tells us he goes someplace and he does these bad things to me, and he gets the point across of what happened.

We're trying to get him to describe the place. His story becomes very bizarre at this point. He says, "Well, I was in a bed on a mattress and it was raining on the bed." "I don't understand." "I was on a mattress, like this"—he points to the hospital bed—"and it was raining on top of the mattress." I said, "Well, were you inside or were you outside?" The little boy said, "We went in through the wall. The wall opened up, and we went in through the wall. And you could see airplanes." And I said, "What kind of airplanes—little ones, big ones?" He said, "*Real* airplanes. You could see airplanes flying in the sky." I asked him to describe the inside. "Well, there were a lot of yellow doors with numbers." "What kind of doors?" "Car doors." He said, "We had McDonald's to eat, and I left my shoes there."

He tells us about the offender. It's a white guy. And he was wearing a T-shirt, a "beep-beep" T-shirt. "What do you mean by beep-beep?" "Beep-beep like the Road Runner." "Is it a picture of the Coyote and the Road Runner?" "No. It says beep-beep. That's all it says."

So—the yellow car doors, the airplanes, beep-beep. The story is just too bizarre. We start looking; I don't know where to begin. For some reason, this little boy has personally affected me because I had a son about his age at the time. I spent a lot of time on this on my own.

One day, I went in on my own time and in my own automobile and I went to the neighborhood where the kid was ultimately found and I just started walking around. As it turns out, there's a McDonald's around there. I just started walking up and down the streets and walking up and down the alleys. I went on my own; I wasn't even working, it bothered me so much. So I start walking up and down the alleys. And just by chance, I happen to be going by a garage. I'm looking in the garage; it's obviously abandoned. And I'm looking around the side, and there's a hole in the wall. I don't think anything of the hole in the wall, I climb over the stuff and I go in the garage, and at this point, I'm astonished.

There are probably thirty or forty doors from Yellow taxicabs stacked up in a row, and they've all got numbers on them. Just doors. That's all that's in the goddamn garage are doors from abandoned Yellow taxicabs with numbers on them.

I start looking around. Right in the middle of the place is a mattress. And there's a hole in the roof. Right above the mattress, there's a hole in the roof, and you can see the airplanes going by on their way to O'Hare Field. And I could see—if you lay on that mattress, if it's raining, the rain's gonna come right down on top of the mattress. And there were the kid's shoes.

So my partner and I started, just from there, we started going from block to block, going into every store, knocking on doors and everything else, looking for somebody wearing a T-shirt that said beep-beep. That's all we knew—there's a white guy wearing a T-shirt that says beep-beep on it. And I'll be damned, ultimately some guy says, "Yeah—that guy lives over here"— and he points across the street to one of the apartment buildings. We start going from door to door to door to door; we

ultimately hit an apartment where a woman says, "Well, that's
So-and-so, but he doesn't live here." But it turns out, he's coming over here right now. He was going to visit this woman.

We called, we got the reinforcements. Sure enough, about an
hour later, knock at the door, who's at the door?, Here's the guy,
he's wearing a beep-beep T-shirt. We jump on him and everything else—he turned out to be a kid, about eighteen years old,
but he was mentally retarded. He had the brain of like a ten-
year-old. When he told the kid he wanted to play, that's what
he wanted to do. And he had the suitcase with his clothes in it
and everything else, and he was just a little mentally slow.

And we got him just from the little boy's bizarre story of the
location of where it happened and the description of the
T-shirt. And that's all we had.

A tac team from Twenty-three brought in two little girls, nine
and ten, who accused a sixty-eight-year-old man of giving them
marijuana and toluene for sexual favors. The tac coppers
tended not to believe the story at first.

You know how the guy got convicted? The tac team asked,
"Does the guy have any identifying marks?" The little girls
said, "Yeah, he's got a *P* on his dick"; you know, tattooed on his
dick. And the thing is, it was too painful for him to put the Pee
Wee on, that's what they called him, so he only had *PE* put on
his dick. Soon as they confirmed that, they had him.

You'll find fathers are abusers, grandfathers, stepfathers, uncles, boyfriends, sometimes kids in the same family. In most
cases, in-the-home sexual abuse is an ongoing thing. A person
doesn't abuse a child one time.

Stepfathers and live-in boyfriends are common child molesters.

The mothers of these children are more protective of the guy
they're living with than they are of their own child. I've seen
many cases where the mother comes to court with the person

charged and totally ignores the child—when there's concrete medical, physical, and circumstantial evidence showing penetration.

Why? It's the meal ticket. Especially in lower-income areas. It's the meal ticket. I'm not trying to stereotype that area; we've had mothers from lower-income families come forward to report child abuse, but a lot of times they don't want to see it, they don't want to lose that meal ticket. Or they don't feel what's been perpetrated is that heinous a crime. They don't feel incest or sexual abuse is that heinous. Or they won't admit it, they turn a blind eye to it, even though, in most cases, this goes on over an extended period of time.

When you talk about long-term abuse, the woman usually knows it's going on. She knows.

Sometimes the woman takes part in the child molestation. There was a case on the North Side; again, it was a stepfather, and he'd been abusing the twelve-year-old daughter for three years, since she was nine. And the mother was part of it. And their rationalization was, as they were talking to us about it, they were teaching her about sex; she was getting ready to date, so she needed to know.

Women are involved in the sexual abuse of children, but not nearly to the extent as men. They're involved more than we know, I believe.

The biggest frustration in investigating in-the-home sexual abuse is: What do you do once they've told you what happened? What do you do with the kid? That's the thing that bothers me.

You get a kid that tells you, "My father's been doing this, or my stepfather, or my mother's boyfriend." Now they just told you this, right? And the mother is unwilling to believe it, and you know if you put the kid back in the home with the mother, the mother's going to be coercing that child into not testifying, so what do you do with the kid? What do you do with the victim?

If you yank the kid out of the home—now the kid feels pun-ished for telling what happened, and you're really screwing the kid up because you're putting him or her into an institutional-ized setting. If you yank them away from the only thing that they have, which is their mother, now that they've told on their father, it's a terrible thing. It's a real dilemma. I don't know what the answer is.

Or what if the story doesn't wash? Say a kid tells a teacher, the teacher calls the hot line, she comes in, the police get in-volved, the police don't believe the story, there's no physical evidence. . . . Now that kid has to go back home and live with the person she just snitched on. What kind of relationship is that? Do you think she's gonna come forward to tell again? It's a tough crime.

If a kid tells, his family life is shot. It's over. All the good things are gone. You not only lose your father, but your mother probably has some mixed feelings towards you now. A lot of times, they don't even believe their kids. Or she's not gonna give up her meal ticket. Or they found out about it and figure they can handle it; try to get the guy into counseling or stop him from having contact with the kid. It just doesn't work. So it gets really screwed up.

For the kid, for the victim, it's a no-win. No matter what you do, you're gonna get hurt. Which is the worst hurt? That's the only way we can look at it. Which is worse—to remain in the environment, keep living through that, or to get out of it?

Kids always think *they* did something wrong, not the mo-lester. They blame themselves.

The majority of child molesters I arrest are seeking sex from a child who's the same age they were when *they* were victim-ized. He's focused to the age.

So the pedophile will start grooming his intended victim before he reaches the right age; say he's fixated on ten-year-olds; he might start grooming his victim when he's six. When the kid gets past that age, he won't want to have anything to do with him. He might pass him on to another pedophile.

Child molesters sometimes seek out and marry divorced women or single women with kids, for the sole purpose of molesting those kids when they're the right age. Or they'll marry and have babies; again, so they can molest them when they're the right age.

It's occurred many times. We had a pedophile that we locked up that had joined several computer dating services, specifying that he wanted to meet women with children. We set up an undercover meeting with the man, when he delivered his commercial child pornography. We did a search warrant of his residence and came up with photographs of a nine-year-old that had been vaginally penetrated by a foreign object *by* the offender.

It's a cycle. A lot of psychologists and social workers will tell you that pedophiles were sexually abused when *they* were children, and one reason they get fixated on a certain age of a child is they want to sexually abuse the person at the age that they were sexually abused at. That's what they say. That's a crutch, and a lot of offenders will tell you that. I don't know if it's true or not. The reason people do things shouldn't be any of our concern except to help us figure out how to catch them.

Child molesters gravitate to areas with a high concentration of multifamily dwellings, single-family dwellings. And they're basically taking lower-income children and paying them for sexual gratification. So hypothetically, a lot of child sex abuse is, by statute, classified as child prostitution, but, in reality, it's the farthest thing from the truth.

Children are lured into prostitution by bicycles and games and trips and different things like that. Some are lured because they're getting psychological things they don't get at home.

* * *

The majority of child prostitutes that I've come in contact with have started out, at eight or nine years old, as sexual-abuse victims in their own families—by their actual father, by their mother's live-in boyfriend, by individuals in the area, uncles, grandfathers. There's a loss of self-confidence and self-esteem. The child is ultimately placed as a ward of the state and bounces from family to family. These are the types of children that are vulnerable, because there's no real, solid, concrete outcry in their lives.

Child molesters recognize this. They gravitate toward children whose credibility is tainted.

They're experts at seduction. They work at it. They develop their techniques, just like a man who goes to singles' bars develops his technique. A pedophile will too. He'll try something; if it works, he'll keep that in his little bag of tricks. If it doesn't work, he'll never try that again.

I mean, they actually have rules. We've met with them in undercover capacity. They've said things like, "Number-one rule: Never hurt a kid." Okay? Because if you hurt him, he's gonna tell on you.

They have rules set up—we've recovered rules, written rules that these pedophiles would have kids sign. When they can come over, what they can do in the house. I remember one we recovered—it was a "boy lover" letter—it starts out: "This is to let you know that I am what they call a 'boy lover.' And that means that I like to have sex with boys. It's not that I have sex with *every* boy that I know, but I would like to. This is to let you know up-front what I'm about."

The pedophile will have these kids read this, and it goes on with rules about what they can eat out of the refrigerator, when they can watch TV, what hours they can come—because he doesn't want to be bothered all the time, because he's gotta work too. And he'll have them sign this.

The real slick ones will pick a kid that's about thirteen that has no sexual experience, so he's got nothing to base his judgment on. So he'll ply him with marijuana and beer, get him some *Playboy*s, make sure it's real dark in there so this kid can't see what's going on. And then when things start to happen—you know, the sexual drive is a very important part of life—and these kids have no experience to know what they should be doing—and thirteen, that's the age kids experiment.

So these pedophiles—another way to look at it, this one pedophile that's eighty, and he's been arrested in about seven different states, he's been doing it for fifty years. If you can't perfect something in fifty years, then give it up. So he's had fifty years of learning techniques to get kids to do what you want to do.

He's in the pen now. We had a tip that a young boy was being kissed on the head by an older man. So we went and watched his house. We set up on his house, there was all kinds of rock music blaring, laser lights coming out the window. So we went up there, knocked on his back door, and asked him to please hold down the music, and there were three kids standing behind him, about fourteen years old. We said, "Who are these kids?" So he gave us their names and he gave us his name and we left.

The next day, we went back and interviewed all the kids and found out what he'd been doing, and we ended up with seven or eight different kids. He printed a magazine, he wanted to open a boys' club, he wanted to get funding from the mayor. He was actually what you call a "boy worshipper."

And when you walk in the man's house, you know that something's wrong, because first thing you see in this eighty-year-old man's house is pictures of boys sitting in a tree, pictures of boys here, pictures of boys there, and they were all between eleven and fourteen years old. Some people have pictures of their kids. Well, he's got pictures of all his victims. He hung normal pictures on the walls; the pornography he took was hidden.

There's a great picture we got of this guy. We use it in training seminars. There's a picture of this eighty-year-old guy in his bedroom, and he's standing in front of an AC/DC poster. Now what eighty-year-old is going to be into head-bangin' rock 'n' roll?

What's the payback for these kids? Crash pad. It's like when we hit this old guy's house, it's nicer than any YMCA you would ever want to see. There's a weight room in there, there's a punching bag, there's model airplanes, there's AC/DC posters on the walls—this is an eighty-year-old man's apartment! So these kids can go there, and there's *no* fee, they don't have to pay like at the YMCA. Plus when they're done with the workout, they go to the fridge and get a beer. So what better setup?

Mostly, the kids think of it as a hangout. They're getting money out of it too; they're getting a few dollars from this guy; he buys all their beer for them, gets their reefer for them. . . .

These people are tricky. If they have a lasting relationship with a kid over a period of time, they'll take the place of the father. They'll supply some psychological needs that this kid has by giving him the love he's not getting at home, and then this kid is *all* mixed up because, you know, he has to do a few physical things, but he's getting back some psychological things that he really needs. And when it comes time to give this guy up, it's real hard for him.

They have their little collections. That's another interesting thing about pedophiles—their collections are—their whole *life*. When you're talking about a child pornographer—if you hit him and he hasn't been hit, and he's been collecting for sixteen years, you're gonna have to have a truck to carry it out. He'll have kids in underwear ads—he'll take the Sears catalog and completely cut out every picture of a kid in underwear and paste it into a scrapbook. We recovered pictures of kids taken in Uptown—and the kids are now thirty years old, and the pictures are of them when they were *eight* years old. And these were passed on from one guy to another guy.

Pedophiles keep souvenirs from kids. They're recordkeepers. They keep diaries and talk about what they've done. We've recovered diaries where the guy will write about having sex with a boy, and then a month later he'll be writing about the boy having his twelfth birthday. So when you have a diary like that, when you get to court, there's no denying that he knew how old the boy was; you've got his diary. There was one that we blew up and used in court.

They're great savers. There's pedophiles that will build their own little environments; they'll have secret rooms, where only they can go, with all their collections.

We haven't run across any women pedophiles. We've run across women that would help pedophiles. We had a funeral-home director that used a woman to entice the young boys out of game rooms and then get them into the van, and she'd be kissing the boys, and then he'd all of a sudden get in the middle of the action. They'd take the kids back to the funeral home.

This guy's in jail now. Our investigation of him started with a kid that was in a group home, that told us that this guy was Dr. Mengele. He told it to youth officers in Area Six first, and they gave it to us. We went out and picked the kid up in the group home, and he's telling us this on the way in. We're look-ing at each other like, How much of this can we believe? The kid's telling us, "Yeah, he takes pills so he never gets old. That's why he looks so young. He's Dr. Mengele from Germany, and he's hiding here and he's been here since the end of World War II." And we were saying, "Uh-huh."

So we get a search warrant and hit the guy's apartment over the funeral home. He had a lot of things up there about being a Nazi, being from Germany. And that was one of the things he used with kids that would work, like when they're twelve years old. He'd tell them he was from Nazi Germany, and if they didn't behave, he'd get the Nazis to kill them. Kids don't know a thing about it; they think he's for real.

It's amazing the way that pedophiles can communicate with each other. It's something that I still don't understand. By look-ing at each other, they'll know.

I think that the way they read each other is they watch the way the guy reads other people on the street. If you're standing on the same corner as some other guy, and every time a kid comes by, his eyes start following that kid—every time a woman comes by, nothing, or an adult gay comes by, nothing. . . . They see that little spark in the other guy's eye and they say, "Ahhh. He's another one." Kindred spirit.

Juice bars are notorious hangouts for pedophiles. A juice bar is a nonalcoholic establishment that allows both adults and juveniles into the same area; it's a perfect setup for pedophiles.

I investigated one juice bar after the police department received allegations of adult males hanging around with runaway children and children beyond curfew hours. I went undercover. I observed drug sales, I purchased narcotics, I observed men picking up boys, leaving with them.

One February evening, a fourteen-year-old boy solicited me for sex. I'd observed him leave with numerous men before, and now we had some substantiation for what was going on. We placed him in protective custody, and he began giving us information about a large number of men from the suburbs who were picking boys up, taking naked photographs of the boys, having sex with them. Out of that case, we ended up with seventeen men that were charged and indicted with sexual abuse of children.

You know who's out there actively looking for missing children? I mean, actively looking. Pimps and pedophiles. They're looking for them. They're cruising all the time. Absolutely.

There's two different ways that they work. The pimps will take the kids and put them on the street. The pedophiles will take them, give them a little love. . . .

And a lot of times it's not the runaway kid so much. It's the kid where the parents don't care if he comes home or if he stays out. Say this kid lives in an apartment with ten other brothers and sisters, he's got some guy that picks him up in a Mercedes-Benz and takes him home or to a hotel and lets him have a shower and sleep in a bed by himself, and all he's gotta do is close his eyes for a couple minutes. . . .

That's why they do it. And it's real hard to break into that, because you can't offer them anything. What are *you* gonna offer them? You gonna offer to take them away and put them in a group home?

A lot of times, it's not so much the parents don't care about them, but it's gotten to the point where they *can't* care about them anymore because they've got so many other worries. Unless you grew up in a poor area and know that kind of atmosphere, anybody that comes out then and criticizes that kind of parent is wrong. Because a lot of times the parent does care about the kids, but it's out of control. It's beyond them. So the kids are out in the street.

With runaways, there's an underground of pedophiles that will take care of them, pass them from person to person. They'll live with one guy until it gets a little too hot, maybe, and then that pedophile, he'll pass him to another person. Usually, the reason is the kid gets too old for their particular preference, so they pass him on.

I had a kid in Uptown tell me that he couldn't walk out of the apartment without some fat guy pulling up in a car and blowing his horn at him. And it's not the same fat guy. Different fat guys. He'd go over there, and they all wanted him to climb in the car with them. So it's tough. Real tough on kids.

Child prostitutes. There are streets in Chicago where it's like being in the Indy 500, where you jockey for position. We've been doing undercover work on some of these strips, and the cars are so tight in there, the guys are honking these kids so bad, you gotta kind of force your way in. It's like being in a race.

A guy by the name of Joe, who's now in the penitentiary; we caught him three times picking kids up in the city and bringing them back to his house in the suburbs to perform acts of sex. This was a retired high school teacher.

One night, the first time we met him, we observed him pick

up a boy. We followed the gentleman up to an exclusive area in the northern suburbs, watched him go into the house with a fourteen-year-old boy, and then, through an imperfection in the blinds, we were able to see him performing acts of sex with the boy. We gained entry to the house and placed him under arrest. We executed search warrants on the man's house, coming up with hundreds of naked photos of children.

When the man got out on bond, rather than getting psychiatric treatment, he went out and bought new blinds.

Child prostitution is what they call a cottage industry. There *are* children working the street. Oh, absolutely. This year alone I've been solicited by fifteen children. But, for the most part, you have to know somebody to gain access to a child. Lot of times, child molesters will cruise areas frequented by male and female prostitutes, and use them as the medium, so to speak, so that they can link up to a younger child. A lot of prostitutes who don't believe in this act as our informants.

These kids are hard-core sexual-abuse victims—that's what I call a prostitute; I don't label a child who's working the streets a criminal; that's a hard-core sexual-abuse victim. Every child prostitute that I've come in contact with is a victim, not a criminal.

A lot of times when the child is taken into custody, we'll learn from the child who the adults are who are manufacturing the child pornography, urinating on them and tying them up and different things like that.

If you don't get to a kid within the first couple months of being out there, forget it. If the kid's been out there for over a year, if he's been there two years, it's impossible. They're into that life. If you pull them out of it, they'll go back to it as soon as it's over.

For them, it's freedom. They're shooting all the dope they want, going to all the rock concerts they want, they're staying out all night long, don't have their parents telling them when to come in. For them, it's not a hard life. It might be hard when the pimp beats on them for not giving up their money. . . .

When you start at their level, and grow up poor, don't have anything, even when you got this, you got something. They're gonna do it however they can.

That's what a lot of policemen don't understand about children prostitutes. They refer to them as whores. One time, my partner and I went into a district, this thirteen-year-old girl had just finished telling the tac team about how she had this pimp who put her on Lincoln Avenue for two, three months and made money off her, and they gave her a cigarette. So the old-time youth officer walks in and sees her smoking a cigarette and knocks it out of her mouth and says, "This is nothing but a little whore. I'm gonna put her in the Audy Home." Because that's the way police departments traditionally were taught to handle that kind of crime. Instead of looking at her as a thirteen-year-old victim, she's a thirteen-year-old offender.

The real scary thing about child prostitutes is the AIDS. It's not just the sex, because a child prostitute, a lot of times, will become involved with drugs, too. So they've got the needles and they've got the sex; they've got both ends of it. They're *really* at risk.

You ever heard of a gump with tall bank? One night, my partner and I picked up two child prostitutes, maybe twelve and thirteen, and put them in the back of the squad. They're talking back and forth. We hear this one kid say to the other, "Yeah, he's a gump with tall bank." We're like, "Boy, we never heard that one before." Turns out that's the street term for a fruit with a lot of money.

A lot of child prostitutes live at home. They go home with the money. The parents don't care. The parents are drunks and narcotics users. Example I can give was a girl in Uptown we heard was involved in prostitution; we pulled her referral card to see what kind of record she had. We found that her five-year-old brother had suffocated when her two parents in a drunken stupor rolled over on top of him. Suffocated. Now if the parents

do that to their son, do you think they really care if their thirteen-year-old daughter is out there being a prostitute? They're
happy to get her out there. You know, she's making her own
money then, and they don't have to worry about giving her
money; she's not in the house, so they can do whatever they
want to do.

What we see a lot is women that get their children involved
in prostitution. Their own daughters, and then they'll get other
kids involved. It's not uncommon at all. I've sent some of the
mothers to the penitentiary when they have arranged a situation in which I personally could have sex with their daughters.

Some of the mothers, and I think we're gonna see more of it,
they're narcotics users and they're getting older; they can't
work the street anymore because they're no longer desirable. So
they take the child, who's now thirteen or fourteen, and put
them out there, and they start working the street, start sharing
the narcotics with the mother. We had a mother in Uptown who
put three different girls out there, who were thirteen and fourteen years old, so she could get her T's and Blues to shoot. She
had all the kids using narcotics too.

I've sent over twenty female prostitutes to the penitentiary
who have sold us children and who were actively recruiting
children and selling them, including their own children, for
prostitution. We work undercover in the adult-prostitution
field. Many times, we'll be solicited by adult prostitutes, and
they will actually arrange a situation where we're offered sex
with their daughters or their neighbors' daughters. Several
cases I've done, the victims have been under the age of *nine*.

One case, the girl was six years old, and the mother sold her
daughter to me for $150. A woman met with me in a hotel in
Area Six, and there was her six-year-old child laying naked on
the bed. The mother requested $150 for an hour of sexual activ-
ity with her daughter. I gave her the money and made the
arrest.

* * *

We do photo-lab contact. The last case we did, a gentleman dropped off photographs to be developed of a seven-year-old and an eight-year-old girl who seemed to be unconscious and he was performing sex acts. We staked his house out, placed him under arrest, and found out that the girls were his daughters, and that he was drugging the kids after the mother went to work.

These people who say child pornography is a harmless crime are wrong, because we meet with these people, and even if they haven't stepped over that line yet, they're thinking about it. They just haven't got up enough nerve to do it yet. And God forbid they discover how to drink and get their inhibitions gone and then they can step out and do what they want to do. Every person who's involved in child pornography—even the ones who haven't sexually abused a child—has fantasized about it. Just the pornography itself shows an act of child abuse.

In most cases, when you've got a child pornographer, you've got a sex case to go with it. Most of them are also child molesters. Absolutely.

The commercially made child pornography, like *Kinderlieb* and *Ballbusters,* is foreign-made and has mostly dried up now because of aggressive enforcement.

Here, it's a cottage industry. Child porno is made by pedophiles for use by pedophiles. The money is unimportant to them.

I'll give you the extent—in 1986, my partner and I alone locked up six Chicago schoolteachers, two of which were manufacturing child pornography right in the classroom.

The sexual exploitation of children is a whole different crime to investigate than a robbery, a burglary, a murder.

These guys, some of them, believe they did *absolutely nothing wrong.* Child pornographers, child abusers—you arrest them red-handed and they act like—"You're kidding! For this?" They'll tell you the kid asked for it. It's amazing.

Child molesters don't think they've inflicted damage. You talk to a child molester, and many times he'll tell you the child wanted it. I talked to one molester who told me that this child was being provocative and exposing parts of his body, that the child knew what he was doing, and that he just couldn't resist. Now this child was two years old and wearing diapers.

If you talk to the offender and the victim, you'll see two very different points of view about what happened. The offender will describe this very loving, tender relationship in which the kid was a willing participant, while the child will tell you about how they put on four pairs of pajamas when they went to bed so that Daddy wouldn't come and bother them.

They don't think they've done anything wrong. Always a rationalization. They love this child. They wouldn't hurt this child. That's why they lie so good. They lie so good because, first of all, they're lying to themselves. They lie to themselves about this being wrong. So, when you go talk to them, they're convinced, they're enraged, they're incensed; they want to take lie-detector tests. They couldn't possibly do anything terrible.

If you've got a child molester, you get up right next to them, you put your arm around them, tell them you understand what's going on. Let them shed a tear or two. If you can convince this guy that you understand where he's coming from— and I think I can honestly say I understand where these guys are coming from—you'll get a statement.

If you want to tell him he's a motherfucker, tell him that on the way to lockup after you got the statement.

A lot of police don't want to work in Sex Crimes, or the Special Investigations Unit, because it's such an ugly crime. A lot of people don't want to look at it. We had one supervisor come down; he didn't want to have anything to do with it—"It's nasty; it's dirty; it's filthy. Leave me alone. Let me out of here."

Not too many people want to hear about it. There's a couple problems with doing this kind of work. Other policemen—we do a lot of training seminars to try to teach them that you don't beat on these people. A lot of people have that first instinct that they want to hit somebody that molests their child, not only policemen—civilians. That's not the answer.

We're up-front with offenders. We tell them our main goal is to put you in the penitentiary; if we can't do that, we want to get you psychological help, but we're gonna stop you one way or the other. But we don't yell at them and scream, "You dirty pervert. What are you fucking these kids for? Are you crazy?" So you've got to protect these people from other policemen sometimes, not so much physical abuse, but verbal abuse, because that will shut the offenders up, keep them from talking.

Most of them *want* to talk about it. That's the amazing thing. We've had people shake our hands when we put them in jail. They'll shake our hands—"Thank you, Officer. You know, I've been living with this for so many years, and it's so good to get it off my chest. You understand and you're not beating me for it."

Even among the worst offenders, the short eyes are isolated because it's a taboo. Especially with policemen.

They're the worst because they play a front like they're a coach, they're everything America stands for, they're everything we're supposed to look up to, and they take advantage of their position to obtain sexual favors. It's hard for us.

You get very emotional. You get attached. I guess you wouldn't be human if you didn't get attached. Especially you get the infant cases or early childhood cases.

The sexual abuse of infants—hardest case to make. Because you don't have a victim who can tell you anything.

* * *

It affects you a lot. An awful lot. Maybe you get overly protective. I watch people all the time. And when I look at people and see how some people act in certain situations, from what I know from my experience, I wouldn't let my kid go anywhere near him. And I have no concrete evidence against that person; it's nothing you can pinpoint; it's an instinct. It could be a Sunday school teacher, or somebody they're going on a field trip with, and you've got some evidence of how that person acts, and all of a sudden it sets off the alarm system. You don't want your kid near that person.

It's not paranoia, that's not it. *But I watch people.*

I'm one who believes that the sexual abuse of children is not on the rise—it's always been around. It gets reported more now. It's been going on for years, but people used to hush it up— "Let's keep it in the family. It's a family problem, a family problem. Don't worry about it. You didn't get hurt."

I've spoken to groups on exploitation of children, and a lot of women come up afterwards and say, "Some of the things you were talking about, that happened to me when I was little. I was too scared to say anything about it." Never reported. That even surprised me, the extent of it.

Statistically, this is an underreported crime. In cases of sexual abuse, there usually isn't an immediate outcry—it's a year later, even years later. Children do not report their sexual victimization for a multitude of reasons.

The primary reason is that the offender transfers the blame. Children need love and affection. And the pedophiles use the seduction process to gain legal access to the child, and in doing this, they negate any kind of outcry.

Or the victim is financially dependent on the offender, or the offender is in a position of authority over the victim: Scout leader, clergy member, parent.

Or the parent will ask the child not to come forward, because of the stigma. I'll give you an example. Your child comes home from Girl Scouts and you find out that the Girl Scout leader's performed oral copulation on your daughter. Now if you live in a nice area, that's gonna make the news. Would you want that stigma attached, that your daughter's the one they're writing about?

Those are some abbreviated reasons children don't report their own victimization.

Here's a perfect example of what can happen to sexually victimized kids—Danny, a twelve-year-old kid, who was murdered and hacked into pieces and tossed out into the garbage by a pedophile named Larry.

When we were interviewing that fourteen-year-old from Joe's Juice Bar, he also told us about some runaway boys. One of the runaways was a boy named Danny.

We found Danny in an apartment outside the city. In the apartment were multiple naked photographs of boys and Danny, all of whom had been molested by the occupant of the apartment, known as Ron. Danny was staying with him; he'd met him in Joe's Juice Bar in Chicago. Ron was placed under arrest and charged with a multitude of crimes.

Danny was a runaway. He was a throwaway and a runaway. He'd been sexually victimized since he was nine years old, and by the time he was twelve, he was so entrenched into this, it was difficult. So we placed him. We got back in touch with him in 1984, when this Larry guy was a suspect in a series of killings in Indiana. Danny had been missing for some time, and they actually sent for his dental records to match them against the corpses that they found.

We found Danny in High Point, North Carolina. We found him involved in a child sex ring run by funeral-home directors. We brought him back; again they attempted to get the boy into traditional placement, but he didn't fit in, because adults had molested him over the years.

Danny was subsequently back on the street, where he met Larry and was dissected into eight pieces.

And there's many stories about boys like Danny. It's not been the first time; there's been many times where young child sexual-abuse victims have met their demise at a very early age.

* * *

There is no bottom. There is no low. You never know what you're going to see next. There's no worst—it does amaze me what people do to other people, that's what's crazy about it—but there's no worst. You know what I'm saying?

Sex Crimes:
Contributing Police Officers

OFFICER TOM BOHLING, Organized Crime Division, Vice Control Section. Bohling is one of the United States' foremost experts in pornography and obscene materials; in 1986, he testified before the Meese Commission. Bohling joined the CPD in 1968, was assigned to the Fourth District on patrol, served in Vietnam in the U.S. Navy, returned, and was assigned in 1973 to the Intelligence Section, Subversives Unit, for a year, and then went to the Fifth District on patrol. In 1975, Bohling was assigned to the Conspiracy Unit within the Vice Control Section, and has been with Prostitution/Obscenity for the past fourteen years. Bohling has a master's degree in criminal justice.

SERGEANT SAM CHRISTIAN, watch commander, Special Investigations Unit. Christian came on the force in 1973 and was assigned to the Twenty-third District, where he worked tac for five years. Then Christian served as a patrol specialist, training recruits on the street. In 1980, Christian went to Area Five, Youth Division, where he was assigned to the crime car. Christian was assigned to SIU in 1981, where he worked with Brian Killacky and the late Michael J. Dolan. In 1985, Christian was promoted to youth officer in the Area Five Youth Division. Christian has spearheaded a program to investigate interfamilial abuse. Christian returned to SIU in 1989.

CAPTAIN TOM CRONIN, Fifteenth District. Cronin was selected by the CPD in 1985 to be trained in investigative profiling by the FBI's National Center for the Analysis of Violent Crime. Cronin joined the force in 1969, worked patrol in the Thirteenth District until 1971, when he became a crime analyst. In 1973, Cronin was promoted to detective and worked Robbery in Area Two for two years and Robbery in Area Five for two years. Cronin made sergeant in 1977, lieutenant in 1985, and captain in 1990. Cronin, who holds a master's degree in social justice, is one of twenty investigative profilers in the United States.

DETECTIVE PAUL HAGEN, Area Six Violent Crimes. Hagen joined the police in 1971, was eight years on patrol in the Eighteenth District, was promoted to detective in 1979 and assigned to Burglary on the West Side. Two months later, Hagen went to Sex Crimes North and served in the Sex Crimes Unit till it was disbanded in 1981. Hagen has been in Area Six Violent Crimes for nine years.

LIEUTENANT ROBERT HARGESHEIMER, Fifteenth District field lieutenant. Hargesheimer joined the CPD as a cadet in 1969, was a patrol officer in Twenty-three from 1972 to 1974, and on the tac team in Twenty-three from 1974 to 1980, when he was assigned to the Special Investigations Unit as a patrolman. At his promotion to sergeant in 1981, Hargesheimer served as the administrative sergeant to the commander of the Youth Division until 1983. Hargesheimer worked as supervising sergeant in SIU from 1983 to 1988 and has been a field lieutenant in Fifteen since 1988. Hargesheimer also has experience as a hostage negotiator.

DETECTIVE SCOTT KEENAN, Area Six Violent Crimes. Keenan became a police officer in 1971, worked eight years in the patrol division in Twenty-three, spent one year in the Preventive Programs Division, was promoted to detective in 1978, assigned to Area Five Burglary. In 1980, Keenan joined the Sex Crimes Unit. Keenan has worked Area Six Violent Crimes since 1981. In 1988, Keenan was detailed to the Detective Division where he designed a Sexual Assault Investigation Protocol, which contains procedures for all officers who come in contact with sexual-assault victims.

YOUTH OFFICER BRIAN KILLACKY, Special Investigations Unit. Killacky is a nationally recognized authority on the sexual abuse and exploitation of children; he's frequently called on by the Justice Department to lecture to police departments across the country. Killacky worked in a suburban police force for two years before joining the CPD in 1976. Killacky worked Vice and tac assignments and was promoted to youth officer in 1981 and assigned to investigate the sexual abuse of children in Area Four. In 1982, Killacky, along with Sam Christian and Michael Dolan, was selected to implement the Special Investigations Unit, designed to target child pornography, child molestation, and juvenile prostitution and pimping. Killacky and his partners have developed hundreds of cases involving the sexual exploitation of children.

DETECTIVE CAREY ORR, Area Six Violent Crimes. Orr came on the CPD in 1978, worked patrol in the Fifteenth District until 1980, when he was promoted to detective and assigned to Area Six Violent Crimes.

LIEUTENANT CINDY PONTORIERO, Twenty-first District. Pontoriero, the first woman detective in the CPD, was assigned to Area Five Homicide in 1972, to the Sex Crimes Unit in Area Six in 1980, and to Area Six Violent Crimes in 1981. Pontoriero has twenty-three years on the force and seventeen years' experience as a violent crimes detective. After being promoted to sergeant, Pontoriero served as Area Six sex crimes coordinator from 1985 till 1988. In 1988, she was assigned to the Detective Division. Pontoriero joined the force as a policewoman in 1967.

DETECTIVE DAVID RYAN, Area Six Violent Crimes. After joining the force in 1977, Ryan was a patrol officer in Eighteen for three years and was promoted to detective in 1980. Ryan worked in Area Two Property Crimes for two years and then was assigned to Area Six Violent Crimes in 1982. He and Scott Keenan have been partners for five years.

DETECTIVE JAMES SPENCER, Area Six Violent Crimes. Spencer has been on the force since 1971; he worked as a patrol officer in Fifteen till 1973 and then was assigned to Special Operations in Areas Five and Six for seven years, and has been in Area Six Violent Crimes since 1980.

NARCOTICS

Eighty percent of all the paper money in the United States has cocaine residue on it. That fact's from an international symposium the FBI held in 1987 on drugs. In Florida, *any* money that's in Florida, can be analyzed and found to contain drugs because there's so much drug action down there. Here in Chicago—if you walked into the Crime Lab and you took off your jacket and subjected it to a minute enough analysis, we'd find drugs on it. It's everywhere.

**–Lieutenant Jim Nemec,
Chicago Crime Lab**

They swallow on us a lot. As soon as they see us come up, they swallow. Condoms full of cocaine, tinfoil with coke, heroin, little cut-up Baggies full of the stuff. If their stomach acid eats the package away before they retrieve the dope, they're dead. We tell 'em, "Don't take any plane rides."

–Area Six tactical officer

It used to be homicide detectives had all the rep. The cool. The toughness. The ability to walk into a room freshly festooned with blood and body parts and say to the district cops, "This ain't nothing."

Homicide dicks even get to dress well. Murder-rich Area Six has long had the tag "the Hollywood Division" for its bizarre, press-getting homicides and the flashy style of its homicide detectives. What could match Homicide for gritty glamor?

Narcotics. Especially Narcotics now, when, police say, the addict's need for drugs is the driving force behind roughly 75 percent of robberies, burglaries, and acts of prostitution; the addict's response to drugs fuels the most wantonly savage homicides, and the drug dealer's greed supplies both the addict and spiraling crime.

Narcotics cops move within this strung-out cycle, sometimes crashing in on dope dealers like storm troopers; sometimes slowly insinuating themselves into the dealer's confidence, stringing the game out, passing from what the cops call the bag guy to the kilo guy.

There's a phrase for much of what narcotics cops do—they "go through the doors"—meaning, they execute search warrants by kicking in doors, or smashing them open with sledgehammers or battering rams. This alone has given them a gutsy rep; running into rooms with well-armed dope dealers waiting on the other side is considered, next to walking up to a bomb, the most dangerous job in the police department.

"Narcotics has the biggest collection of ballsy coppers I've ever met in my life," says an ex-narcotics detective who now works Violent Crimes, "because it takes a lot of balls to walk up to a door where you don't know nothing about what's behind it and start swinging at it with a sledgehammer."

Narcotics cops go through doors of all sorts, the ones they smash open, and the ones that open for them once they've made the right moves and created the right role. They learn to mimic different kinds of junkies: the slack-jawed slur of the whore who's high, the swivel-headed jumpiness of the heroin addict in need, the constant nose-fiddling of the coked-up. They create elaborate identities for themselves when they move among dealers, going full dress in a studied con game leading up to the big buy-bust.

There's something else that marks the narcotics cop, whether he or she works in a district tactical unit on the street, or in the citywide Narcotics Unit—an almost insane relish for the job. They talk about tough doors, cockroaches, dead rats, rat-ass attorneys on dope-dealer retainer, shootouts on stairwells, not with horror but with hilarity. "This was great," said one narcotics cop after discussing over lunch various ways to induce vomiting in an addict who's swallowed a cocaine-filled condom. "This has brought back so many of the good times. Working dope is just so much fun."

Seven members of an Area Six tac team, skilled in the ways of the street and at breaking into dope houses, a former commander of city-wide Narcotics, and nine citywide officers, who do everything from going through doors to impersonating high-line drug dealers, and two ex-narcotics officers now working Violent Crimes, held forth on the intricacies of fighting the drug trade for this chapter.

The narcs interviewed include two women, one a former Area Six tac-team member and one who currently works citywide, both of whom have gone in on raids and buys. The citywide narcotics officers are divided into General Enforcement, which concentrates on street buys and search warrants, and Special Enforcement, which specializes in long-term investigations and undercover work. In reality, though, as one Narcotics Section cop put it, "We all end up doing everything. We roll with the best case."

Through all of it runs their conviction that Narcotics is the only game in town:

"When you go in on a raid, you always have to send somebody to watch the back door, and you can never get a volunteer for it. Every-body wants to be in on the action. Everybody likes living on that edge, you know what I mean? There's a high to it.

"The reason is, the average cop gets maybe one or two things a year where he's got a lot of action. In Narcotics, it's every night.

You're either knocking down people's doors or chasing guys down alleys.

"Working dope is as much of an addiction as being on dope."

"Street eyes": cop for the ability to read what's happening on the street. Crucial for narcotics cops, whose success and health depend on knowing who's selling what to whom and how they can disrupt the convoluted world of addict and dealer. . . .

One night, I had just started working in Narcotics, I'm with my team and we're watching some dealers on the corner. All of a sudden, they say, "Okay, kid. Go on out and make a buy." And I thought to myself, Oh, God, I'm just a middle-class kid. I've never heard of this stuff before. All I'd seen about drugs was what I'd seen on TV, with the addicts being sick and shaky and that.

So I go up to these Puerto Rican guys on the corner—they were working out of a little restaurant; you'd go up to them on the street and they'd motion you inside—and I walk up, shaking as hard as I could. And they look at me like I'm nuts. We go inside and we're sitting in a booth and the guy goes, "Okay, mon, what do you want?" And I'm "Uh . . . uh" and I'm shaking. And I don't know if he thought I was nervous or what, but I'm thinking, This is what they do on TV. This is what I gotta do. The look on this guy's face. It was like, give this guy something for nothing; calm him down. That was my first buy.

Then I went out and explained it to my surveillance team. "Yeah," I said, "I shook." And they're looking at me, and they've got these smiles on their faces like "Oh, kid."

Street dealers carry their drugs in their mouths or down in their undershorts. And what they're hoping is that the average street cop is not gonna search them there. Some of the guys from Narcotics would take them in the alley and make them drop their pants, and there it would be.

We had a young policewoman that had just got transferred into Narcotics. She was just perfect for it—a blonde Polish girl, very strict upbringing, in other words, didn't really fit as a cop—and this was a whole new world for her.

Well, the first time we sent her out to make a buy by herself, we're watching from across the street. And we all break up laughing because, as she pulls up to the guy on the corner and gets out of the car and walks up to him and hands him the money for the drugs, he goes down into his crotch and pulls out the balloons. She's supposed to put them in her mouth—the idea was you swallow them if the police come up. But she takes her purse and sticks it about two feet out in front of her and says, "Oh, you pig! Put it in here." So we tell her later on, "You know, you've gotta be a little more street-wise than that." "*I* wasn't going to touch those things," she says. "How do I know what he was doing before?"

We used to go and get mortician's wax from the neighborhood undertaker. We molded the stuff to manufacture scars on our hands and arms to look like dope tracks. We'd build the wax up on our veins with this stuff and darken it up with some ink and dirt and make it look like we had tracks from using dope. Because a lot of times, dope dealers, when you go to buy dope, they want to see tracks to make sure that you're a junkie and not the police.

You have to get yourself into a mindset to buy drugs on the street. It's hard. You go out there and you have to be something that you're not. I'm the mother of two children, I have a husband, I've been married eighteen years—I don't go out and buy drugs on the street. But I have to get myself into that mindset.

This one time I go out there, right? My partner goes, "You have to get out of the car"; I got out of the car. I'm trintzing up and down the street. My surveillance is down the street.

So this guy comes up to me and says, "Hey, baby, what you want?" And I tell him I want a quarter bag. He goes, "Well, I can't get it for you, but I know another guy."

Now, the other guy comes up. So I tell him I want a quarter bag. And he says, "You look like you're a cop." And I say, "Cop!" And he says, "Yeah. You look just like a cop." And I say, "Hey, I don't know about *you,* but all the woman police officers *I* ever saw had big fat asses."

I turn around and stick my ass out at him. And I go, "You ever see a cop with an ass like this?" And he says, "No. No." And he sold to me. I never said I *wasn't* a cop. I just asked if I had a cop ass.

We got a tip about this cabdriver that was selling coke out of his taxicab. He was a fairly hefty dealer. And I met up with him at this little coffee shop at about two in the morning. A whore tipped us off to this guy and set up the meeting. So there was the whore, and me, I was acting like a whore, and this cabbie dealer. It happened real quickly, so I didn't have much time to whore myself up; I was just wearing my blue jeans, what I wore into work that night.

We met at this horrible little coffee shop, and my backup is sitting a few booths away, just merrily eating bacon and eggs, reading the paper, eating away, eating away. So this guy comes up and we start talking. And the horrible thing is, I had to have coffee with this guy, and because he thought I was a whore, here he had his hand on my upper thigh and I couldn't flinch. So there I was—this man's *hand* on my thigh, drinking coffee. Oog.

We finally got around to—I wanted to buy an amount. He says, "Well, you know, how do I know you're on the up-and-up?" So I took out a flash roll—I had about $200—and I gave him twenty bucks. And I said, "Look, I don't know you either." And I was gonna eat the twenty if the guy skipped.

Before that, though, we also talked about prostitution. He asked who I worked for. I said, "I work for myself. I don't work for anybody." And he said, "Well, you know, if you worked for *me,* I pick up all the conventioneers . . ."—and this cabbie had a list on him from like the Department of Tourism for Chicago listing what dates all the conventions were, where they were—and he says, "I can suggest your name. Think of all the people you can meet that way. You're too pretty to have to stand out on a street corner." "Well I'll have to think about it. I don't know. You're sounding *good.* I can understand the *business* of this. But I never like working for people."

So it got to where I gave him the twenty—he was gonna have to go somewhere to pick up the dope; he wouldn't tell me where—and he drove off in his cab. That left me and the real whore and my backup. We're waiting and waiting and waiting, and no one was coming back. So finally we called off the surveillance, because we figured he just took the twenty and ran.

And as soon as one of the tac cars pulled out of its position—it had a good hiding place—the cab showed up, with this guy driving. And he spotted the tac car right away and took off. He had a guy in the backseat of the car. We saw him toss a packet out the window. That was the coke. So we retrieved the coke.

In the meantime, I just kept walking to the police station, because it was just a couple blocks away. They got this cabbie and the other guy, an enforcer whose nickname was Hammer.

What the cabbie did when he left the coffee shop was, he got the coke. But he also picked up his enforcer. And Hammer told us that the cabbie told him that there was this white girl he wanted working for him and she didn't have a pimp, and he was supposed to beat the shit out of me and God knows what else—and they were gonna keep me until I said yes, I'd work for the cabbie.

My partner and I were making some undercover buys around Wrigley Field. This was in the early seventies.

One of the guys that I purchased from sold me a burn bag, which happens sometimes. I got what I thought was a bag of heroin wrapped in a balloon, and as I was opening it to check it, the guy I had purchased from ran into the building and got away. I found it was a cigarette filter—so he burned me with a cigarette filter.

We were making all these buys in the area, so I had to go back, because if I didn't go back and say anything, this guy would think, This is awful strange. I just sold to this junkie, and he don't seem to care—I was acting like a junkie then; real dirty and nasty; long hair; I had a goatee, always acted real nervous, looking around all the time—so I had to go back and confront this guy; otherwise, he'd know I was the police.

So the next day, I went back there with my partner and found this guy that I had bought from. And I confronted him on the street. This guy and I got into a fistfight. And while I was fighting with him—my partner was down the street on the corner—another guy ran out of the building and jumped in on me also. He was a friend of the guy that burned me. So my partner and I ended up fighting with these two people on the street.

It turned into a pretty good fight—this guy picked up a house brick and was whacking me over the head with the house brick—and my partner and me got separated. He was about fifty feet away from me with the one guy, and I was with the other guy, and at this point they didn't know we were the police.

Now the one guy my partner was fighting with pulled out a knife and got my partner down on the ground and stabbed him several times. I was able to get free from the guy I was fighting and get to my partner's aid. I tackled the guy and threw him off my partner, and he came up at me with the knife and I had to shoot and kill the guy.

There was a crowd of about a hundred people that had gathered because this was right in the middle of the daytime, right in front of this old flophouse where a lot of junkies hung out, right down the street from Cubs Park.

So a big crowd had gathered, and after it was over, my partner was bleeding on the street. He was stabbed in the stomach, slashed across the hands, stabbed in the arm. I went to show my star to this crowd of angry people, right, I had to identify myself, and the whole back of my pants was ripped away from fighting with this guy. I couldn't find my wallet with my star; it had fallen out of my pants in this fight. That was pretty scary.

But we had surveillance officers that were in the area, and when they heard the shot, they came right up to us. Then a 10-1 was filed, an officer needing assistance. I'd only been in Narcotics about a year when this happened.

You work the street and you see kids walking around in slow motion. They've got severe, irreversible brain damage. Their brains are just fried. They're on toluene.

Toluene is *the* most dangerous drug out there. They call it tollie on the street. It's a paint thinner. It's big with Appalachian white kids; twelve years old on up; you don't see black kids doing it. They pay one dollar for a four-inch-by-four-inch rag soaked in toluene. Or they pick up a half-pint bottle on the street, they bring it to the tollie supplier; he buys a gallon of paint thinner. He pours it in the half-pints, fills it with three, four ounces for five dollars. This stuff is good for a lot of people. The hillbilly kids tell us they like to use it on girls because it's supposed to make them real loose. They say they'll do anything on tollie. The big kids give it to the juniors; these little kids take it because they look up to these guys.

You can't buy it in the city; guys bring it in from hardware stores in the suburbs; it's about eight bucks a gallon. They make about fifty dollars on the gallon. These assholes make a nice profit.

Within a year, the kids' lungs and brains are destroyed. It eats your brain cells up. The kids look fried; they're marshmallows. They walk in slow motion. They look like zombies out here. We tell them to smoke marijuana; it's better for them. Sometimes you get them in the squad car and they start coughing on you and you've gotta get out of the car. It's like you're snorting it yourself.

How many tollie dealers go to jail? Nobody. They treat it very lightly in court.

If you see a guy walking down the street, throwing punches in the air, knocking out windows, you know he's on PCP. It's a very violent high. We came up on another team once subduing a guy on PCP, and they had broken this guy's arm; it's just hanging there; he didn't even know it was broken.

You grab a guy you think is using coke—"You use coke?" "No, I don't use coke." First thing you do is tilt his head up and look up his nose and say, "You're full of shit. You're using coke." Because cocaine absolutely destroys nose hairs; that's the tell-tale sign.

Junkie whores don't like to have tracks. They don't like their customers to know they're junkies. So they shoot heroin right into their groins. Or they use liquid Vitamin E to take away the tracks.

A junkie whore told me about it. She used to do ten guys at two bucks a blow and then she'd go and buy her twenty-dollar bag. I said, "How come you don't have any tracks?" She said, "I squeeze Vitamin E capsules on my arm after I shoot up."

Junkies age fast and die fast. We know a junkie whore who's twenty-eight; she looks fifty-eight. We knew one real beautiful girl, we started watching her when she was twelve years old, very blond hair; she looked Scandinavian. Her street name was Snow. That could have been for two reasons: her hair and her skin were so white or it could have been that she was a coke addict. She died at seventeen.

With heroin addicts, you can tell right away—just by the complexion. They've all got very sallow complexions. They sweat a lot. They're itchy, scratchy. If you see a heroin addict sitting, in a coffee shop or something, his head's on a swivel; he's always looking around; he's jumpy. They're antsy. They need something.

Dopers borrow needles from each other the way other people borrow cups of sugar. They don't care. Once they shoot it into their veins, they don't give a fuck. They might take a precaution, put it in some alcohol and some cotton, or shoot it through a cigarette filter. They think that helps, but not enough; they don't care enough. They want it in. They got a needle; they don't care where the needle came from. They don't even wash the needle off. They pass the needles around. They use used needles laying around the floor of a shooting gallery; they don't care who was there. They never wash them off. Never.

Sometimes we come across a shooting gallery. You just happen on them; usually, it's an apartment or a room in an abandoned building, with maybe a mattress on the floor. Word gets around that here's this empty room; dopers come in and shoot up; they use the stuff that's lying around.

You usually see a lot of cotton balls and wine bottle caps on the floor. The junkies use the caps off cheap bottles of wine to cook heroin in; they like these caps better than pop bottle caps because they're deeper. They call them cookers. They put some water and heroin in the cap and heat it up with a match—a candle is being sophisticated. They take a syringe and draw the liquid out. There may still be a drop or two inside the cooker; that's why you see so many cotton balls; the cotton ball gets it all up. Junkies don't want to miss a drop of that stuff. Then they inject it.

You see a lot of kits on the floor—heavy rubber bands to tie their arms; needles lying around, or eye droppers with needles attached, caps. It's not uncommon for ten or fifteen junkies to share a kit. It's real common for a junkie to come into a shooting gallery and use whatever's lying around on the floor. He don't know who left the needles and he don't care.

Everybody has this image of the heroin addict as somebody who lies around sweating on a mattress or puking in the gutter. Not true. They do just fine when they're on the stuff.

We set up an operation once where we'd watch the heroin addicts come and buy, and we'd let them get a couple blocks away and then we'd stop them and arrest them. Among the people we stopped, besides the regular junkies, was a female accountant for a major airline who was a heroin addict, making $45,000 a year, dressed to the nines in a three-piece suit. She'd shoot down the highway from O'Hare on her lunch hour every day, go buy her heroin and shoot it up, then drive back to work.

See, once they get that heroin into their system and they get off that nod which lasts about fifteen minutes, half an hour, they now can do any other function in a completely normal way until the drug starts wearing off and they start getting sick again. A lot of productive people are heroin addicts.

You watch for junkies first thing in the morning. Heroin addicts always cop first thing in the morning and late at night. They have to go for a cop first thing in the morning, because when they wake up, they start getting sick because it's been eight hours since they last shot up. And once they shoot up, they're fine.

Ten years ago, all we saw on the street was brown heroin from Mexico. Now, it's all cocaine. Heroin's still there, of course. Heroin always was and always will be. But cocaine is the drug of choice now.

Chicago has crack, but it's nothing compared to New York, D.C., and Detroit. Jamaicans are the ones who bring in crack; they set up the crack houses; they run everything. They're very, very dangerous people.

So far, they haven't been able to get a foothold in Chicago, we figure, because Chicago's a very volatile gang area. Chicago gangs are not going to be willing to let anybody else in without a lot of bloodshed, and they're used to it, they've been killing each other for years. This is not an easy-play city. You're not gonna have an outside gang coming into Chicago and taking over any territory without a lot of bodies rolling. This territory is staked out, and they'll defend it. They'll die for it. They always have, and they always will.

Crack is the fast food of dope. It's ready-made; ready to go. Freebasing is the same thing as crack, but you have to be a good chef to freebase. They call them the "cooker"—not everybody can cook.

You know what a couple crack addicts told me? They say crack is like the devil's breath. You become instantly addicted. Crashing is terrible. That's why there's so much crime with crack. They'll do anything to keep that five-minute high.

In citywide Narcotics, we go by two measurements to see what drugs are moving: the total seizures we make of a given drug, and overdoses. Heroin seizures have pretty much stayed the same. But cocaine seizures have increased four-hundred-fold since 1984.

You find out that the overdoses are always about the same consistently for heroin, no increase, no decrease. But what has happened over the last several years is a dramatic increase in overdoses for cocaine. That shows two things: that you're getting a better-purity drug, and a lot more people are using it.

On the street, heroin is "boy"; coke is "girl."

Heroin is cheaper. Heroin is cheap. It's fifty dollars a gram for heroin, one hundred dollars for cocaine. Most of the transactions on the street are less than a quarter of a gram, a twenty-five-dollar bag for cocaine. See, they want to make it affordable to the junkies. With heroin, it's eight-dollar bags, ten-dollar bags. You can get some heroin for a sawbuck. But with coke, they start at twenty-five dollars; a bag could be thirty dollars, fifty dollars, on up. If you're buying, you don't say, "I want two bags of heroin or coke," you say, "I want two boy or two girl."

There's a new kind of white heroin now called Karachi, like in Pakistan. It looks like raspberry Kool-Aid. Karachi's even more expensive than cocaine, about $3,000 an ounce. It's smoking heroin. You don't mainline it, because it's not water-soluble; you snort it or you put it in a cigarette and smoke it. It's an immediate rush to the brainstem, very potent. White heroin is extremely more addictive than brown heroin. It's much more pure.

Nigerians import it. They fill condoms with white heroin, get on a plane, stick it up their rectums on the plane, get off, go to the delivery place, and excrete the stuff. What they don't realize is, if that condom breaks, they're dead. It's immediate death. Nobody can take that amount of heroin in their system. They're walking around with a time bomb inside of them. If they don't get it out, they die.

* * *

We did a search warrant one day in Area Six where four Nigerian women came in. Each of them carried ten ounces of white heroin apiece. Probably you're talking about $200,000 to $300,000 street retail for each ten ounces. It comes in 100 percent pure; you break that down to street level where it's usually 5 percent pure, you can imagine the profit. This has been going on for years.

So these women come in; they're right off the tribal reservation in Nigeria. They're very poor people. And the smugglers give them $2,000 each, more money than they're ever going to see in their lifetime, to bring the stuff in. So they come in; they go to the location where they excrete it.

What these women do, after they're done excreting, they go to grocery stores and load up on disposable diapers to bring back to the reservation. They always go back loaded with diapers.

Sometimes you'll ask, "What are you looking for?," you know, to some of the girls who are strung out, some of the guys who are strung out, and they say, "If I could be put in a room, and intravenously be shot with Demerol or morphine or heroin, I'd just stay in that room; I'd just exist right in that room." That'd be it. If they could stay in that room their whole life, intravenously be there, and not move, and keep that high where they have it, just keep it, that's what they'd go for.

It's a class thing. Heroin still carries a certain negative or lower-class connotation. Cocaine is the drug of choice of the middle and upper-middle class, and it carries a certain panache to it, a certain status to have cocaine. Because of that, you have people who will use cocaine and will look down on someone using heroin. But they're every *bit* as addicted, if not more addicted, than the heroin addict.

A heroin addict can adapt to a daily life. A heroin addict shoots only so much and doesn't need more. But a coke addict is progressive.

The coke addict comes down harder than the heroin addict, because the heroin puts you on the nod, but coke is a very speedy high. You're very alert to what's going on, and once you reach that point, you want to come down.

So the coke user will use heroin too, a lot of times, to come down off that high. And that's when you use heroin or you go to a downer or you go to a barbiturate, you go to the 'ludes—or whatever. The one habit feeds the other when you use cocaine. Because you're at such a point of anxiety, you've got to come down. And that's when they shoot heroin usually. That's one other reason why cocaine is so deadly.

I've seen and arrested people that are addicted to cocaine, and the lust for it is so great, they'd probably sell their souls for it. They will do *anything* for their dope, especially when they start freebasing it. They can go through an ounce a day for personal habit. That results in the expenditure of a lot of money. If they have a good steady source, they can probably pick it up for $1,000 an ounce. If they're buying it at sixteenths or eighths, they'll probably end up spending $1,500–$1,600 an ounce for it.

The middle-class coke addict will bleed his family dry. Their victims are everybody they know—they will use their mother, they will use their brother, their friends; they will lie, they will cheat; it's one vicious circle, anybody who's close to them, they'll end up using them. When they can't use them anymore, then they'll go on to somebody else. They'll soak everybody they know—and when everybody's soaked dry, then they'll go into crime.

The lower class can't bleed their family and friends. There's nothing to bleed anyway—no collateral. They go right into crime.

Junkies are conscious, man. They gotta do what they gotta do. If they gotta go suck a prick to get the shit, they'll suck a prick. If they gotta rip somebody off, they'll rip him off. No matter what they tell you, they only care about one thing, and that's getting that high.

There was this junkie kid, always hitting his mother up for dope money. He ended up killing her for it. This was a woman who found a baby abandoned in a garbage can in Puerto Rico, saved the baby, raised him as her own. The kid becomes a junkie, always asking his mother for dope money. She'd give it to him. One time she said no. She fell asleep on the living-room couch; he stabbed her to death and took the money out of her purse.

Drugs have revolutionized crime. There's been an enormous, and almost totally unrecognized, boom in shoplifting—it's an easy crime, low risk.

Another change—criminals of the past had something that they wanted to *do* with the profits from crime. Most of today's criminals, though, just want to convert their contraband into cash to buy dope.

We knew a forty-nine-year-old junkie, a true heroin addict, he did heroin for forty years. He was a great shoplifter, retail-theft man, he'd go into liquor stores, steal bottles, bring it to the guy, and get his money for his fixes. He died about a year and a half ago. They said his heart burst.

Dominic was fascinating to listen to, the way he'd talk. We could listen to him for hours. Real nice guy. Good-looking guy too. When he was cleaned up, he looked good.

His mother died; she left him the house. He ended up selling the house for dope money. Him and his brother—his brother was a cocaine dealer—went through everything their mother left them and sold the house.

He was an excellent shoplifter. All booze. Because you can always sell a bottle of booze. He had shoplifting down to a science. He told us, "You don't go by nothing twice. You see it the first time; grab it on the way in."

He went to prison. They played a joke on him. They circumcised him. Legit. Now, he's in the infirmary; they bring in the fruits, the transsexuals, and they do an erotic dance in front of him. He says he blew twelve stitches. I says, "You got excited?" He says, "You're in prison, you get excited."

We asked him about drugs, and he said he would rather do drugs than anything. We said, "Than fuck?" He says, "Yeah. You're with a girl; then it's over with. But the drugs last." Boy, he really analyzed it though, the heroin. He said it was better than anything you could do. It was like a mistress to him.

Dominic liked everything about being a junkie burglar. Planning the score, going to the score, copping, thinking about when he was going to get it in his vein. The whole excitement. You could see he was excited when he was talking about it. It was all part of the same ritual. The escape. The risk. It gave him a high. If you gave him the dope, if you came and gave him dope, I don't think he'd appreciate it as much as what he had to go through for it.

In the police, if you've got two flaky guys in a district, somehow they'll end up with each other. It's the same with junkies. You can take two junkies—they don't know each other, put them in a party of a thousand people, all of them straight, and somehow they'll find each other. They can be at a Bears game and they'll find each other. It's an inner magnetism.

The average habit costs between $200 and $400 a day. Junkies on the street aren't out there buying a gram. They're out there buying twenty-dollar bags. As soon as they get their twenty dollars, they go and cop. They don't wait. They've got to get it into their veins as soon as they can.

We're sitting on a dope house one night, and within half an hour, we see a whore spend sixty dollars. She'd turn a twenty-dollar date, go buy dope, turn a twenty-dollar date, go buy dope, turn a twenty-dollar date, go buy dope. Half an hour. Back and forth. We couldn't believe it.

We ended up busting that house. There was a girl selling

cocaine for her brothers at the door. The whole family was a drug family; they set the girl up and they told her not to sell to anybody except girls so nobody could rob her; if she sold to a guy, a guy could take her out. So we had a prostitute go up there to cop, and then we hit the joint. The dope was hidden in one of the baby's toys. It was a little mechanical dog, and the mouth was stuffed with cocaine.

VCRs are *the* big things to steal now. A VCR will get maybe fifty dollars on the street, enough for two bags of coke. Shithead burglars will take an $800 loss on a VCR to get a bag of coke.

You knock over a good dealer's house and there'll be all kinds of property in there, because not only do they take cash, they take merchandise too.

Dealers aren't very compassionate people. If they're selling twenty-dollar bags and a guy came with eight bucks, they'd tell him unh-unh. So the guy walks down the street and breaks into the first car he sees and brings back a car radio and gives him the eight bucks *and* the radio. Then he'd get his bag. It's amazing when you think someone could break in your house and steal your computer, your VCR, or whatever, and probably get five or ten dollars for it. The most important thing to them is the dope. And the dealers adjust their prices according to their read on how bad these guys are hurting.

Cocaine addicts tend to be violent criminals. They're much more aggressive than heroin addicts. Coke makes them think they have more balls.

Everything I see now with robberies and homicide is coke. I don't know the last time I saw a heroin perp. And now, when you see a particularly vicious murder and you pinch the guy and you say, "How the hell could you do that?"—"Oh, man, I was high on coke at the time."

* * *

Every criminal that used to have to climb a roof to burglarize a place, pull a pistol to stick up a place—they don't have to do it anymore. There's big money in drugs. All you have to do is deal.

Anybody can play. There are enough customers for everybody. On the street, it's not like an organized crime type thing, though the Outfit is in on it too. Everybody is trying to get themselves a piece of the action, whether it's Puerto Rican street gangs, black street gangs, kids, adults on the commodities exchange.

There's just so much money to be made. Especially with cocaine. Cocaine has made even black dope dealers that for years dealt only heroin rich beyond their wildest imaginations.

We did a raid on a white guy in the suburbs once. We seized $1 million cash. We brought it in to headquarters, had it all counted out and stacked on a table; it took hours and hours to count it all out. The guy's sitting there, and he says to the copper who's just sort of looking at the table, "You get your rocks off looking at this stuff?" The copper says, "Hey, I never seen this kind of money before." And the guy says, "Let me tell you, kid. That ain't shit." And it isn't.

The vast amounts of money are on the street level, where they're breaking the dope down into ten-, twenty-, twenty-five-dollar bags.

Now don't get me wrong. There's *nobody* making more money than the Colombians with cocaine or the Mexicans coming out of Durango with heroin. They have probably billions of dollars. And the Colombians are making more money than anybody. I mean, what's it cost them? By the time they put it together, it might have cost them a couple hundred dollars a kilo. By the time it hits Miami, it's worth fifteen thousand. By the time it hits Chicago, it's worth twenty-two.

I mean, a guy may be selling hundreds of twenty-five-dollar bags at street level. And the cartels are selling a hundred *kilo* bags. They're pushing out so much of this coke.

The only thing is, your profit margin is so much greater if you're a street dealer. You can buy ounces of high-grade coke, high-grade heroin, cut it down for bag-level sale and make $3,000–$4,000 an ounce.

So here's a guy that has three or four dope houses going; he's got twenty people on the street working for him, and he's pumping out three, four, five thousand bags of dope a *day*.

Maybe he buys kilos or multiple ounces. His profit margin is so much greater, the markup is so much higher for him than for a middleman or even the guy who's dealing in kilos, because he's whacking it, he's putting a lot of mix on it. He may cop an ounce for $1,000; by the time he mixes it all up and dishes it out at street level, he's getting $5,000 return.

The guy selling kilos is making 20 percent; the guy running this string of bag houses is making 500 percent profit. There's a lot of people in this city driving Mercedes, Cadillacs, and everything else, and they ain't working.

The beeper has been the greatest boon to the dope business, followed closely by the mobile phone. It's allowed for instant communications and allowed them not to be confined to one location.

The mobility—they can now reach out for . . . whoever: their source, their runner, their middleman, their packager, all by beeper. They use codes on the beeper for who's who—eleven might be their runner; twelve might be their supplier—they're using the beepers as identifiers, to take orders and everything.

They've been banned in Chicago schools; the kids were getting beeped in the classrooms by their customers.

When you buy heroin, what you're buying is about 5 percent pure; the other 95 percent is shit: they cut it with baking powder, quinine, powdered sugar, brown sugar, whatever's handy.

Coke's a lot purer, anywhere from 60- to 97-percent pure. You cut coke with pharmaceutical powdered milk, like Mannitol, a powdered milk sugar—we've gotten it right from the pharmaceutical company, and it's expensive, thirty dollars a pound; at a head shop, it's sixty dollars a pound—they use that, or they use inositol, a powdered milk.

You get more ODs with cocaine than you do with heroin, especially today. A lot of people don't know how to test it properly when they buy kilos; it's a lot purer now, and they start cutting it according to how they cut it in the past, and people OD on the stuff.

New York junkies are accustomed to stronger dope. In New York, heroin is about 10 percent pure; here, you're looking at 3 to 5 percent. If a junkie from Chicago cops in New York, he'll get sick; he could OD.

The only Americans who have ever accepted the metric system are the dope dealers. Here are guys who probably couldn't get a D in grade school math, and they're converting grams to ounces to kilos at the bat of an eye.

In the seventies, dope was sold by different ethnic groups in different forms. Hispanics put heroin in toy balloons that they'd cut into tiny pieces, easy for swallowing. Blacks used tinfoil. And you never arrested a black with a balloon and you never arrested a Hispanic using tinfoil.

Now, we've entered the Age of the Ziploc. All the dealers—black, Hispanic, white—use minifreezer bags, about as big as your thumb, to package cocaine. That's one way of doing it.

The other way that they do—they get small Baggies, they bring the dope over to the corner of the Baggie, down to the lower corner, press it all the way down, then tie a knot, as tight as they can, and cut it—so it's a very small, tight little package. It's a lot simpler than cutting balloons. And they can use two corners of the Baggie, where with the balloon they could only use one part. Another thing, too, with the Baggie, is nice, because it's clear, so whoever's purchasing can see the product.

You see all kinds of ways with heroin. You'll see heroin in aluminum paper, in the Ziploc, in the Baggie. These are the three most popular.

They used balloons in the old days, and they use condoms and Baggies now so they can deliver dope in their mouths, without it being noticed by the police, and so they can swallow if they *are* discovered.

You get some of these mules coming in from South America—they have them swallow five or six condoms full of cocaine, put them on a plane, and fly them up to Miami. If enough time goes by, the stomach acid can eat away at the condom and it'll break and they'll die. These guys must live in mortal terror of holding patterns.

We were in a house once; we did a search on this guy; he had the dope hidden in his crotch. The copper who found it goes, "Ah ha *ha!* I found it," and the junkie gets the balloon back and swallows it.

This one guy on our team is so mad that we finally got this dealer and he swallows on us, he gets a bottle of baby oil and pours it down the dealer's throat. Then he takes a dildo that was lying around and starts ramming it down his throat, trying to make him vomit. He was frustrated. We had a new guy on the team; he had to help hold this dealer, he was a big guy, to pour baby oil down his throat. It was his first week on the team. He was in shock.

If you use, you deal. That's an automatic. But a dealer doesn't necessarily use.

Anyone that has a cocaine habit is also likely to be a dealer, because he or she is looking for any way in the world to support their habit. If they know they can build up a clientele to where they can pick up an ounce for $800 to $1,200 and then make $200 or $300 on that ounce, they're paying for their own habit.

Or they'll fall behind in payments to their dealer. Then the dealer makes *them* a dealer, has them sell around to their friends, maybe, as a way to pay off the debt.

In the drug business, they've got a couple sayings: "Don't get high on your own supply" and "If you use, you lose." They're successful as long as they don't use. It's about fifty-fifty who uses, who doesn't. Any dealer who uses his own product will never last. He'll either OD because he has access to too much pure shit or he'll become sloppy about business. He gets careless, especially when he sees the opportunity to make a lot of fast money. That's when we can get him.

We knew this one family, Cubans; they were doing all right till they started using. We used to hit the house, they had thousands of dollars just laying around. They sold heroin, and they would chip cocaine. They sold the dope because that was bad and that was crap, and they'd sell it to blacks. The parents had their children sell at the door while they slept. But the old-man dealer started using cocaine himself, and he ended up getting his whole family hooked: his daughter, his son-in-law, his brother, the whole family. Before they got knocked out of business and went to jail, they were all fucked up.

You'll have whole families of dope dealers. They sit around the kitchen table and cut dope together. They hide dope in the baby's diapers and money on the little kids. They'll have the kids sell dope at the front door.

All these dope dealers—there's not *one* of them that lives like *Miami Vice*. They live like rats. They live like shit.

We hit a three-room apartment once. The floors were buckling from the weight of all the new furniture. They had a forty-

inch color TV, a dining-room set with the china cabinet and all
that, a fifteen-hundred-dollar double refrigerator-freezer combination. It was all covered with cockroaches. We were search-
ing in the furniture, all brand new, and all of it was filled with
cockroaches. A year later, they were evicted; they couldn't fit
the furniture down the stairs, so they just threw it out the windows.

They live in squalor and they dress in style. One of the big
symbols for having money in the drug culture is having a Troop
jacket, a designer jacket that's a combination of leather and
suede, they run between $300 and $500. You have to chain the
jacket to your body, because you know about fourteen other
guys have worn it that day.

Not all kids who have them are dealers, but all dope dealers
have them.

We ran an operation once, out of a van, on the South Side near
the University of Chicago. And all these guys dealing, we could
easily identify them because they were all wearing this $500
jacket. And behind them was this backdrop of poverty, kids
with holes in their shoes, abandoned buildings, vacant lots.

With dope dealers, it's money; they blow it. They have no idea
what money could do. They don't use it to upgrade themselves.
It's show. It's flash. They don't leave the turf. They'll have tons
of money and live in a place with rats in the closet. Not everybody, understand. Not the big distributors. But a *lot* of dealers.
It's a mentality.

We hit this real scummy place. Roaches all over. A dead rat
in the closet. When we hit the door, everybody inside scat-
tered. They left this little Easter egg trail of dope, these little
knotted plastic Baggies with half an ounce of coke in each of
them, all leading to the bedroom, where we found $12,000 on
the bed.

* * *

It's the American Dream. A flashy car. Nice clothes. Enough money to take care of your girlfriend. Enough blow to stick up your nose.

Dope dealers have attorneys on retainer. The average, just for preliminary hearings, these attorneys are averaging $1,000 a day to defend basically street dealers, for small amounts of drugs.

I know an attorney—one of his clients got hit on the near Northwest Side. We confiscated four houses, a safety-deposit box, a bank account, and at least a pound of cocaine. I happen to know that the attorney was on a $10,000 retainer so he can drop everything and defend this scumbag.

I've arrested offenders that have admitted that they paid their attorneys in drugs.

The Colombians are the most vicious dealers around. They'll cut your throat out, go home, and have lunch. The Cubans are the next most violent. They're rough people. Mexicans and blacks are just so-so on violence. And the Puerto Ricans are the least violent.

You don't mess with Colombians. You don't back out of their dope deals. Colombians will kill you; they'll kill your family. On a big deal, they'll hold one of your family till the deal is down.

They have another signature, the Colombian necktie. If you've reneged on a deal, say, or informed on them, they'll slit your throat and pull your tongue out through the slit. It's just a thing they do to show it came from Colombians.

We were talking to an informant one day, and he told us when he was dealing really heavy, some Cubans came to his house one day. They were going to rip him off. And he wouldn't tell them where his stash was. He had a real good hiding place. He had cut a hole in the floor and put a board down and put the drugs in there. When they started beating him up, he wouldn't

tell where it was. One of the guys took a pot of water, put it on
the stove, went over to the crib, grabbed the baby, and held it
by the feet over the boiling water, and said, "Now, you want to
tell us where it is?" And he said, "Yep. Over here. Under the
floor." Boom.

It's dangerous to be a dealer. A dope dealer is *the* most likely
candidate to be robbed or burglarized for two reasons: the
money or the drug.

These bag houses may deal to two hundred customers a day,
or more. Each one of these junkies knows that there's a lot of
money and drugs there. A guy will rob a shoe store for $200.
That same guy knows the dope dealer has at least $5,000 laying
around. Some dope houses have $50,000, $60,000, $70,000 in
cash, it's more money than you have in a lot of banks or cur-
rency exchanges. If I can rip off a dealer for $50,000, I'm set. So
junkies rip them off all the time. And other dealers—a rival
gang might come in, wipe the guy out to eliminate him.

What's he gonna do—call the IRS? The police? What's he
gonna say—"They broke in and stole my drugs and my drug
money?"

That's why—I don't think we ever arrested a drug dealer that
didn't have a gun. They all have guns. And the more they're
into drugs, the more ridiculous they get with guns. It's nothing
to go into a house and get ten guns and a thousand rounds of
ammunition. You say, "What are you doing with all these
guns?" and they say, "Man, it's dangerous."

**Narcotics officers hit dealers where they sell, by impersonating
junkies and making buys, by discovering the dope house and then
running in and getting the dope, or through a complicated series
of maneuvers that gain cops the confidence, the secrets, and
finally the arrest of dealers themselves. . . .**

You've got some really sophisticated operations out there.
When they do something like surveillance, they don't go
to Radio Shack, they go to Motorola. They go where the big
guys go.

They have better equipment than we do. I wish we had the

equipment they have. They've got better weapons than we do—
anybody will tell you that. And they pay better.

We basically work on the greed of the dealer. The drug
dealer's biggest downfall is greed.

You can be with a dealer, say, in a bar. And you know he's
looking at you and he's thinking *police.* It's like he sees COP
emblazoned on your forehead. You bring out the money. He
might still be thinking COP, but what you see on *his* forehead,
and really, you can almost see it, is GREED. Greed always wins.

There are two types of dealers: One is the discreet dealer,
where he has a select clientele and he doesn't deal with anybody else—he's real hard to catch; and then there's the indis-
creet dealer, the street dealer—he'll sell to anyone. Those are
the houses and the street narcotics.

The big thing about narcotics is, it's always an introduction.
Like any other business, they're all looking for new customers
all the time. So even though they're going to be wary of people,
they still have to have new customers to stay in business, and
therefore they take chances, and that's how we get into them.

If you know some drug dealer and you and I are friends, if you
introduce me to this guy, if he trusts you, he'll trust me.

A lot of times that middle person is an informant, and he's
setting this drug dealer up with a policeman. The dealer may
not know this middle guy very well, but he sees the chance to
make that big, quick money. He might think, I don't know this
guy real well, I don't trust him, but he sees the chance to make
big money, and greed takes over. And they do it. And they get
caught.

* * *

The biggest asset that we have as a working tool is informants, but you have to be careful with informants.

Informants are probably the least trustworthy people in the world. They'd flip on their mother. You have to realize that up-front. But these are the people you need. So you have to worm the truth out of them, because the reason they're informants is they all have a motive *behind* giving information on someone. Always. It could be they'll knock out the competition; it could be revenge because they got screwed by one of these guys before; it could be they're under the gun and they're about to go away for forty years; it could be a sexual thing. It could be money. Sometimes you get police groupies—we had this one fruit who was begging us to sign him up as an informant; it was like "Yoohoo, sailor—tighten your gun belt—pistol-whip me, you stallion."

You never want to give up an informant. They die if you do. We had a case where an informant tipped us off to a dope house, we hit the place, arrested everybody, brought them back to the station. Then the informant called. We had a new guy on the team. He said, "There's a phone call for you, Sarge. It's Stacy." That was the informant's name. Everybody from the dope house looked at each other. Now they *knew* who gave them up. The new guy had signed her death warrant. The sergeant made me drive around for hours till I found Stacy. I told her she'd been made, and she left town that night.

As soon as possible after the initial meeting, we try to take the informant out of it altogether. I'll ask the bad guy for a phone number, a beeper number, some way I can get in touch with him on my own. Usually, I'll tell him some kind of story; I'll say something like, "You know, every time Johnny introduces me to somebody and I buy some drugs, he always wants part of the bag for himself—he's hard to get ahold of—I really don't like dealing through him or with him—can I get ahold of you on my own so I don't have to deal with Johnny anymore.' " Anything to cut the informant out of any further negotiations; after a while, the bad guy tends to forget Johnny did the introduction in the first place, so Johnny stays safe.

So once the guy's willing to do that, then you're rolling. Then you have several meetings where you meet and do nothing except talk—to gain the guy's confidence. Once he gets to the point where he thinks you are who you say you are, he sees nothing but money.

When I started doing undercover in the early seventies, the way the Narcotics Unit was structured then, there wasn't that much money to operate with as there is now. They used to give a team, of like six guys and a sergeant, $100 a month to make buys with. So you tried to stretch that $100 out and to get as many raids as you could. What you'd do is you'd make ten-dollar-bag buys. So you had to act like a junkie then, because you didn't have the money to play the role of a high-line dope dealer.

Now, we have as much money as we need to make buys with. If you're gonna work undercover now, it's usually you're more high line. We've got nicer cars that we use—we've got a Jaguar available to us, a Cadillac Eldorado, a Lincoln Continental— when we're gonna meet a guy and do a multi-ounce drug deal. And we'll pose ourselves as a fairly good-size dealer. You have to have that look and that rap about you.

I pass myself off as a rich Italian kid from the suburbs that's got Outfit connections. That's usually my undercover scam. I got borderline Outfit ties and a lotta money and I want to get into the dope game.

I did an undercover operation in the Board of Trade using my rich Italian kid scam. It was in a lounge across the street from the Board of Trade, where a lot of the girls and guys who work at the Board would go after work—they were selling dope on the floor of the Board of Trade and in this tavern. I was introduced, then I kept going back myself and making more friends and making more buys.

* * *

Undercover work is basically a case of manipulation. Dealers know the heat's on, but you give them a lot of different looks, different angles, different profiles, and sooner or later someone's going to get caught. It's just figuring out who's gonna bite on what profile.

Mine is to play dumb, like, Yeah, I like to party, I'm blue collar, and I love to cook, and you push them from many different angles. Or I can do the child-of-the-sixties route, I *am* a child of the sixties, so I can talk hallucinogenics, peyote, mescaline, it's Professor Zarkov here.

It takes you years to become a policeman. It also takes you a while to stop acting like one. And that's what Narcotics is all about. You've got to unlearn what you *already* learned. You gotta stop being the police. You don't want to act, walk, smell, talk, or *be* a policeman. If you do, you tip people off.

Here's the female point of view on undercover work. When I was growing up, as a civilian, when you walked down the street, you would never look at a guy because it would look like you were trying to put the moves on him. You pull up to a light, and you know the guy next to you is staring at you, but you don't look at him.

When I became a police officer, I had to lose that. I *had* to, when I pulled up, look at the guy. I *had* to talk to these people who were going crazy and yelling and screaming and acting like idiots. I *had* to make eye-to-eye contact.

Now I come to the Narcotics Unit, now I'm not supposed to be the police anymore, right? Now I'm impersonating a drug buyer. So now I really have to force myself to put my eyes down and look away when I talk to them. I have to go back to acting the woman. It's hard.

There's three things you do if a dealer asks you to sample. One is, "Man, I don't use. I used to, and I was losing all my profits by using. I don't do it anymore." The other thing is, "I don't do it. My old lady does." And the third thing, you tell them you have some kind of illness. "Man, I almost died. I was doing it last year and I had to go to the hospital and the doctor told me, man, if I do that shit anymore, I'm dead." And you come up with a heart murmur or something. And you know what they all do? "Oh yeah. Yeah. I understand. You . . . you better be careful."

We work out a signal for the buy-bust, so when the officer gets the deal down—say, he's in a car or on a corner with the bad guys—the backup can come in and bail him out. Make the arrest.

The big thing is with the signal, you want to have the undercover officer do what *isn't* natural. If he or she never takes their hat off or scratches their head, that's what you give them. But if you give this to somebody who always scratches their head or fiddles around with their hair and that's the signal, it can really goof things up.

We did a buy-bust one time where I was gonna take off my hat when I got the dope. But my backup didn't see the signal. My backup didn't see me at all.

We had it set that I'd get the bad guy in the backseat of the car—the informant was driving; I was in the passenger seat—so the deal would go down on the street where my backup was waiting. Then I'd take my hat off, and we'd grab the guy.

But the guy wants to leave the street and go into the alley. He goes, "Look. I've got it. It's all set. But I don't want to bring it out to you in front 'cause I just took a three-ounce pinch and I'm scared to do it out here. Why don't we do it out back?" I told him, "Okay, go get it."

The guy comes back, gets in the backseat. The informant lets the car die in the middle of the street to give everybody time to make their turns and get behind us.

We go into the alley—and there's *another* guy back there. The bad guy says, "Stay right here." He gets out, goes up to the guy in the alley; the other guy gives him a can. The bad guy takes the can over by me, shows it to me while I'm sitting there. There's the half-pound of heroin. So now he goes, "Give me the money."

I don't see my backup. I tell him, "Get in the car." So I get *him* in the car, *I* get out of the car, I take off my hat.

They're not coming. And he's saying, *"Give* me the money."

So now I'm out there like Fred Astaire; I'm out there taking my hat off, swinging it in the air. I have to say, it was not my team; I was loaned out to a different agency—if it was my team, that never would have happened.

They're not coming. And the guy's going, *"Give* me the money." So now, I get back in the car. I'm hanging my hat out the window. It's just me, the bad guy behind me, the informant in front, and the other guy is still standing there in the middle of the alley watching—and I don't know if he's packing a gun. The informant's just sitting there staring straight ahead, holding on to the wheel, because he knows it's falling apart.

The bad guy pats me on the shoulder, kind of forcefully— "Come on, man. Give me the fucking money." So now I toss it back to him; I let it spray. He goes, "Goddamn!" He's picking all the money up. I say, "Don't you want to count it?" He says, "No."

Now the bad guy wants to get out of the car and leave. I figure, Fuck it. I gotta take them down myself. He gets out of the car, I think, Well, all I can do is put him as a shield between me and the guy that's in front of me. So when he gets out, I tell him, "Police!" and I banged him against the garage—I tried to put his head through the fucking garage, just to stun him, just to get his attention, you know. But, you know, he was very obedient then. Then I turned him around with his arms out facing the guy in front of me. And that guy, he just stood there; he just can't believe what's going on.

By that time, I hear the greatest sound in the world, *vroo-ooom,* the cars, the rush of the motors, as the backup comes in.

My partner and I, neither one of whom knows anything about planes except they go up, once ended up at the controls of a twin-engine plane while two drug dealers are waving at us, waiting for us to take off.

It started one night when we were off-duty, sitting in a tavern. One of my partner's informants spotted us. He was sitting at another table with a bad guy. He sent over a couple rounds of drinks; we sent over some drinks; finally, the informant comes up to our table with the bad guy.

He introduced my partner as somebody he'd been in prison with. For narcotics. The bad guy had been in prison too. It's smart to introduce somebody as an ex-inmate, because ex-inmates always trust each other, far more than they trust straight people. And the informant was sharp enough to say that my partner had been in a prison his pal had never been in.

They sat down, and we were just bullshitting; we were saying we were kilo guys who had a regular run from Miami to Chicago. My partner said I was a defrocked American Airlines pilot—defrocked for selling drugs, so now I ran him everywhere. It was just a way of explaining my presence; I didn't think anything would come of it.

It ended up the bad guy had friends who were interested in buying dope on a big scale. We went to the bad guy's tavern that he owned, and so he'd think we were legit, we asked if we could do a dope deal in his tavern. He thought we were flying drugs into Chicago and they were going to meet us at Midway Airport at three-thirty on the day we were supposed to do the transaction. So we had a DEA pilot in a DEA plane meet us at Midway Airport. This was at three in the afternoon. He flew us around for half an hour, we landed at three-thirty, and the bad guy and one of his buddies meet us on the ground.

We told him we asked some guys to meet us in the tavern for a $40,000 coke deal. He clears the tavern of all patrons, puts us in the basement, and two more of our guys show up. We had a kilo of white powder in a briefcase, and our two other narcs brought $40,000 in a briefcase. So we're dealing with each other—the whole sham is so he thinks we're for real and introduces us to his people. So here's this poor mope watching five law-enforcement people go through this little game: four cops and a DEA agent exchanging money for dope; he's the only bad guy in the room.

Now him and his buddy are driving us back to the airport. He says, "I know you're for real now, and I'll put you in touch with my people." We get to the airport, and our plan was just to walk in the airport, hang around for a while, and then go home. But they don't drop us off. They both get out of the car and come in with us.

They want to see the plane; luckily, DEA had a twin-engine parked there; we're all standing around looking at the plane, waiting for these guys to leave.

But they don't leave. It becomes obvious they want to watch us take off. I'm thinking, Oh my God, they're not leaving. We're gonna have to do this. While everybody's standing around looking at the plane, the DEA guy pulls me to one side and says, "We can pull this off. Just get in the pilot's seat and I'll sit next to you."

So now we get into the plane. I get into the pilot's seat, the DEA guy is next to me, and my partner is sitting behind me. Here are the controls—they're confusing enough anyway, but this plane had special surveillance equipment, so the controls are loaded with all kinds of extra stuff—I'm real nervous. I'm afraid to touch *anything.* The only way I can talk to the DEA guy is through the headset, and I have to press a button to do that.

The DEA guy hands me the checklist; it's four or five pages of instructions, and I start reading it off like I know what it means, while the DEA guy does everything. This was the opposite of how it's usually done. The bad guys are standing right outside the pilot's door—it's still open—listening to all this.

Just before we take off, they say they want to see the dope we said we had. So my partner opens the other door and shows them four kilos of powdered sugar we brought with us.

So now we've gotta take off. The DEA agent says. "Put your hands on the yoke, make it look real, but don't put *any* pressure on your side." And we fly out across the lake; it was a bitterly cold winter night, three in the morning, and it looked like we were flying into a black hole.

I'll never forget—as we lift off, these two bad guys, standing at the end of the runway, waving good-bye to us. It looked like something out of Laurel and Hardy.

The plane really sealed it. They introduced us to the big drug purchasers, and we got into them big.

* * *

Drug buying is a matter of salesmanship. We're not selling a product; we're selling ourselves. You sell a concept. You paint a picture of what they want to see.

Sex sells. If you have to get next to somebody in a hurry, sex sells. Now, the law forbids us to go ahead and partake of the pleasures of the flesh, or the pleasures of the nose, but you can paint a picture. . . .

We got a van one time and went with two girls and two guys in it—all armed. Normally, you don't like to pile a lot of people into any vehicle, because it scares people off. But we rolled up as a party van; we turned the music way up.

So we painted a picture of sexual perversion which was absolutely fantastic. It almost got *me* excited. Basically, what it was, we had one policewoman in the back of the van with her legs spread up on the ceiling—she had her jeans on—her head in another guy's lap, and her gun concealed between her legs. Both of them had revolvers. I had my cat-o'-nine-tails up front with me.

We pulled up to a street corner, it was a street buy, operating out of a building. A very tough place to get into. Very, very suspicious people.

We pull up, music blaring. The guy on the corner comes up, and I say, "My baby needs some coke. My baby'll do anything if she has some stuff. You rub a little on this; you rub a little on that—she'll do anything; she'll do anything."

The officers in the back of the van opened the side door, the guy saw her legs up in the air, and he literally fell right into the truck. So he falls into the truck and he says, "Okay, I'll take you to the place where you can get the dope." So we took him and we scored. That was the first time.

Then we went back another time. It was snowing and stuff, and he had a real big broom to clean up the snow on his corner. So he's straddling this, and our policewoman is trying to be helpful, so she lifts it up, and cracks him in the balls. Then she's real apologetic. The poor guy falls for it, lock, stock, and barrel. I told him I was taking my baby down to the lake and showed him the cat-o'-nine-tails again. He was just bedazzled.

He kept saying, "Can I go with you?" And he did, but not where he wanted.

Undercover work is an act of betrayal. It *is.* You become friends. They tell you their private lives, how they don't have jobs, how they're looking for something better maybe; how the big score's coming in.

I mean, I used to get recipes that these guys would get from their grandmothers; I'd tell them I was really into cooking; Puerto Rican foods; they'd get their grandmother's recipe for *sofrito.* They'd take me shopping.

You become close. There's security in it. Because if they like you, they're not gonna kill you, for the most part.

I did an undercover operation once on a big street-gang dope operation. I dealt with the middle guy.

I made about two, three buys from this middle guy—one for a half-ounce, another one for two ounces, finally one for fourteen ounces, and then we arrested him.

This guy liked me so much and trusted me so much. He used to call me at home all the time; he found out I had a girlfriend; he wanted to meet my girlfriend. We used to go out for dinner, party all the time; he invited me to a family party. You develop a relationship with these people; they start to like you.

When he was arrested, all the surveillance officers were in the area. I gave the bust signal. I forget what it was exactly; I think I ran my hand through my hair or tapped the brake lights. My backup couldn't see me for some reason. So nobody was coming up to grab us.

I turn to the kid and tell him, "Look, I'm the police. You're under arrest." He starts laughing. "No, really. I'm the police." "Cut it out. You're always goofing on me. Will you quit it?" He's cracking up. "I mean it. I'm the police." He's still laughing; he thinks it's a huge joke. "Come on. Let's get going." "We ain't going nowhere. I'm the police."

Finally, I had to put my arm around him and get him in a

lock. I didn't want him running away when the cars pulled up. "I'm the police. You're under arrest." I'll never forget the look on his face.

Then the backup comes up. He just couldn't believe it. He didn't believe it even after everybody was on scene and placed him under arrest. As they're taking him away, he's turning around, shouting back to me, "Johnny, you gotta talk to me. Call me. We gotta talk. I can't believe what you're doing to me."

I felt real bad about this one. He liked me so much. I liked him too. He got five years in the fed pen.

We've brought as much as $200,000 to a buy. When you're bringing that kind of money and they know you're bringing it, there's always the possibility that they're not gonna come back out with the dope but with a couple other people. With machine guns.

We had a dope deal for about a pound of cocaine. We were paying $25,000. We were doing it in the parking lot of a rib place on the North Side.

It turned out that a street gang, a little group that goes by the name of the Thorndale Jag-Offs, showed up to relieve us of our money. One brought an Uzi. And told the undercover police officer that he was gonna kill him. "Give it up or I'll kill you." But another officer, behind the gangbanger, seeing the problem, yelled, "Police!" The gangbanger turned around, and that gave the undercover guy a chance to get away—actually, he dove under a car. Then the guy just sprayed everything with his Uzi. We later found bullet holes in the cars in the lot; our undercover van got shot, the houses surrounding the lot, but not in any people.

Then they tried to make their escape, shots were fired back and forth, and finally there was a car chase, and a crash, and they were all arrested.

They beat the attempted murder charge. They were all convicted of armed robbery, but not of attempted murder. The jury didn't believe that the guy spraying the parking lot with his Uzi meant to hurt anyone. Now, this guy had just gotten out of the joint for murder. This ain't no choirboy.

But the jury said, If he had meant to hurt a police officer, he would have done it. No, he was just firing it in protection of his own life.

One component of Narcotics, undercover work, means always living off the perilous security of the role, knowing that you're alive only so long as your particular act goes over. The other major component of Narcotics, executing search warrants, offers no security at all. . . .

If you look at the statistics, the vast majority of slayings of police officers have taken place during drug raids. You can't be a narcotics cop for any length of time without being shot at at least once. Everybody who's done raids has been shot at—he may not have been hit, but he's been shot *at.*

You can be as careful as you like, you can be conscious of the danger all day long—and that's not gonna stop somebody from shooting at you. If you go through enough doors, you're gonna get it some time.

The search warrant is the most complicated and most dangerous thing you can do in the CPD. A warrant is the most power a police officer has—it's a document that gives you the right to knock someone's door down.

Doing a search warrant is a real art. First of all, to get it approved, it has to go before a state's attorney, and they scrutinize them pretty good. In addition to that, you have to have the expertise to get the people in there who are sharp enough to get into position, get in the place within thirty seconds, get the dope, bring it back, arrest all these people, and have the finesse to put it down on paper, bring it to court, and then testify before the judge—and not blow the case. There are all these steps you have to do. You leave one of those out, and *you're* out. The whole thing for nix. Nothing. It's gone.

You better be 1,000 percent right when you hit that door. If somebody ends up getting popped or whatever else, you better be right.

What makes search warrants so dangerous is that a great deal of the time, probably 70 percent of the time, a forced entry is involved. Ninety percent of the time the people on the inside have weapons.

In any other type of warrant, you can sit and wait. Say you're going after a stickup man they say is armed and dangerous. And you know about him. You find him, say, in a third-floor apartment building. You can get on the loudspeaker and say, "We got you surrounded. Come on out." The worst that can happen is the guy kills himself. And that ain't too bad either.

But with us, it's a totally different thing. We have to go in and we gotta break that door down and get that dope before they flush it. And that's what makes it so hard and so dangerous.

The dope house is always the best-protected house in the neighborhood. They've got bars on the front and bars on the back, gates, case-hardened locks, pit bulls, peepholes, lookouts, walkie-talkies, electronic surveillance, the apartment's not registered to anybody, nobody knows who the hell is in there—you know that they've been through the mill, all these guys are so well versed.

They're not worried about us so much, because they know we're gonna lock them up, but at least we're not gonna kill 'em. They're worried about each other.

We go in on raids and we find caches of automatic weapons, higher caliber, higher power, more sophisticated. We're seeing Uzis. Machine guns. Sawed-off shotguns. You'll recover them in different locations: on the kitchen counter near the kitchen window. On the windowsills. Next to a door. They have communications equipment. They do countersurveillances.

It's almost like they have a fortress there, and they're one army and they're protecting themselves against another army trying to invade them.

You only have thirty seconds to get into a dope house. Thirty seconds. You've got to be *in.* You've got to get to them before they throw it out the window, flush it down the toilet—now, they keep a bucket of bleach on hand, and they toss it in and it just dissolves.

Not only do you have to get in on two or three rams at the max, you've got to be able to get in howling.

We call it our tumultuous entry. There's no other way to describe it. It's our biggest advantage.

You never give a guy a chance to think. It's like, you're sitting in your living room reading a book, the next thing you know, your door is down and guys are running in at you—you have no time to think.

Sometimes our tumultuous entry even sends the guard dogs in retreat. Dogs aren't used to doors coming down and four or five guys shouldering each other to get in there.

Defense attorneys sometimes try to get us on a no-knock. But we *do* knock—we have to knock and identify ourselves, wait for a response—and then we're out there knocking with a battering ram or a sledgehammer. And we *do* identify ourselves as police—if you had a tape recorder on one of these things, you'd hear "Police!" yelled about twenty times on entry. It cuts your chances of getting killed by about 90 percent. We don't want them to think we're the stickup men. We want them to know we're the police so they don't kill us.

We've had guys, when we hit the door and yelled "Police," they'd run into a room and come out with their hands up and say, "Dope's there. I got a gun there. Let me get in and call my lawyer." He says, "Man, I thought I was getting ripped off."

And you go in on some places and as soon as they find out you're only the police, they get a little cocky.

I've seen guys on my team, instead of shooting, when they get in the place and the guy's pointing a gun at them, just snap it out of the guy's hand. Now that's restraint.

We had one dope dealer that was armed on the couch when we came in and he unloaded a .357 at us, because he was just coming out of his sleep and he didn't know what was happening. Maybe he didn't hear us say we were the police—all he hears is somebody breaking the door down from his sleep. He pulls his weapon, and he starts to shoot.

The Mad Doctor of Lincoln Avenue. We did a warrant on this doctor who ran a weight clinic on the North Side, very nice building, a series of offices, his own pharmacy, his own living quarters there. He was manufacturing and selling Quaaludes from his office.

Six of us go to his apartment; we're at the back door. We ordered him to open the door; he wouldn't. We knock the door down. It's totally dark in there. And he opens up on us with an Uzi from the end of the hallway. We found out later the doctor had barricaded himself with his two little boys and his wife in the bedroom at the end of the hallway. He had a peephole there, and when he saw us come through, he just shot through the door with his Uzi. And just tore up the entire hallway.

So this guy's spraying us with an Uzi—bullets are flying through the door. Luckily, from the angle he was shooting, they were bouncing off the ceiling. Dry wall and plaster were raining down all over our hair and faces.

We got back outside. Now we're on the back porch. I have a little snub-nose, and I shoot into what I think is the hall, but what I hit was the burglar-alarm system. The guys say, "What did you do that for?" And I said, "I just want to make sure that the donkey on that end knows that there's a gun at *this* end. I don't want him rushing down this hall like we've got some fools down here."

This guy's got us pushed down on the back porch with an Uzi. Periodically, he's sending bursts down the hallway. We're there with out little portable radio, but we couldn't receive. But they could hear us.

And later, when we listened to the tapes, you could hear it—the shots, the guy on the radio cursing because it wouldn't work, and all of us laughing. We were so scared, we were laughing all over ourselves. And none of us had anything more than our little snub-noses; the goddamn little things only have five bullets, and I had just killed the burglar-alarm system. So we're saying, "Shit, I only got five rounds. Give me three." "Unh-unh. You go get your own." And we're all laughing.

Finally, police surrounded the place. The Mad Doctor gave up. He came out wearing a bathrobe, slippers, and a German helmet.

At the end, we brought the door the doctor had fired through into headquarters as evidence. One guy on our team made a little sketch of the apartment, and he had little stick men attached to it, showing the doctor's and all of our positions.

So here's this door with all the bullet holes in it, up in the Narcotics main office, along with the sketch with stick men, and the guy who made it put names on everybody. Then he's got "Lincoln Avenue" in front of the doctor's office, and he put one of the little stick men running away, with the arms—one out in front, one out in back—and my name on it.

The newspeople come in and they're taking pictures of the bullet-riddled door and of this sketch, which we didn't know they'd do. So on the news that night, here's this little stick policeman with my name on it, hoofing it down Lincoln Avenue.

We did a search warrant on a guy, and he ran out the back door on us. Inside the apartment were narcotics and a gun, so some of us had to stay behind with that.

The rest of us chased after this guy. It just so happened, the street we were on, right behind that in a parking lot was Mayor

Jane Byrne, giving a community speech to the neighborhood. About street crime.

And this guy ran right through the crowd with four of us chasing him with our guns out. We're yelling, "He might have a gun! He might have a gun!" And he's running right in front of the stand the mayor's on giving her little pep talk—"Street crime is down."

Her bodyguards never even assisted us, right? Here's a guy running through the crowd with men chasing him, with guns, and they're kind of ignoring us, you know, as we apprehend him. He turns around, he has a knife in his hand. "Drop it or you're dead," we're yelling. It turns out he has an apple in his other hand; he was paring it when we kicked the door.

We tried to hit a place once that had gates and twenty-four-hour lookouts. We had the warrant in hand, but we had to figure out a way to get in this apartment building without being spotted in the first place.

Sarge figured out, okay, this is what we'll do. It was a shitty building, we'll dress up as painters, you know, as workers, and we'll surround the front and the back. And we'll conceal our weapons in our painters' clothes.

I had some horrible old green paint laying around my house, it was like a park-bench green—rusting, shitty paint. And I brought some old brushes; the hair was coming out of the brushes.

We got in, and we're painting the whole thing; we're plastering; one guy was doing a little spackling. We figure they're never gonna make us. But the owner of the building happened to call over there, to the dope house, and they say, Well, we got workmen out here.

So in comes the new owner of the building, and he says, "What's going on here?" The first guy he talks to says, "Go see the boss-man! Go see the boss-man!" He's down there with the brush; he wouldn't even look at him; he was afraid he was gonna crack up.

So the owner comes up to me and the sarge and says, "What's going on here?" And the sarge says, "We got a contract." And

the guy goes, "When'd you get the contract? I've had this building since December." "We got this contract in November to do
this building. This is the soonest we could get to it"—this is like
in March.

"What you guys doing?" "Well, we're filling up the holes
and painting." "Who authorized this?" We gave him the name
of a guy back at the station. All the guys are laughing. "Who's
gonna pay for this?" "It's all paid for; it's been paid since November."

So now the guy really starts looking around—there are old
brush hairs all over the walls. We painted all over the holes.
They had oak banisters; we painted all over them. And the
brushes just kept shedding their crummy hairs. "What kind of
paint is that?" "Well, mohair. Mohair paint." "Oh. That don't
look too bad." And he left.

So we were out there about two hours, waiting for somebody
to come in; there was always a lot of traffic going in and out of
this place. Finally, we go in, and they're all just sitting on the
couch, smiling at us. And nothing's in there. Our informant,
who was in there, later told us that a he-she at one point looked
out the peephole and says, "I know them all. They're all coppers." They flushed it all.

We were scouting a dope house that had twenty-four-hour
armed lookouts, front and back. We decided to raid the place in
uniform, because dope dealers aren't looking for uniforms;
they're looking for plainclothes coppers.

We pretended we were answering a call of a man with a gun.
We're running all over the yards behind the apartment building; yelling back and forth; we're running up and down the
stairs; making ourselves as obvious as we can.

Six of us went running up the back-landing stairs to the
third-floor apartment, right above the dope house.

Only three came back down. Us other three waited inside the
apartment upstairs. The people there were accommodating;
they knew the people below were selling dope, and they were
glad to help us. So we're just up there for about an hour, an hour
and a half, as quiet as can be.

We had our own lookout in an apartment across the alley,

he's got binoculars and he's watching the bad guys. Their lookout's sitting on an old sofa on the enclosed back porch. Our lookout would radio, "He's sitting down. Whoop! Now he's standing up. He's looking around." Finally, he radioed, "Okay. He's down. Now's a good time."

So one of our guys starts creeping down the stairs; he's inching his way down, trying not to make any sound on the stairs. He's creeping down the stairs, creeping down the stairs, trying to be so quiet.

He gets to the point where he has to make the turn on the landing. So he just charges around the corner real fast. The lookout doesn't say a word. He just sits there with his mouth open, great lookout that he is. And our guy just charges down the stairs right at him. And this lookout runs away, through the entire apartment, and hurls himself out the front window. The other guy in the apartment follows the lookout's example and jumps out the window—he lands on the lookout, breaks the lookout's leg, and runs off down the street. We didn't get him, but we got the guy with the broken leg.

One time we had a guy wearing a hard hat and a tool belt go up to the dealer's door and knock on it right after the rest of us had poured water all over the floor right by the guy's door. He knocked on the door. "Who's there?" "Maintenance." "I didn't call maintenance." "Well, we're getting complaints of water coming in from the ceiling." And the guy goes, "*Shit!* There's water all over the floor!" So he opens the door, and we crack him.

Most of the time, you can't bluff your way in. You've got to go in and break down that door.

You hit a lot of tough doors. A heavy, solid door is gonna be tough—the door's not hollow; it's wood. A steel door is tough. A lot of the projects have steel doors. According to project regulations, they can't have any gates, but with the fire regulations, they have steel doors and they put locks on them. Those can be tough.

We're seeing a lot of double-gated doors now. So if you rip off one set of gates on the outside and start banging that door, figuring you're okay, you're gonna find another set of gates on the inside.

Gates. Bars. Braces behind the door—we call them T's or New York T's. They nail a two-by-four right on the inside of the doorway and then they brace another two-by-four into the back of the door, down into the two-by-four that's nailed into the ground, creating a T-effect.

If we know we're gonna have a real tough door and if we have the room to operate it, we'll bring the ram. A battering ram. A lot of times, though, you're in a small hallway and you don't have the room to swing the ram, so you use the sledgehammer and the Chicago bar—that's a long tool we have: On one end it looks like a crowbar and on the other end it's like a forked prying device. You use the Chicago bar between the door and the doorjamb, or if there's gates, between the gates and the doorjamb. Then you hit it with the sledgehammer and it pries the door open or it pries the gates open.

We like to get the heavier guys behind the door swinging the hammer. You always have two officers there just for the protection of the officers working the equipment—the guys on the ram or the hammer are very vulnerable. They can't have their weapons out; if somebody wants to fire through the door, or once the door is taken down, they're kind of at the mercy of whoever's on the other side.

You usually send somebody out on a scouting mission on every warrant to locate the joint. We want to determine if it's a case-hardened lock or whatever.

We were gonna hit this one place; we send the scout; the scout comes back. "What kind of lock is it?" "Oh, it's just an old brown rusty one. No problem."

We go up there. And here is this case-hardened lock. You couldn't attack this thing with a hacksaw.

One of the guys found a snow shovel on the first-floor landing. We're on the second. They've got the gates, the locks, and chicken wire over the kitchen window.

Sarge is so hot at the scout, he takes the shovel, notifies the unit in front, he says, "Now!"—breaks the chicken-wire, breaks all the glass—dives through—onto this little table they had under the window. The table collapses. Sarge is on all fours on top of the table, he looks like a fucking cat. The next guy has his leg poised at the window; he just misses Sarge. The third guy dives through after them.

They get up, start running after the dealers, but they're slipping all over the floor because the dope dealers were frying chicken on the stove and the pan got knocked over, so now there's grease all over the floor. And blood from the sarge. He got cut going in. About ten of us came in; the guys in front kept yelling, "Come on in" and we'd dive in and fall all over each other. We finally got to the front. They already flushed. Sarge needed thirty-three stitches that time. Was he hot.

The toilet is our biggest enemy. If we can, we'll try to have an officer by the bathroom window. He'll throw something through the window or create some kind of diversion at the window so that if the guy was going to run to the toilet and flush, he might be able to discourage him.

If we know the guy already flushed on us, we'll take the toilet out and try to catch the dope while it's still in the pipe. That takes a lot of luck. Once it's in the drains, good-bye.

This is what people will do to try to defeat you. They may have their stash on the first floor, rent an apartment directly up on top—and just deal the bags out of the top floor. They might drill a hole in the floor and when the police come drop the bag down to the first floor, or send the bag up on a string to the second floor if the police hit the stash house. They have intercom systems set up between the levels.

We hit a very fortified dope house on the South Side. There was only one entrance. There was a fire escape that was guarded. The windows out to the main street were watched. They had double gates, they had a door, and they had a railroad tie braced behind the door and one braced up against it into the floor. So it took us an incredible amount of time to get in.

We get in, we see cigarette smoke dying out in the ashtray, the cigarette's still lit—and nobody's in the apartment. We radio the guy out front. "Nobody came out the window"—this is on the second floor. The fire escape's watched. They had to be in there, because the railroad tie blocking the door couldn't have been set unless someone was in there. It's like they disappeared into thin air.

So after about ten minutes into the place, I look under the sink. And it looks unusual, and I find a piece of paneling that was up against the wall. I pull it down, and I notice a hole in the plaster wall of the apartment. And behind that hole is another panel of the same material. I push that down. We crawl into the next apartment, and there's the toilet all backed up and two guys trying to flush. One guy, he was a black guy, it looked like he was powdered white, he had so much coke all over him.

What they actually did was rent two apartments. One on the south side of the building; that's the one we hit. And one adjoining it on the north side. When we hit the door, they crawled through a panel under the sink into the adjoining apartment. Yet our informants knew nothing about that apartment because every time they went up there to buy dope, it was always from the apartment on the south side. Nobody knew about the other apartment.

It makes you crazy when you can't find the dope. You start tearing down walls. Now you're looking at places where everybody else on the team is looking at you like, There's no dope in *there.*

We hit one place where they had four ounces of cocaine sewn into the bottom hem of the bedroom curtains. The left curtain had the coke; the right curtain had $600 sewn in.

* * *

We hit a place when I was on tac, we went through, searched it, but we couldn't find any contrabands. We found some wrappers and all that, but we couldn't find it. We knew he was holding it, because of the informant.

So we're talking to the guy, you know, we're interrogating him in the apartment. And one of the officers takes a two-by-four that was used to bolt the back door, and he's just kind of tapping it against the wall. And another officer noticed that it sounded hollow. And sure enough, it was hollowed out and was packed with several ounces.

Then we started feeding the dealer's ego. And we said, Hey, pretty good, how'd you do that? We figured now that we had him, he might as well show off. So finally he showed us his hammer kit and this little pounding device he had to bat it all in—and he'd put turning screws in it and start jiggling it up and put a couple bolts in there. He got a big kick out of the fact that we admired his creativity.

If you're going into a bag dealer, he'll flush. With ounces, you can flush. But with multi-ounces, or pounds, they don't have time to flush. So they keep it in stash houses. The stash houses, a lot of times, are exactly where you would never expect large-scale dope to be. They'll rent a $5,000-a-month apartment on the Gold Coast or go into small, quiet white neighborhoods and buy a house.

I have an extreme fear of dogs. We were gonna hit one guy who had a three-legged pit bull; one leg got bit off in a fight. The informant told us this guy had his stash in the basement, and the pit bull was down there too.

Now I ain't getting *near* this dog. So we called for the city dog handlers. The plan was, my partner would have the sledge-hammer; he's gonna hit the door. The dog will come up to get my partner, and the dog handlers will take the noose, get the dog by the neck, take him out. Then we do the search.

Okay, fine. We arrive with the dog handlers. We knock on the front door. We go all the way through the house. We're at the three-step landing leading to the basement door. My partner hits the door with the hammer. The dog comes charging up the stairs, just as we planned, but the dog handler misses the dog.

Now, the dog has one end of the sledgehammer. My partner has the other. They're twirling round and round with this thing. I run through the swinging doors into the dining room. My partner yells that the dog has run out the back door. I'm peeking through the swinging doors into the kitchen, ready to hoof it if the dog comes back through the back door. What I forgot was we busted down the front door, and the front door is wide open. And the dog ran all the way around the house and back in through the front door.

So I'm standing behind the swinging doors, peeking into the kitchen. Suddenly, next to me, I hear pant-pant-pant-pant-pant. I look down—the dog is sitting right next to me. So I run into the bathroom, I'm thinking, Feet, don't fail me now!, and I lock the door. And I say, "I'm not coming out of here till you promise me you got the dog in the car."

My partner swore to my kids lots of times, "Kids, your Daddy's a coward. Someday we're gonna have to take him out and put him against the wall and shoot him for cowardice."

One thing we'd always do, when we searched apartments, we'd always hang our coats on the light fixtures while we searched, because there were roaches all over. And when you got home at night after hitting apartments, you'd take all your clothes off in your backyard because, let's face it, there'd be roaches all over, and you don't know even how good your coat is doing on the chandelier. You'd throw your clothes outside, run in the house, and go get them the next day to make sure all the critters were out of them.

This was back in the seventies, we hit an apartment and a shot rang out and caught my partner on the arm. We couldn't see anybody, and we just kept firing back into the apartment.

To show how chauvinistic-thinking we were back then, finally we were yelling to throw the gun out, and we see a gun come out into the hallway. And we run into the apartment and here's a woman and her fourteen-year-old daughter. And the first thing out of our mouths is, "Where is he?" We run to the back of the apartment and there is no back door, and we start, "Where *is* he?"

Then it dawns on us. It's not *he.* It's *her.* This was a stash crib where her boyfriend would stash dope, and he had told her, "If anybody comes through that door, shoot them." And that's what she did, and she went to prison for it.

One of the worst things, and I think everybody who's worked Narcotics or done any kind of search warrant will agree, are the babies and the kids. We've actually found drugs in diapers. Not only that part of it, what really gets me is, I have kids. And you see the look they get on their faces when they see something scary or horrible on TV. Your heart goes out.

And when you go through a door and there's children there, *you* feel terrible because *you're* a bogeyman. You're like a *monster* coming through the door. So as you're coming through, they're *running* from you; they're in horror because you're tearing their door down, you're screaming, glass is breaking, you're using profanity, you're telling everybody, "Don't move!"

And most of these people, they don't scramble for their kids; they're scrambling to dump their dope. They leave their kids out there in the middle of the living room, or these kids are running for the back door.

It always hurts with the kids. They don't understand what's going on. They're crying. With kids under ten, you try to tell them that you're looking for something in the house, that Mommy called the police, or Daddy called the police, and you're trying to find something and they're helping the police.

What bothers me the most is, you go into these houses and there will be this load of kids under five, six years old. Cute as can be. And you find drugs, guns in the house, money, just what you went there for with the search warrant.

And you now have to take their father out of there in handcuffs. And as you take him to the door, this two- or three-year-old runs up and grabs Daddy's leg and starts crying. And, you know, we always look at ourselves as the good guys, and you look down in the eyes of this three-year-old kid and you can see the hatred that is building up there for *you,* because he doesn't understand that his Daddy has done anything wrong. All he knows is that this man with a gun is taking his Daddy away, and he knows now you're the police, and that's probably his first impression of the police.

Plus, you gotta realize that no matter how rotten of a person the father is, the kid sees him as the idol of his life. He doesn't understand that the package of brown powder is wrong; he doesn't see his dad doing anything wrong; he doesn't see his dad beating anybody up or anything; he doesn't understand what's happening. That's real hard to handle. We all talk about it.

Dope houses are like hot-dog stands. They spring up every other day. They're all around. You close one guy down, and two days later—it's called being back in the box—he's back in operation again. He just went to court and he's back. Already.

The judicial process is a laugh, a fucking joke. The public is completely unaware of how the court system is run in Narcotics Court. These people are let go left and right, not by lack of evidence or by the police officer screwing up somehow, but just because the judge thinks it's an insufficient amount. That's the travesty. If you don't catch them with a large amount, then the judges look at it like you haven't got them big, so we're gonna let them go. Even though it's listed as a felony, they still throw it out. Time and time again.

I don't see anything drying up. We're left to do the most dangerous task of breaking down these doors, or having to make tumultuous entries into fortified houses.

And you know what? Sometimes you wonder. I've done narcotics work—six as a tactical officer, in gang crimes, and in Narcotics for six-and-a-half years.

I've seen friends of mine that I've worked with get killed doing narcotics work. I remember one friend especially, got blown away doing a narcotics raid, and his wife and family got just petrified, they were destroyed by the whole thing.

And you look back and you try to count and you say, How many raids have you been on? And you wonder sometimes, you know, when are the odds gonna catch up to you?

You know, you've totally lost two generations to drugs since the sixties. Two generations almost have been lost.

To think that we're gonna solely win it by knocking doors down every day—you can't. You gotta keep the dope dealer on the run. Somebody will always be there to take his place—you get an eighteen-year-old dealing on the street; while he's waiting to go to trial, somebody else is out there waiting to take his place.

Whether they put the bars up again the next day—we'll be back. We have to go there. We have to break down that door.

We *have* to break their door down and go in and get it. We can't let them bar up a flat, cut a hole in the door, and just let them deal openly. We can't let them take over.

We have to beat them to the toilet. We have to beat them to the sink. We have to hit them as fast as they open up, and if they reopen, hit them again. And we'll hit them again and again.

Narcotics:
Contributing Police Officers

DETECTIVE ANDREW ABBOTT, CPD/DEA Task Force. Abbott joined the force in 1970, and has worked patrol, tac, and Gang Crimes South. Abbott's experience in Narcotics totals sixteen years, going back to the mid-seventies, when Narcotics had only forty men in the entire unit. Abbott was detailed to the DEA Task Force for two years in the late seventies, and served in the current Narcotics Unit, General Enforcement, from 1980 to 1989, when he was again detailed to DEA.

SERGEANT JACK BROWN, Narcotics, Special Enforcement. Brown, who joined the CPD in 1971, has worked in Special Operations, Intelligence, and as a detective in Area Four Property Crimes. Brown made sergeant in 1982, and masterminded a Thirteenth District tac team for six years till he joined Special Enforcement in 1988.

LIEUTENANT PHIL CLINE,   field lieutenant, Eleventh District. Lieutenant Cline has fourteen years' experience working citywide Narcotics. Cline joined the force in 1970, was promoted to detective in 1972 and assigned to the Narcotics Unit, where he served until 1977, when he made sergeant and went to the Tenth District. Cline returned to Narcotics later that same year and stayed until 1985, when he was promoted to lieutenant and assigned to the Twenty-first District. From 1986 to 1989, Cline was a detective lieutenant in Area Two Violent Crimes.

SERGEANT JOE D'ANTONIO, General Enforcement, Narcotics. D'Antonio and Abbott have worked together most of their twenty-year careers, in patrol, tac, and Gang Crimes. D'Antonio was a gang crimes specialist in Gang Crimes South, starting in 1978. D'Antonio made sergeant in 1982 and came to Narcotics, where he heads up an eight-member team.

LIEUTENANT RALPH DEWITT,   commanding officer, General Enforcement, Narcotics. DeWitt's nineteen-year career includes four years with the Area Four Special Operations Group, work in Area Six as a patrol sergeant and a tac team sergeant. DeWitt came to Narcotics in 1984 as a supervising sergeant, and has been commanding officer, General Enforcement, since 1988.

SERGEANT ALAN ISAAC, Twenty-fourth District. Isaac, in the CPD since 1976, worked patrol and tac before becoming an Area Six property crimes detective in 1982. Detective Isaac joined the Narcotics Unit in 1984 and worked Special Enforcement assignments until 1989, when he made sergeant and went to the Twenty-fourth District.

LIEUTENANT GENE KARCZEWSKI, commanding officer, Special Enforcement, Narcotics. Karczewski is a twenty-five-year veteran of the CPD. He's served on the Area Four Task Force, worked as a burglary detective, as a sergeant in the Fourth District and in the Special Operations Group, as a tac lieutenant, and has worked in Narcotics as a unit commander since 1984.

DETECTIVE WILLIAM MARLEY, Area Two Violent Crimes. Marley worked in Narcotics a total of ten years. He has been a homicide detective in Area Two Violent Crimes for the past six years. Marley has also served in the CPD's Task Force, in the old Robbery Unit, in Gambling, and in Intelligence.

OFFICER WENDY MARRELLO, Special Enforcement, Narcotics. Marrello, a police officer since 1982, was in patrol and tac in the Eighteenth District until 1987. She's been in Narcotics, Special Enforcement, for three years.

DETECTIVE BILL PEDERSEN, Organized Crime, Asset Forfeiture. Pedersen was a narcotics detective in the old Vice Control Division, Narcotics Section, from 1973–83, and has been on the force twenty-two years. Besides Narcotics, he's worked in Auto Theft, the Special Investigations Unit, and for six years as an Area Two Violent Crimes detective before joining the Organized Crime Division in 1989.

CAPTAIN RAY RISLEY, commander, Eighteenth District. Risley was the commander of the Narcotics Section from 1988 to 1990. Before being detailed to that post, he was administrative assistant to two police superintendents (Risley was one of ten finalists for the position of superintendent in 1988). Risley has been on the force since 1961, interrupted for two years by a stint in the army, and has served in the Traffic, Patrol, and Detective divisions.

SERGEANT ROBERT ZAVALA, Special Enforcement, Narcotics. Zavala, who has been with the CPD since 1977, worked patrol and tac in the Fourteenth District till 1984, when he went to the Internal Affairs Division. Zavala joined Narcotics in 1988.

Special thanks to the Area Six tac team, six men and one woman, who contributed a great deal to this chapter but requested anonymity.

Property Crimes

Burglars think they're so smart. We brought one into Area Six; we're questioning him. He tells us, "I've got everything at home." So we say, "Okay, can we go over and get it back?" "Sure. But I've got to call the wife up first."

We let him make the call from the other room. The sergeant picks up the phone. This burglar goes, "Hello, Mary. The police are coming over to get all the stolen goods. Listen, this phone might be tapped. So take the G-U-N-S out of the drawer and put them on the porch."

–Sergeant Carl Menconi,
former burglary detective

I think if Joe and Jane Citizen knew how bad it was out there, they'd get their family in a rowboat, row out to an island, surround the island with a brick wall, and put cannons all over the walls.

People don't realize how bad it is out there. They have no idea. And it's all around. There's always somebody out there trying to beat somebody out of something.

–Captain John Hinchy,
cofounder, CIU

Burglars. Cat burglars. Windowcrash burglars. Home invaders. Boosters. Con artists. Stickup crews. Safe burners. Jewel thieves. Embezzlers. Nightcrawlers. A day-and-night army of opportunists and pros devoted to detaching people from their property.

Cops divide them basically into two groups: the "good burglars," the ones who plan and execute scores with so much finesse that it forces admiration; and the "shithead burglars," dope addicts made frantic by their need for money.

CPD property crimes detectives handle all the permutations of thief except for robbers, who confront their victims with the threat of force and are handled by the violent crimes detectives.

Professional thieves, a.k.a. career criminals, major criminals, those who make a high-line living by pulling down big scores on jewel thefts, cartage thefts, home invasions, bank robberies, safecracking, commercial burglaries, used to be the province of a unique arm of the CPD, the Central Investigations Unit (originally the Criminal Intelligence Unit), formed to target and tail career criminals exclusively. CIU was disbanded in 1985, for reasons, they say, having more to do with frugality than common sense, and now the professional thieves are sometimes caught by Property Crimes, sometimes by Violent, and many times not at all.

Cops make distinctions among thieves—"A burglar doesn't want you home," says one veteran burglary detective. "But if you come home unexpectedly and that burglar's in there—and your house has a gun— the burglar finds the gun; you come home unexpectedly, he puts the gun on you, now he's not a burglar anymore, he's a robber. A cat burglar and a home invader come in *wanting* you home."

They make these distinctions among thieves. But, based on years of following known thieves around, analyzing their habits, hearing about thieves from informants, and interviewing thieves once caught, property crimes dicks hold that the thief is a unique species unto himself.

"They're strange, these guys," says a former CIU sergeant. "Very strange. Of course, everybody's strange. Everybody's got their little foibles, but it just seems that thieves have *more* foibles. . . ."

The true thief is the guy who wakes up in the morning knowing he's gonna steal, and he goes to sleep at night figuring out what he *did* steal, and when he wakes up the next morning, he's gonna go out and steal again. He's gonna beat somebody out of it.

Thieves will steal anything. They'll steal anything from bridges to xylophones. They may not even have any use for it—they just do it to have something to *do,* I guess. It never ceases to amaze me—they'll go after things they have no possible use for.

The most notorious professional thieves Chicago has ever seen, the Panczko brothers. They pulled off scores in the hundreds of thousands of dollars, but they'd steal *anything.* Pops, Butch, and Peanuts. They had a sister, Louise. Pops lived with her, her husband, and her junkie son, Richie. Louise's husband was the only straight one in the family; he worked in a factory. They made him stay in the basement. The working member of the family had to stay in the basement; they brought him a plate of food if he was lucky. Pops, Louise, Richie the drug addict, they had the run of the house. The old man had to be in the basement like a prisoner down there.

Pops didn't want to pay for nothing. He had slugs, he'd use them in phones, newspaper boxes, cigarette machines. He took a conviction once for using slugs in telephone booths and stamp machines instead of paying the coins. Old Pops—there's a guy that hated Sundays because all the businesses and all the salesmen were off the street on Sunday. That was the one day he couldn't steal.

They just loved to steal. Butch stole a cement mixer one time.

You know, instead of stealing a candy bar, you're going down the street, there's a cement mixer—Butch just took off with it. That's the way they were. True thieves.

Thieves are optimists. They seem to feel that if they get caught 50 percent of the time, they got away with it. With thieves, the glass is never half empty, it's always half full.

The thief's whole attitude is "Easy come, easy go." There's always another score tomorrow. Spend it today, with broads and what have you.

They live high on the hog. Some have an abundance of property, live in nice houses, drive nice cars. But they also have a lifestyle where they spend money faster than they make it. So they put the pressure on themselves. They have to go out and steal.

We heard of this one thief through a stickup guy cooperating with the G. He was part of a crew that worked down South, home invasions, sticking up coal miners and businessmen.

And he told a story about one of the bad guys that was running with them, how nutty this guy was, to the point where if they got lucky with a particular robbery, they'd come back to the hotel—this guy would actually throw his clothes away and then go out and buy all new outfits. He'd just take whatever he had and pitch it; you know, whatever he had with him. Because he had this newfound wealth.

There is no honor among thieves. They steal from each other, they shortchange each other, and if they think it's getting too hot, they beef on each other.

You can forget honor among thieves. I remember there was one home-invasion crew, they were going for precious-coin scores, stamp collections. They went into a place up in the northern suburbs, the coppers were waiting for them and killed one of them, a kid by the name of Phillie Polito. And Phillie

Polito, out of the whole crew, was the only one that had any concern, I thought, for his family. I mean, he left them with good insurance policies, his kids, his wife.

His widow had a big hoop; it was about a five- or six-carat diamond ring. She came home one night, walked into her hallway, there were two guys with ski masks on. They were in there to rob her of her diamond ring. Who do you think *they* turned out to be? Her dead husband's partners.

You know, as much as I hate thieves . . . if a guy sits down, and breaks bread, and eats, fucks the same broads, steals, shares in the profits of their thievery, and then, when a little steam comes down, he turns around and beefs on them to save his own worthless ass . . . he's the worst of all of them. He's the worst of all of them. Just rats. Rats.

Being a bad guy seems to skip a generation.

When I was growing up, neighborhoods were neighborhoods. You had good guys and bad guys. But the thing that struck me—with some of the guys I went to high school and that— their fathers were thieves. And they would kick their ass if they ever caught their sons doing anything wrong. They wanted their kids to grow up straight and nice and get a good education.

If you look at some of your higher-echelon Outfit guys, the organized crime guys, you'll see this. I mean, you'll see them and they're connected with the juice rackets and stuff, but their kids may be lawyers. Because they don't want them dirty. I don't want to sound like *The Godfather,* okay? But it almost seemed, when I was growing up, like it ran in generations. You'd take the father, then you'd take the son, and then you'd take *his* kid. And this kid would be a wiseguy, because he wanted to take after Grandpa. So the grandfather would be bent, the son would be straight, and the grandkid would be bent.

No one starts at the age of twenty-five or thirty doing crime. They start early. They start with petty stuff. It might be the guy has an anti-social habit of defying the system, hanging around the corner, not going to school. They might start out by stealing tires, joyriding, and then someday they realize if they take the tires off the car and sell them, they can make some money. It goes from there.

I've always been surprised by the boldness of the thief. I mean, I've sat and watched them break into places, with buses and cars going down the street, because maybe the only place they could get in was on the main entrance side where they were kind of exposed. And they'd actually work on the door, to gain entry, with traffic going by and everything else.

If you didn't stop and look, pay attention to them, you'd think it was a guy maybe standing in a doorway trying to light a cigarette. They are very bold people.

A thief thinks—and he's right—that the most conspicuous is the least obvious.

I remember a thief, he was the lookout on scores, burglaries, and what have you. And he would get a broom, and he'd be sweeping up the sidewalk out in front of the fur store, while the other guys were going through the roof. A squad would go by, and they'd think he was the janitor sweeping up the front sidewalk. This would be at three in the morning.

I remember some guys in Pops Panczko's crew that were after a jewelry salesman, and they knew his car had an alarm. So they went and they got a power saw, and they cut a hole in the side of the car so they wouldn't set off the alarm. Then they just reached in for the case. They did it right on the street. Broad daylight. Guy came out, there was a hole in the side of his car.

The thing with thieves is, they make it so obvious that nobody notices.

Thieves specialize. Even in auto theft, there's different specialties. You might get a guy who steals a car and cuts it up for the parts. You might get another guy who steals a car and re-tags it, and sells the whole car. It takes only thirty seconds to break into a car.

We recently put a guy out who was a tagger, which means he changed the VIN number, the Vehicle Identification Number. He specialized in exotic cars. When we grabbed him, he had a brand-new Mercedes and a Rolls-Royce and a Ferrari that he had stolen, and he had them stashed in a garage. He was in the process of getting the VIN numbers changed and the titles changed.

Then he would sell them. He'd discount the price, which would make it attractive to a buyer, but not so low, because that would scare them away.

This guy owned a villa in France.

Hotels have another form of thief. We refer to them as night-crawlers. A nightcrawler generally is a hooker who's had a bad night, or it could be somebody who specializes in hitting hotel rooms.

She'll get into a hotel at four, five, six o'clock in the morning. She'll walk the halls, and she'll push on doors. You'd be amazed at the number of people who don't push their doors closed.

Or she'll look for one of those plastic Do Not Disturb signs. Well, that Do Not Disturb sign works just like a key—you can slip the lock with it if the chain or deadbolt's not on.

The nightcrawler gets in. Slip the lock, push the door. And then she'll crawl on her hands and knees over to the nightstand. Go through the purse, go through the man's pants, take his watch, wallet, her wallet. Leave the room.

People might wake up, see a light in their room, see a door open. Many times, they think nothing of it. Go back to sleep—think they're dreaming. If they do see something, they think it's room service or the maid or housekeeping. It doesn't register. They go back to sleep.

They wake up next morning and find their things are gone.

In the lobby of a hotel, you've got what we call "ball knock-ers." These are gals that come in, they follow a guy into the

elevator. Maybe one woman, maybe two. One of them grabs the
guy in the crotch while the other one goes into his pants pockets
and grabs his money. It totally takes you off guard.

Gypsies are great thieves. They have an uncanny ability to
con their way into people's homes and then to find exactly
where their valuables are. It's almost like they can smell it.
They're uncanny.

One of the worst days in the police department is Good Friday. An awful lot of Gypsies steal on Good Friday. What's
taught to the young Gypsy kids is that when Christ was put on
the cross, they had four nails to nail him to the cross. A Gypsy
kid came by and stole one of the nails. That's why, on the
crucifix, Christ's feet are nailed with one nail and the other two
are in the hands.

That's passed down from generation to generation. So, according to the Gypsy lore, Christ on the cross is supposed to
have said, From now and forevermore, Gypsies can steal and
it's not a sin.

Good Friday's a big day for them. When I was working the
Gypsies, we worked them for ten years, we would never take
Good Friday off because it was a day we'd have to get up early
and be on the run with them because they would be everywhere.

There's guys who make a living just picking the right victims.

In financial crimes, offenders make victims of other offenders. And that's the truth. If you're gonna defraud somebody, like
in an investment scheme, you don't want to pick somebody
that's lily white. You want to know something about this person
that can dirty him up. Wouldn't it be nice if you were partners
with somebody and you decide to defraud him, if you and he
had had conversations about defrauding Uncle Sam, or if you
knew he was involved in some other illegal activity? That

makes it very difficult for the prosecution to put your victim on the witness stand.

There's a real self-destructive streak in a lot of financial thieves. God, I've noticed it probably hundreds of times.

Usually, when you see the fatal flaw—the fatal flaw being not stealing in moderation, not embezzling or defrauding in moderation, there's a driving force behind it. A substance-abuse problem, a gambling problem, a problem with trying to maintain a standard of living beyond their means. You can't say somebody is discovered being an embezzler because they like more money. What caused them to like more money? Well, they have a thousand-dollar-a-day cocaine habit or they have a penchant for young boys—we've had a lot of those—or the guy has to have a couple of girlfriends on the side or he's got to have a swimming pool in his basement, those types of excesses.

It's almost an axiom in police work: What gets somebody in trouble is their greed. Rather than being a conservative thief, most thieves get caught because they don't know when to stop.

There's an old police adage about burglars: "It's like chasing a ghost." They go in when no one's home, or no one's around. No witnesses. No evidence, unless they slip. But there is a trail, of habits and associates, police can pick up on. . . .

We had a string of cat burglaries in high rises along Sheridan Road. During the winter months, people in the high rises were reporting burglaries, during the nighttime hours, fur coats—sometimes very trivial stuff: a comb and a lantern.

It was really goofy. We'd check, and they all had double-locked doors, deadbolt doors, no signs of any forced entry.

There was a detail put on it, and we had guys stationed on various roofs of these high rises. Middle of winter—it was *cold* up there, and we got the wind coming right off the lake. You'd get two or three buildings close together, and we'd get a guy on a roof across the way, with the binocs, trying to see anybody coming up.

So one night, a guy appears on one of the roofs, about two o'clock in the morning, a cold and windy night—carrying a bike. We later found he came up through the high-rise stairwells. Takes the bike, puts it on the roof. Then he takes out one of these . . . a rope, like mountain-climbers use, hooks it on the roof, and he—*rappels*—down three floors off the top, and drops onto the balcony. And he goes in through the sliding doors. The majority of people never leave their balcony doors locked—who's gonna think somebody's gonna come in from outside on the fiftieth floor?

He came back out with some camping stuff, climbed back on the roof. That's when we caught him. He's going to the bike he rides to and from the burglaries. "What'd you bring your bike up for?" He says, "I don't want nobody to steal it."

There's only three ways you're gonna catch a thief. It's one, through surveillance, find out who they are, and watch, and be patient enough to wait for them to do something wrong so you can grab them. You catch them in the act. The other way is, they go to do something, pull a score, and they make a mistake, or somebody spots them, and the police come upon them and grab them. And the third way is, they complete the score, nobody's watching them, they just go out and they pull that score, but they make a mistake—maybe they leave prints there or somebody drops a dime on them, beefs on them, and the police get them.

Say we lock up a guy for burglary. We'll say, "Where are you fencing? If you tell us, we'll try to help you. Now we can't promise you, but we'll talk to the state's attorney. And if they find out you're cooperative, it might help you a lot." "All right, I get rid of all my stuff at So-and-so's place."

Then all we gotta do is sit on the fence. We use the van so they can't see us, and if you see one or two guys, in a matter of three days the same guys going in there, you *know* they haven't got that much jewelry at home to get rid of. So—follow them, find out where they live, get background checks—then we go *on* 'em.

Everybody we arrest, we always give them the b.s.: we can help you out—"Who's going out every day?" "Well, you know . . . Jimmy Jones is." Gives us an address—then we start our investigation from there.

We might get an address for a dope house. So all you do is sit there undercover, watch the dope house. All you do is get plates. Go back to work with a hundred plates. You run all the plates, do a background check.

If you sit on a dope house three or four days, if one car's there twice, three times a day buying dope, you know he's out stealing. You follow him. You find out where he lives. You sit on him. He leaves his house, *you* leave his house.

I think the best thing is informants. Anytime you arrest somebody, always give them an off, always give them a deal. Even if you *can't* help them in court, you say you're *gonna* help them in court. So in front of the judge, you tell the judge, "Well, he *did* give us some good information that we were able to work on." And the judge plays the game too. "Oh, thank you very much, I'm glad you cooperated. Twenty years." Boom. He's gone. Who cares? Because when he leaves, there's eighteen guys taking his place. There are more *thieves* out there. . . .

And I don't feel bad about lying to an informant. I could care less. Some I really like—they're honest guys; they do you a favor. But some are rat junkies. They're lying to you. Half the things they tell you are b.s. Or if they *do* tell you something, they told it to five other guys already.

You get a detective with good informants, he's gonna be the best detective.

For the most part, property criminals are so much smarter than murderers. The murderer is usually brutal—or he commits the murder without preplanning. But with most property criminals—they don't want to get hurt, they don't want to hurt anybody, they want to do their thing and get out—they're the proverbial thief in the night.

A burglar is a sneak thief. He just wants to get in and get the hell out. A burglar usually isn't violent. If you were going to get hurt, it would be by a street robber more than a burglar. Robbers have got a different personality than the burglar.

Burglars never go in armed. Very, very seldom. That's their nature, that they don't want the confrontation.

Your having a gun, that won't stop a burglar. What's gonna stop him is if he thinks someone is home. More often than not, that's what's gonna stop him.

Put a pair of construction shoes outside your door. It looks like the guy came home from work and took his shoes off. Put out a big dog chain. Put a dish outside your door with some dry dog food in it. What's it cost to buy dog food?

Most burglars, if they see a Beware of Dog sign or they see a dog chain, they don't want nothing to do with it.

The basic burglar M.O. is to get in the easiest way. Break the window. Kick the door in. They might use the Wonder Bar, it's a small tool, easily concealed.

A lot of apartment buildings are empty during the day. They get in, go up and down the halls, knocking on doors. No response? They go in.

Once they're in there, it's theirs. They can do whatever they want. Anything. No one's home; they own the place. They'll have a beer; make themselves a sandwich.

Usually, they go right for the bedrooms, collect the jewelry, rifle the bedroom drawers.

It depends on how they feel. With some burglars, it's in and out. Others feel the place is theirs.

Some of them do weird stuff. I had one, he used to go to the bathroom on the kitchen tables. He'd crap on the kitchen tables. It's not all that unusual.

If you have the chance to sit down and talk to a burglar and you ask him, "How come you went into this house at this time?" he'll say something like, "Well, usually the police are changing shifts at this time. So the patrol cars are on the way in, or they're not really looking for something." Or you have burglars who go in eight, eight-thirty in the morning. "Why'd you go in then?" "Well, I saw the person leave his house. So I *knew* the house was empty." So they're putting some thought into it.

Burglars are a little more inventive than robbers—they've got to look to where they can go, and then they have to figure out how to dispose of their property. Some thought has to go into it.

The most observant person in the world is a burglar coming out of a house. He may not even *come* out of the house if he hears a car, any car, coming down the street.

That's why, when you're on something, you might have to just park that car and kind of like hide in the car, lay down on the front seat, using the mirrors, the rearview, the sideview, to see what's going on. We do that a lot.

I've hugged a guy I've been in a car with on surveillance. When somebody is driving by, you grab him like you're making out or something.

You might pull up in somebody's driveway and walk up to somebody's door if you think the guy's spotted you.

One guy we worked with, he'd take his dog. Somebody sees a guy in a car with a dog, they don't think they're a cop.

I got a Cannonball Express sign I put in the front window,

people just think you're loafing or something. I should really put a City of Chicago sign in the window.

A lot of times, you don't stop people when you watch them. You just let them go. By you stopping them, you scare them from doing a burglary. Whereas if you lay back, he'll do that burglary.

People have a misconception about, you know, why don't you grab 'em before they go in? If you don't get them doing something, all you end up with is a gun pinch. You gotta show an overt act. So we're forced to allow them an overt act.

We've had guys come this far away from doing scores. We had two guys out on a Friday night, they went to a hardware store, they bought a Wonder Bar, that's a small pry tool they use in opening doors, they were out in Elmhurst, looking around, in rural areas. . . . They were so close. . . . And then something turned them off.

And I wish we could have gone up behind them and just pushed them, and said, "Go ahead and do it, Bruce."

The thing about burglars, excluding the professional ones, the majority of them are narcotics users or gangbangers.

Most burglars—you know the old thing how burglars would watch houses? They don't have time for that. The real good ones do, the pros. But these junkies—they've gotta do three, four burglaries a day. If they knock on a door, if you're not home, they're coming in.

It used to be, the majority of our arrests for burglary were heroin users. You don't see that many burglars that are heroin addicts anymore. They're all on coke.

Cocaine addicts will steal more than heroin addicts. They use up more money than heroin addicts because they almost *can't* overdose on cocaine. Heroin, you can only use so much, you're gonna OD. I'd say anybody that shoots good heroin, you can't use more than $200 a day. Cocaine you can burn up a lot more. And then you get the dopers using both, so it's compounded.

Most junkies, if they've got a $300-a-day habit, they gotta steal like $1,000 worth of stuff. Like with cigarettes, they get three, four dollars for a twelve-, thirteen-dollar carton. A VCR, you might get forty dollars.

Video cameras are big now. VCRs and CDs are really hot to steal. They're portable and instantly saleable. Jewelry's always big; it's easy to snatch up, to conceal, and hard to trace.

A VCR will get maybe $35–$40 in a pawnshop. That's the going rate. The rule of thumb is ten cents on every dollar. The street may or may not bring more, depending on how you impress your customer. The guy who steals a $600 VCR may get $60. He's still got his $200-a-day habit to support. So he goes out and burgles some more. Or he might do a burglary today for a fix tomorrow.

Bars are *the* biggest receivers of stolen goods. Not lounges—neighborhood taverns, shot-and-a-beer joints. Far more than pawnshops. With pawnshops, you bring something in to pawn, you've gotta show identification. And if it's stolen, we're gonna find out about it. But with a bar, anyone can walk in.

Shoplifters go into bars all the time, they bring in steaks a lot of times. Meat's a big thing to boost. Cigarettes and liquor are the two biggest things to steal. What does a bar sell? Liquor and cigarettes.

❊ ❊ ❊

A true burglar, even if he's a narcotics user, never wants a confrontation. He doesn't *want* you there. The majority of burglaries are committed during the daytime hours on residences.

We found out that the burglar that goes in at nighttime, especially a residential nighttime, is a different animal—because he has to know in his mind that he may have to confront somebody. It can turn into something else so easily.

The guy that goes in at night—you can't classify him just as a burglar. The violent crimes dicks come over to us all the time, say they're investigating a rape. They come over and ask, "Do you have any cat burglars?" And they've had rapists that we've known for years as cat burglars.

That's a different breed of person, a cat burglar. They're sick people. Anybody that prowls a house when someone's home at night is a sick person. Some people believe that they're getting a sexual gratification out of it, the excitement of it, they're pumped up so high. They're right in the house; people walking around, laying in bed, and the cat burglar's just pumped up high.

Years ago, we were working on a detail up in West Rogers Park where a guy was coming in and out of houses at two, three o'clock in the morning—these are all residential houses, the people inside, the majority of the time, were sleeping.

And he'd take maybe raw meat out of the refrigerator, chew it up, and spit it on the bed where the people were sleeping. How'd you like to wake up and find you had a raw chicken chewed up on your bed?

Or he'd defecate on the bed. That's real common with cat burglars—a lot of cat burglars defecate on the floor, on the living-room rug. He'd really get his cojones off out of going into the house, knowing somebody was there, and doing something to let them know that *he* was there.

* * *

Cat burglars are very daring. They think they're so good that they get on a little ego trip. They feel the more daring they can be when they're in there, the better they are, man. I've heard of them walking in bedrooms—they like to go in with the people in there—they get the money; they get the jewelry.

I talked to this one cat burglar, Torrance. He said, "I've been in bedrooms, and the bitch is lying in bed and I just pull the sheet back and look at her, man." Cat burglars will *do* that. They won't touch them or nothing, but they want to see what the women look like.

This guy was an unbelievable cat burglar. This was a very, very active guy. He was telling us a story—he did a burglary and he had been up all night, two nights in a row. He went to this house, it was about eight in the morning. He thought no one was home; he got in through a sliding patio door.

So now he's prowling around and he hears somebody move, so he goes and hides in the closet in the kitchen, it's like a pantry. He had been up all night, for two nights. He told us that when he was high on coke he'd go for two or three days without sleeping. He was on a roll.

So now he's in the closet. There's a man sitting at the kitchen table, having his breakfast. Torrance is standing in the closet. He fell asleep standing up. And when he fell asleep, he fell against the door, and he fell out onto the floor. He's half on the floor and half in the pantry. The guy just about had a heart attack. He's screaming. To be sitting there eating breakfast and have some guy fall out on your floor.

He did another one, on the Gold Coast. Late at night. He goes to the apartment. He's rooting it real good. He tells us, "All of a sudden, I hear somebody coming. I hear the key in the door. Shit!"

He jumps under the bed. He says, "It's late. I'll wait till they fall asleep and I'll sneak out of here." He's under the bed and two people get *in* bed, and then they're making out, and he says, "Holy shit. I gotta get out of here!"

So he jumps up. He thinks it's a guy and a girl, and it's two fruits in bed. They almost die of a heart attack when they see this black guy crawling out from underneath the bed as they're locked up in an embrace.

He pretends he's got a gun. He says, "I got a gun. If you guys try anything, I'll kill you." Right? Now he finishes rooting the apartment. He says, "I made the faggots *walk* with me back to State and Division because I didn't want them to call the police while I got in the cab. And then I went." God, he was a bold son of a bitch.

A lot of house burglars used to be professionals, career-type criminals. But now burglars have gotten a little more frantic and let their guard down because a lot of them are involved with the cocaine. Where in years past, guys that might have been their brothers, or guys they looked up to, fathers even, were also house burglars. But they were careful.

Those guys—I mean, they would go to do a house burglary, they would go four- or five-handed; they'd have walkie-talkies; they'd have work cars, what they call work cars, fictitiously registered. And they would target people. They always like professional people—doctors, lawyers, people who owned their own businesses—because they felt these people were hiding stuff from Uncle Sam.

It was a Thanksgiving Day, probably fourteen years ago. The beat car got a call of a burglary-in-progress. He answers the call. He goes there and the neighbor says, "Hey, listen. I seen some guys come out of the house there. I think the door's open. I think they did a burglary."

The beat man walks in the house, and he sees money laying on the floor. The house is messy, but he says, "There's money here. Are you crazy? There was no burglary here." He closes the door and he leaves.

After the beat cop leaves, the burglars come back. Now the neighbor calls the station again and says, "These guys came back. There were four guys went into that house. They were carrying bags out. The car was dragging, it was so heavy, the trunk of the car, that it's making sparks."

What happened, there were four bachelor brothers that lived there, they were dentists, all of them. They didn't believe in banks. They invested in silver coins and silver dollars. All their money. Supposedly, the attic of this house was loaded with between $100,000 and $300,000 face value in silver coins, which, at that time, was a lot of money.

And these guys came in there, made the one trip, left, and came back again. The car was dragging, it was so loaded.

When the dicks came, the brothers were really playing it down. "I'm not sure what we lost. We didn't really have that much here." They made a claim for like $1,500 cash that was taken in the burglary. They would never claim what was actually taken. I think silver was way up at the time, they were paying about 400 percent then, so the burglars made like $600,000 on this burglary.

Most of the good burglars got out of house burglaries when they changed the sentence a few years ago on residential burglary to a mandatory four-year sentence, even for a first offense. So they've gone into boosting—unless you have a previous conviction, shoplifting's not a pen offense—or commercial burglary, where you might get probation for a first offense. And if you boost, it's hard to catch you.

You know how boosters do it? They're obvious about it. And they create a diversion.

They keep going back in. They'll make several trips, just come right out, dump the stuff in the car. That's if they have cars. Others take buses. Call cabs. They'll get done for the day, load the cab with all this stuff. The cabdriver knows they've been boosting. He doesn't give a shit.

We watched one guy—first time he went in, he came out with seventeen cartons of cigarettes, six or seven steaks. And he didn't have fat clothes on; he didn't have loose clothing.

That was the first trip. Went right to the car, dumped them in. Right back in. He must have made three trips.

* * *

Gypsies are great shoplifters. We once had a girl who carried a twenty-pound ham between her legs out of the store.

What they do in stores is almost like a magic act. You're watching their hands, and with their feet they're kicking something out the door.

They know how to feign sickness. It's part of their stealing. They go into supermarkets, twenty or thirty of them, some are passing out, falling down, the managers are running to help. In the meantime, the other part of the group goes into the manager's office, the safe is usually left open during working hours, and they grab the money in the safe.

When they did their thing in California in the seventies, they hit a town called Verago, 150 miles south of San Diego. They hit every store in town. They came 150 strong, using CB radios for communications, they'd pull up in front of stores, it was like an absolute invasion. They did this, convoy-style, all the way from Alabama to California.

Robbers force you to give it up, burglars and thieves take without your knowledge, but the con artist gets the victim to conspire in his own victimization. . . .

The best con is the simplest con.

This con happens every year around Christmas. Usually, they'll pick on the Mexicans or Spanish people—they pull up: "Listen, I got a VCR. Wanna give me a hundred dollars for it?" If they give them fifty dollars, all they're doing is buying bricks.

We had a rash of these last year. A guy got a big box, wrapped it all in paper, he got a magazine and cut out "SONY," then he put plastic all around it, Saran Wrap, so it looks brand new.

The way we got this guy—I was interviewing a woman, I had Levi's on, a sweatshirt. I walked out of the house. Here comes this guy. He pulls up and he goes, "Wanna buy a VCR?" I knew right away. I dug in my pocket for my wallet. Out comes my money, and he's hypnotized. "How much you want?" "Give me three hundred." "No way," I said. "I'll give you a hundred."

He went to reach for the VCR, it was next to him, I come out with the gun, as soon as he came up, I put it to his head. Right between his eyes. I could just see his eyes going, "Shit, man."

Victims of cons always have a little larceny in their souls. How do you cheat an honest man? You can't. The reason is, if you're not coveting somebody else's money, you can't be drawn into a plot. This sounds almost religious—if you don't covet your neighbor's goods or the company that you work for, their property, or the insurance company's money, you can't be cheated.

We get this all the time—if you went to somebody with an investment scheme, somebody's got a stash of cash somewhere that they want to make a spin somewhere, invariably they talk to the offender about how they can keep this from Uncle Sam. And that's how the offender is able, of course, to draw the victim in.

It's like the old pigeon drop—"Hey, I found a bag of money. It belongs to somebody; now it belongs to us." There's no question in the victim's mind that he's got someone else's money.

The totally honest person is the hardest to con. Try to find one.

The most expert con guy we ever came across was Anthony Seritella, a guy who posed as a copper, told people he was a North Side tac officer.

He told us he did this con for twelve to fifteen years. He said he's made over a million and a half with this con. What he would do, he'd go into a beauty shop. Have his nails done. Strike up a conversation, mention that he was a policeman; in fact, he'd show them a star. And he'd tell them a friend of his owned an electronics store and the guy had a fire. And he had some equipment that he had to get rid of because the insurance company was gonna pay it off and he had to get the stuff out of there, and he could get them a good deal on it. He'd get them to come up with the money up-front, come up with cash. Then he'd leave to get the property, and he'd never return.

Once, he had purchased a car from one guy, and after purchasing the car, he came back later on and conned the guy into buying stereo equipment, VCR, TV. The guy paid him with the same money he got for the car two hours before.

He had two guys just met him on the golf course, he played golf with them. They said he golfed like shit, this guy. They said he let them beat him for money and everything, gained their confidence. And then he said, "Hey, guys, by the way, I just bought a nice TV set, my wife is so happy, I brought it home yesterday. Nice TV, nice VCR, got a good deal on it too." They said, "Oh yeah, where?" "I have a friend who owns a small video store, he had a fire there, he's gonna make a settlement with the insurance company, but he's getting rid of stuff, you know, out the back door for a little bit of money." And they say, "Yeah?" They're looking for a deal. "Could you get any more?" "Sure, but you've got to give me the money up-front. I'll meet you there."

The guys for the bigger amount—fifteen, twenty TV sets—he said he'd take them to a trucking outfit where they have loading docks. He had one guy rent a truck and everything. "Wait here. I'm gonna go in. I'll settle up and we'll go." The guy backs the truck up to the loading dock, right? Two hours go by. No Seritella. He's gone. He went out the other door.

Loading docks are great business places for cons to meet their victims. You can walk in and out of them. They say, "Pull into the loading dock, I'll get your stuff." And they never come back.

He didn't always want to pose as a police officer. But if he thought that would put you over the hump, you know what I mean?, really gain your trust, he'd let it slip. He'd let them see his handcuff case. "Are you . . . ?" "Oh yeah."

He had one guy down at Eleventh and State. Police headquarters. They were driving—"Hey, let me stop here." He had him double-park the car, he ran in and started talking to the desk man like he was his friend. "Yeah, that was my buddy. I had to check something out with him."

He got caught when a victim spotted him downtown. He was meeting his wife for lunch. A tactical unit pulled up—he almost had them conned.

He told us that the people he conned the most out of never reported it. Twenty thousand, thirty thousand at a time. These people never reported it because they can't cover the money. They're conniving somewhere—the businessman hiding money from Uncle Sam, gamblers, dopers, they could never report their losses.

Gypsies are the most ingenious con artists. Gypsies have an uncanny ability to read people. And they have incredible acting ability. I'd say eight out of ten people that I talked to who fell for Gypsy cons would always come up with the same words: "I was mesmerized." "Didn't you realize what you were doing? You were going through this con with them and you were giving your money away?" And they'd tell me, "Officer, it was like I was mesmerized, hypnotized or something, I don't know what. But at the time I thought it was the right thing to do."

One of the superintendents of the Chicago Police Department—his aunt was taken for $15,000 by American Gypsies. She was a recent widow, Italian. And during this con, they sent her back to Italy to dig up her husband's body and take a button off his vest. International phone calls were made between Chicago and Palermo, Italy, continuing the con on this woman, warning her that she must do these things in order to keep her three grandchildren safe. It was five thousand dollars for each grandchild.

Now, this con went on for several months before it came to our attention. She, her daughter, and her son-in-law went to Palermo, to the church of St. Michael's, where they did some praying or whatever. Then, the next day, they were going to the cemetery to get this button—you have to realize that the people that the Gypsies deal with are under some type of pressure or some type of depression, hoping that somebody will give them one little thing that will make the world better.

So they went to this woman's brother in Palermo—now here's the corker. Her brother is the chief of police in Palermo, Italy. They're staying at his official residence. So the next day, she asks her brother could he get them some shovels, they're going out to the cemetery to visit her deceased husband. And he asks why do they need shovels? She then explains the reason for it, and he immediately calls the police back home and insists she make a report, which she does.

My partner and I had been watching a certain Gypsy house for months. New people had moved in; we were just laying back watching them. That night, I got a phone call from the superintendent through my lieutenant—"You're getting everybody else convicted and recovering their loss. A member of my family's been taken for fifteen thousand dollars."

I went over to the house we'd been watching where the Gypsies just moved in—I knew the family they came from—and I said, I want all the money returned to this woman.

We opened negotiations, and they said they only took $10,000. I wasn't successful at this, so I got warrants for the man and woman who did this. And the judge told me, "If you bring these people into my courtroom, it's going to be very difficult to prove. It's like 'Let the buyer beware.' "

This went on for six months. The man and woman had fled Chicago and were on the run. But I had contacts in Detroit, Los Angeles, and Florida. I find out that they're now in Detroit. I would call up a detective friend of mine and say, "Listen, do me a favor. Go to this address. Knock on the door. If a Gypsy comes to the door, tell them I want them back in Chicago." Did the same thing in Los Angeles, did the same thing in Florida.

Finally, I got a call from their attorney, a big-name attorney downtown, this is like six, seven months after we found out about the crime. He said, "The Gypsies think you're everywhere. What can we do to settle this?"

It was arranged that the victim, my partner and I, and the offenders would meet in the attorney's office. My promise to the attorney was that I would not take them into custody. They would write two certified checks for $7,500 apiece with the stipulation that the warrant dies. I then went back to the judge, he said I think that's the best way we can go on this case, and it was done. And the woman got her money back.

They had done everything with her. They did "the devil in the egg." The devil in the egg is, they'll tell you to bring an egg with you from your home. They'll take a little piece of meat and palm it. You give them your egg, they wrap it up in a handkerchief, and they break it, open it up, and there's this little red piece of meat in the middle of the egg. They throw it on the floor, screaming and yelling, "Your money has been cursed, see, here's the devil!"

They also had her bring in a live chicken. It's kind of hard to find a live chicken these days. But she did. She brings the chicken in, the Gypsy holds the chicken next to her own neck— she has a needle concealed in her hand—she hits the chicken in the neck, automatically the chicken dies.

Then they go into all this falling-down stuff and "Oh my God, there *is* a curse on you. Look at how that chicken died. Give us your money, and we'll take that curse off. We'll bury the chicken to take the curse off. It'll cost you ten thousand dollars."

When I first went to the head of the family about this, this was when we thought only $10,000 had been gotten out of the aunt, I said, "Louis, you cost those people ten thousand dollars." He said, "I was taking a curse off their children." "Louis, come on." "Listen, are those children safe today?" "Yeah, they're safe." "Then it's off. The curse has been taken off of them." I said, "Why did you charge them ten thousand dollars?" He said, "It was to take the curse off." I said, "Louis, if you had Colonel Sanders as a pallbearer, it wouldn't cost ten thousand dollars to bury a chicken."

Burglars are ghosts, cons are psychologists, and career criminals are the scientists of breaking and entering. The old CIU studied this science and came up with a counterscience of its own . . .

When we talk about career criminals, we don't mean junkies who go out and steal, even though that may be their career. We mean criminals that are more sophisticated, more professional, more experienced. They're professional criminals— their one and only source of money is crime.

Some of them might be crime syndicate guys, but they're the fringe guys; they might be coming up in the Outfit, or they might use it to supplement their income because maybe they're not deeply involved on the payoff in the rackets.

And I'd say 98 percent of professional thieves are not dope users. Maybe now and then they do a little cocaine and that, but . . . they avoid dope users because they're not reliable. These are your career criminals, your good, top-notch criminal.

You've got guys who only try to zero in on scores, burglaries, robberies, or stickups, where there is a *lot* to gain. I'm not talking about thousands, I'm talking about hundreds of thousands.

There was one guy like this in particular, Paul DiCaro, who only went after the big scores.

We took them down one time, we got Paulie his first conviction, it was right before Christmas. They were doing a safe burglary in a Toys 'Я' Us. It was a four-handed score. They were just about to burn open the safe when we got them. In the safe was about $75,000; they were gonna split that four ways, which would have made a nice Christmas for them.

We got them; they bonded out of jail. Needless to say, they had to go back out and make money. And there was a warehouse that distributed premiums for credit-card companies; there might be jewelry, there might be coins, there might be electronic stuff in there. They went in there, bypassed the alarm, got in, put guns on people that were in there working, tied them up, backed a trailer in, and loaded the trailer up with about $900,000 worth of product.

Being the businessman that he was—inside the cartons they had a bill of lading telling what the actual value was, what the wholesale value was—and the crew was selling this stuff on the street for what it cost this company to buy—so he got top dollar. So what it came down to—they took the score off, they added like 50 percent to it, they'd sell it. So he ended up making a good buck on that one.

If you get good thieves, they put a lot of effort and equipment into their work. The big name of the game is "Don't Get Caught." So whatever or whoever you can get to assist you in not getting caught, you invest in it.

In a good professional crew, you have a driver. You have a guy that can cut through a roof. You've gotta have guys that can climb, that are athletic and not afraid of heights. And you've gotta have somebody that's knowledgeable about alarms, because a lot of these places that they're going after—most of them are jewelry stores, coin stores—and they have real sophisticated alarm systems and these guys are gonna have the stuff to defeat them.

In sophisticated crews, guys will actually become electronics experts. They call them "wire guys." Most of your alarm systems run on phone wires in some way, shape, or form. These guys cut into the cable or the box, pick out the pairs that are alarm wires, hook up to them, and bypass the alarm. And what they'll do is, they'll hire out to circumvent alarms.

What a wire guy would do, he'd go circumvent the alarm, he'd open the place up, he might even serve as a lookout after he circumvents the alarm, monitor the radios, and then after they got through, he'd get his end—probably an equal share of whatever proceeds there were from the score. Usually, these people bounce from crew to crew.

And then you have grunts, guys that actually do the work, that can move the merchandise, but they've gotta be bold enough to be in there—you can't take just any strong-backed guy, you gotta have someone that's got a little balls.

They enjoy it. They get a thrill out of it. Consequently, they're having fun.

You've got to have other specialists on the crew—you might be able to get into a place that's alarmed, but maybe it has one of the best safes around. So you have safe specialists too—guys that specialize in burning, know how to burn the safe open.

A true safe is more than fireproof. It's a container that can't be moved by hand. It weighs more than eight hundred pounds. Doesn't have any wheels on it. Has a circular-type door with a combination. That's why they call it a safe.

If you can get it out, you have time to peel it or work on the combination. Peel is when they turn the safe over on its side and try to rip the back or the bottom open, maybe chisel it out and then literally peel it apart.

When they punch a safe, they knock down the combination

lock and knock it off and then they'll use something to get in there, like a small sledgehammer, and actually knock out the device so the safe opens up.

Sophisticated safecrackers—they'll get what are called "burning bars" from a construction crew. Burning bars can be as long as six feet—they're these numerous metal rods, each about one-eighth of an inch thick, which are connected to an oxygen tank. The bars go through the metal of the safe, and as it burns, it consumes itself, leaving nothing but ashes.

Some thieves are ingenious enough, because they *do* have to have a certain skill in mechanics, to develop their own special tools. Their tools are very unique.

If you look at auto theft—everyone knows the term "slim-jim," this tool. It was probably developed out of the necessity of getting into cars—maybe by a legit guy, some locksmith. And then it fell into the hands of the auto thieves, because now all of a sudden they find out, they don't have to pull the door locks and break a window open—you just walk up with a slim-jim and you pop it.

They take good tools and modify them to fit their needs. For instance, they'll find a tool that would normally be used for pulling up nails, a plier-type tool. They may take these things and modify the jaws to fit over a lock. Then you just bite into the lock and you pull the lock up.

Thieves usually go in through the roof. Your doors—the doors on the perimeter, where you can get at them, are usually pretty heavily barred. It's easier to go through the front door, but that's more visible. If you get up on the roof, you can hide and chop your way through.

There's a kid doing time in the fed pen, Ronnie Jarrett, started out stealing tires and stuff. Then he just grew up into burglaries, where he'd go in and just take whatever property was lying around—then he got a little bit more ambitious, learned the mechanics of breaking into safes, and by the time we got into him in CIU, he had a crew that was going out once a month. They were a safe crew. What they'd do is, they'd go out and hit a Jewel, National, a Walgreens, Osco, they were taking all these types of joints off. We ended up with eighteen burglaries we could pin on them—all supermarkets or large drug-chain establishments.

Before they went in, they got knowledgeable about the operation of the store. They were very sophisticated; they'd send scouts out ahead of time and all that good stuff. What they found out was, most of these stores have hydraulic-lift trucks. Now, the thing with those type of places is the safe is usually up in the front window, and the chances of getting caught opening the safe are very great because of the visual contact with the public driving by. You can see the safes from outside. The reason they do this is by placing the safe in a visible location, the possibility of somebody getting in there and opening that safe is very slim because they're liable to be spotted.

So Ronnie's crew devised a game plan. They'd go in through the roof—chop through, drop down. And because they circumvented the alarm prior to going in, then they had time to break the door open in the back. They'd break out of the place—that's the term for breaking the back door open to get out. Then what they would do is take the existing forklift in the place, go up to the front of the store, pick the safe up, and take it out the back. They'd put it on the truck and they'd take it to a garage, and then they'd—leisurely—open the safe without any chance of being caught.

When they first started out, they stole a truck and a forklift off a loading dock. That was the concept of it. And then they realized that most of these stores already had electric hand forklifts or whatever present. So what they did, they stole another truck with a hydraulic-lift gate on it, so when they rolled the safe on the rear end of the truck, the hydraulic-lift gate raised the safe up, they'd push it in, then put the tailgate up and take off. And they were long gone. They did this over a year and a half. Some of these safes had upwards of $80,000, $90,000 in cash in them.

The way they got rid of the safes, after emptying them, was, they took the truck, and ran over to the Old South Branch of the Chicago River—the safe would still be on the truck—they'd back the truck up at a high rate of speed, slam on the brakes, and the safe would slide right off into the river.

We conducted a series of surveillances on various members of the Jarrett crew. We decided it was too difficult to set up surveillances in the neighborhood where they were operating—they were very elaborate people; when they were about to go out on a burglary, they would go so far as to send scouts out in cars, with walkie-talkies, just looking around the neighborhood to make sure there was no heat.

We ended up realizing that one of the crew, Ronnie Brown, a very athletic guy—his expertise was climbing, he'd do roof entries; he'd climb and cut wires—we realized that this guy lived out of the neighborhood, he lived out in Cicero. So we just surveilled him. It kept us out of the neighborhood and, at the same time, gave us the opportunity to know when they were going. As we went along, we picked up more and more information that made it easier for us to surveil them.

They liked Sunday nights, primarily because, if you look at safe burlaries, you'd realize there'd be more money on a Sunday than on a Friday or Saturday, when Brinks would make a pickup. The store would be open Saturday and all day Sunday, so the safe would be chock-full.

One Sunday, we surveilled them, and they got rolling. We followed them out to Homewood, Illinois, to the roof of a Jewel out there. Unfortunately for them, the surveillance they had apparently conducted didn't allow for the fact that the cleanup people were going to arrive Sunday evening. And lo and behold, they made the roof entry and were preparing to move their truck into position to take the safe out, and the cleanup crew showed up for work. So they aborted.

We took them down anyhow, because we knew they had made the attempt because we had people that had observed them cut the phone wires and stuff like that. So we arrested them out in Homewood; we got five people in custody out there. And then Ronnie Brown started cooperating. He rolled over on Jarrett because, after we arrested him, he expected Jarrett to come up with the bond money, and he didn't. He was looking at some time, so he figured I ain't going down by myself. Honor among thieves.

He started cooperating and we were able to recover about twenty safes from the Chicago River.

The good burglars are gonna have a car. You'll get burglars that walk—they're your nitwit burglars, your shithead burglars.

Your good burglars are gonna have a vehicle. Definitely gonna have a vehicle. May have two vehicles. They may have one—what we call a work car: It can be a stolen car or a fictitiously registered car, and they may have a legitimate car parked nearby. They'll go out to an area, they'll park the legitimate car in a parking lot somewhere, and they'll go do the actual burglary with the worker. If they gotta make a getaway, if there's a chase, they can do it, and they can always go to that cold car, the legit car, if they get seen.

We've covered work cars—four-door vehicles, okay? You open the door . . . the two doors open together. There'd be no backseat in there. There'd be like all plywood flooring.

These are for the windowcrash guys. Professional windowcrash burglars. They back a work truck into the showroom window of a clothing store, and four to five guys run in, grab an armful of clothes, run out, throw them in the truck, and run off. Ten, fifteen thousand dollars a crack. So they had nothing in that car so they could just throw all the clothes in the back, and the door would open real wide, the double door.

Or, other work cars, you see four-door common family sedans with big racing motors in them, souped-up. Some of them have magnetic license plates where you'd have the license plate on there, and it's on a bracket with magnets on it and that attaches to the regular license plate. So now if they catch some heat, they just pull the one license plate down with the magnets, and they've got a different license number on the car.

We've had them where they'll change lights—they've got switches on the car. You know if you're following a car, you might see three taillights? Now, all of a sudden, the guy makes a turn, they hit a switch and it'll turn one of the taillights off. So now you see just two taillights across the back. So you think, Hey, that's not the car.

We've seen them—they've had telephone trucks with 427 racing motors in them. They'd use them on burglaries because telephone trucks don't draw a lot of attention. And with the racing motor, once they get out, they're ready to *go.*

The better guys, some of the good thieves, are kind of leery. They never talk on their own phones. You always see them going into different public phone booths.

And always, always, tail-conscious. Always alert to somebody following them. Drive like maniacs—could be going down the expressway, they come up to where the state police might sight, where it says NO U-TURN—do a U-turn and go the other way.

They do funny things. They park their car and get out and stand on the street and look . . . or they park and crouch down low in there and they get down in the seat—you might think they're out of the car. Now you wait awhile and you go drive by the car. And you're looking at the car, and sure enough, he sticks his head up, and he's looking right at you.

A professional thief, when you start to surveil these guys, if they're going to a restaurant in the city, first they'll drive all the way out to a suburb where there's hardly any traffic on the streets, and they'll drive up and down the side streets just to see who's following them. Or they'll make U-turns, or go the wrong way on a one-way street. This is a matter of course for them. They do stuff like this even if they're just going to the grocery store.

Thieves go through red lights to look for heat. They blow through red lights and stuff to see if somebody's coming, see who might go through a red following them. They look for that; they watch that rearview mirror.

So that's why when you're following somebody, you can't always bust the red light. Then they know they've got a tail. They're not worried about the beat cops. They don't care about taking a ticket. That's the least of their worries.

We had one guy, Butch Petrocelli—he later was a victim in a gangland killing—we stopped him one day in his car. He had a tape recorder with him in the car. We played back the tape— and all it was, was license-plate numbers. It was like "Wednesday night, December 22" and then a string of license numbers. Every time he'd pull up to a stoplight, he'd look at the license numbers of everybody around him and record them.

Then he'd play it back when he'd go home and see if he had any license numbers two or three days in a row, people who were around him and at what times.

He's dead now. He wound up in a trunk. He was looking at the wrong guys.

The main way we get them is . . . People are victims of habit. Like bank robbers with notes. He might walk up and write a note out, "Give me all the hundreds, fifties, and twenties. I got a gun." He might use that same phrase in his note every time— he might vary it a little bit, like "A guy's watching you," but it's always "Give me all the hundreds, fifties, and twenties."

So they *do* fall into these habits. What's successful for them they continue to use. So you *bet* they fall into habits. And if we're lucky enough to find out about their habits, they get caught.

So you research guys. You get their habits down pat. You watch a guy—you watch the way he walks, find out about his lifestyle, what restaurants he likes to eat in, places he likes to drink in, who he hangs with, you can gear off on him. And you can tell if a guy is going out for a social evening or if he's going out for business. And then you mount up. Hit it.

How do you find out what guys to watch? Maybe they took a pinch, and some policeman might feel that these guys are good, and he'll give you information on him. Or you get onto him through an informant. Maybe a score goes down, and they're successful, they get away. And you go out there and beat the bushes, you come up with somebody that's willing to give you some information—he says, "If I were you, I'd take a look at So-and-so, because he's the guy." Previous experience, knowledge of the guy. He did things a certain way, and all of a sudden he goes down. Now he comes back out, and the same business starts up. You say, "So-and-so's back to work." Or you got a notorious guy like Pops Panczko, and all of a sudden he's got a stranger with him. You're gonna find out who the stranger is. Because you never know.

You don't like to tail per se all the time, because if the guy is halfway sharp, he's gonna pick you up. So you may work on a person where you'll start at a certain time and you'll find out he has a regimen—he does certain things at certain times. So maybe after a few days you'll *start* at a location where he goes at a later time of day. You pick up on his pattern.

Mostly, people have patterns. Especially social—guys they hang around with, where they meet.

Career criminals go to restaurants all the time, because they like to see who's around them, and nobody can overhear them.

When you're sitting on somebody, you try and blend in. You don't wear a suit and tie, you wear casual clothes or work clothes, or a jacket and a shirt instead of a suit and a tie.

The type of cars we try to obtain at the department's supply arm—*normal.* You don't go with a Corvette, a Z28—you might go with a two-door Chevrolet that's got a few years on it, and the paint job is nice, but it's not real shiny. You try to blend in. We always used to say, "Try to make yourself invisible."

It's tough doing surveillance. If it's night, you can't smoke. In the wintertime, you freeze your ass off. You can't run the car to keep warm because he's liable to see the exhaust smoke from the car. It can get very boring. But it pays off.

* * *

We took a crew out south of the city. These were active criminals, from the younger set. We eventually took them down on a home invasion out there.

On the way out, we see that they put one of their guys in the back window and he's facing back all the time, looking for guys. We're driving on the tollway and everything else, we take them all the way out there. They have two cars. And we have maybe seven or eight.

We take them out and successfully take them down on the home invasion. We get them in custody, the lookout says to one of his co-workers, who's more or less the leader, "You know, I *thought* I saw those guys at one of the toll stops." And the guy he's talking to says, "You know, what do you think we put you in the back window for?" He says, "You're supposed to tell us that." He turns to me and he says, "You know, you really can't get good help anymore."

There's a term we use—"You can't write the script." You gotta wait them out. And that's what you do, you just wait and wait and wait, and if they go, and you're lucky enough to stay with them, you're gonna get them. Not all the time, but I would say one third of the time.

When we set up on guys, one of us would be the "eye"—"I got the eye"—one guy's got the eye, meaning, "I got the target in my view, I'm the one, I'm watching him."

So one guy had the eye. The rest of us would figure out all the different avenues where he could leave from, and cover north, south, east, west. So we'd be posed in different areas close by where we could cover whatever way he would leave.

You never tail with just one or two cars; you have at least four or five in the tail. That's so you can leapfrog them, one guy goes to the end of the tail if he thinks he's been made. Or you parallel them. If a car's going this way, you've got cars next to him, that's paralleling. Now if the car following him peels off, he looks in the rearview mirror, there's nobody. Next thing you know, there's a red car. Now a blue car. Then you've got the other cars zigzagging.

There are different schools of surveillance. But there's one rule I've always believed in: "It's better to lose a guy than to heat him up." You can always come back.

You might maintain a surveillance on a guy, but you do a loose surveillance because you don't want to heat him up. Once you heat the guy up, his head gets on a swivel and the next thing you know you lose him, or you really have to change your act, you have to get more people out there, more equipment, it really creates problems if you heat him up.

Let's say it's a moving surveillance and it's a situation where you gotta maintain it, you gotta take the chance on, we use the term, getting burned—the guy burns you with his eyes when he sees you. If that happens, you have to remove yourself from the game now, which is really a rough thing to do for a policeman. Go to the tail end, or even remove yourself from the surveillance. It's kind of rough. But if you get burned and you have to jump to the back of the pack, you know eventually you're gonna be up in front with the rest of the guys, locking this guy up. So it's always patience and control.

You gotta be a little bold now and then too. Burn a guy or heat him up a little bit, but just enough where maybe he gets a little cautious. But not so much that he aborts.

The last time Pops Panczko took a pinch, we caught him—he got $180,000 in jewels from a jewelry salesman's car. He was in his early sixties, he had bad feet, he was overweight, and he hadn't quit.

We were on Peanuts and Pops Panczko a long time. When we were on Pops, we had him, Jesus Christ, I bet you for a good month, getting up early in the morning with him. We had him out in Des Plaines, looking for a jewelry salesman's car out there. He was just looking for the right time to catch that car out, to catch the guy moving, or leaving the trunk open or something. Because a lot of these guys would bring their lines in the house—they'd have two big heavy bags, they could only carry one; they'd grab one, walk it in, leave the trunk open—and Pops, this son of a bitch, he'd drive right by, grab the case, and pull away with it. Or he'd take the car. Just grab the keys left in the trunk and jump in the car and go.

Then we had Pops going out to Naperville, way the hell out to Naperville on the East-West Tollway, and every day we're going out there, five, six of us, and Pops is looking around some subdivision. So finally one day we had him out there, and he spots something and he starts moving. Right after the guy he's targeted.

And he has us going down some roads, and we could see that he's following a car for sure. Now, we're way down southwest and he's down some rural roads.

I was on the eye, I was the lead car, and he did a turn on us. They had like a little rural town there—he hit like a highway and then made another turn right away. And I didn't pick up the pace, and we lost him. Now, I'm so mad, I'm saying, "Son of a bitch. Goddamit." I lose him.

So we get back and we put our heads together; so, well, what are we gonna do? Our sergeant says, "Let's go call on the guy's wife." We knew where the house was, so we go out there, and sure enough, we find out her husband's a jewelry salesman and he was going out on some stops. So we find out where he was headed from her. We phoned one of the stops he was headed for, and he had just left there.

So then we call another stop, which was gonna be his next stop, and he hadn't gotten there yet. He stopped for gas in between the two stops. And when he went in to pay for the gas, Pops jumped behind the wheel of the car and took off. One hundred eighty thousand dollars' worth of jewelry was in that car. Pops drives the car about four blocks, takes out the sample cases, puts them in his car.

The salesman calls his house, right? Tells his wife he's been ripped off. We were waiting in the house. So, as soon as we find that out, we set up in strategic locations we knew Pops was gonna go back to. We're way out in Naperville—some of us have to fly all the way back to the North Side of the city where he's living. We've got to beat him back.

So we set up on the different possible avenues of coming back to the city. We have two guys set up on the tollway where we

thought East-West might intersect. I remember going back to
the city, going through the tollbooths, trying to beat Pops back.
We just flew through the tollbooths, like maniacs, the guys in
the booths just watched us—fwoosh! fwoosh!—and we're in the
unmarked cars; I was in an old gray Cougar, my partner was in
an old Chevy.

It was the two guys set up on the tollway that caught that son
of a bitch coming back. They spot him. Stopped him. And he
had the whole load. Man, that was a load off *my* back, because
I was the guy under the gun. I lost him, goddammit. I wanted
to kick somebody. So they got him. He pulled some good time
for that.

If you follow somebody on foot, that's when it gets like a spy
movie. You get people on foot . . . they might park their car,
walk a block, two blocks, whatever, to get to the score. You just
lay back. As long as you can maintain a visual contact on the
guy, you can really lay back.

If someone's out on foot, you have to be more careful, because
they tend to notice vehicles, they tend to notice things more
easily. Their head's on a swivel. They just notice more.

Three guys from Grand and Ogden, the Patch—that's a place
that breeds thieves. We dropped in on them one Friday night.
Within half an hour, we have the one guy out moving, he goes,
picks up two other guys. They get right on the expressway; it's
Friday night rush hour. They go, man, they go in the right lane,
and they go past all the traffic on the left, and they're looking
to their left all the time—they're looking for tails. They're zigzagging in and out of traffic. One of us was just quick enough
to keep up with them and not get made. They get off, make a
left turn, go down about two blocks, go around the block once,
park the car. One of the guys was lucky enough to be on that
street, so he slid his car in behind him.

They get out of the car, the three of them. We set up—one guy
set up a block west of them, I set up to the south, this other guy

sets up to the north. We wait. They're gone ten minutes, fifteen minutes; now when it's gone twenty minutes, I say, "Eddie, they're scoring."

Fifty minutes later they come back, and they're carrying— one of the guy's got a pillowcase and the other guy's got a bag.

So we let them get in the car, and we try to box them. I pull up on the side, Eddie pulls up on the other side, and one guy pulls up on the front. They back up. One guy jumps out of the car. We got him right away. The other two guys come ramming at us in the car.

I pull my gun out, I pointed it right at his head. He was right next to me, so close I couldn't open my car door. I says, "Stop!" and he went right through—even with my gun pointed right at his head—smashed the side of his car, he takes off, driving over the lawn; I mean, it was like a trail of smoke and dust.

While they're driving, they're throwing stuff out the car window: Lladros, crystal, jewelry. They hit an alley, and they dump the car. So we spot the one guy, the driver. The third guy got away; we never found where he was.

We got the furs back, we got the Lladros and some crystal that wasn't busted up, but the third guy got away with the jewelry.

It worked out good. They didn't get the lady's good jewelry. But the one shithead had a tube of toothpaste that the woman had bought that day at a certain store, had the price tag and everything. He stole the toothpaste—that's how funny some of these burglars are, they're out doing thousand-dollar jewelry scores and see something that catches their eye—this guy grabbed the tube of toothpaste and stuck it in his pocket—that's something that could really hurt in court, because the victim can identify it.

We once followed a crew to Watseka, Illinois. These wiseguys went down there, they brought two of their girlfriends with them. Three guys. Went to a real nice restaurant in Watseka, Illinois. Snow up to your ass. Cold, cold, cold day. We tail them; we think they're gonna take a score off close by. We take them all the way down to Watseka, Illinois.

They pull into this restaurant lot. They leave the two girls in the car with the motor running, and they pull the ski masks over their face and they go in—there's gotta be about twenty customers in this restaurant. We look in the window and see the guys with the ski masks and the guns. You can't go in and get them because there's twenty people in the joint.

So two of our guys sneak up, grab the girls by their hair, pull them out of the fucking car—kidnap them. They come over, put them in the squad car, handcuff them, and leave them.

Now the bad guys have got the money, they got the jewelry, they got the wallets, they got everything they want. One of them walks out to tell the girls to get the car; the motor was running. The girls aren't there, and he sees the guys laying—now these are Chicago police officers, with shotguns, rifles—laying on snowbanks. Freezing their asses off.

These guys spot it. Now they take a hostage from the restaurant. And they got her around the neck, with the pistol up on her head. And they said, "We're coming out. We want a squad car. We want our girls back. We want an hour's head start."

We had a guy with us that was . . . we used to call him the Nutty Norwegian. He wouldn't take shit from anybody. And he wasn't about to negotiate. There was none of this hostage/barricade shit.

This guy was an expert shot. He had a .44 Magnum on him. The guy came out with the hostage and made his demands, and this guy said, "Fuck you," and he let one shot go over the guy's head. It hit the restaurant sign, the sign fell right in front of the bad guy, and he ran back in the restaurant with the hostage, and he told the others, "These guys are fucking crazy. We're not going anywhere." Next thing, they said, "Don't shoot! We're coming out." We said, "If you come out with any hostages, you're going to the morgue." They threw the guns out, they all came out with their hands up. There was no HBT.

And what do you think the outcome of it all was? The state police wanted us all to get a reprimand for being out of our jurisdiction and not notifying them. State police got mad at us.

We were in the old Burglary Unit, and we were following an offshoot of a home-invasion crew that we had put away. The original crew, it was a torture crew, would go in and bite off women's nipples, have little girls suck off their fathers; these were the most rotten, dirty motherfuckers you'd ever want to meet.

This offshoot crew would beat people, crack the kids, very violent. They'd put a gun in the victim's mouth and click the hammer. Put a gun to the woman's private parts in front of the husband and say, "You won't be using this anymore," or they'd put a shotgun next to the husband's balls. They'd put a gun in a kid's mouth.

Their ruse was to come up the walk with flowers. Two guys would come up to the door—the third guy stayed in the car, with the motor running. They wore baseball caps and held the flowers in front of their faces. They had nylon stockings rolled up underneath the baseball caps. So when they rang the bell, whoever answered the door would look through the peephole, or they'd crack the chain—all they would see was flowers and a momentary glimpse of the face. "Floral delivery." "All right, just a minute," and as the victim opened the door, the two guys would pull the stockings down over their faces and come in.

We were following these guys for months. This crew had targeted a fellow that was in the furniture-design business, very wealthy. I knew all three perpetrators; one day, one of the perpetrators, who was a barber and a semi-informant, called the unit and said it was important he get hold of me. The unit called my house—and at that exact moment, we were having a meeting at my house as to how we were gonna nail these guys.

So the guy called. He wanted to know what shift I was working. His excuse was to say he was being harassed by some district vice cops and could I do anything about it and when could he come in, see me? I said, "Anhh, I'm tired of shift work. I'm just working days. I work and then I go home, and that's it." I'm saying this, knowing he's one of the perpetrators—we had maps spread out on my kitchen table. And now we know he's planning a score for the evening, when I'd be off.

So the next day, we set up. We had to get heavy equipment: carbines, machine guns, shotguns, revolvers, pistols, into the intended victim's house and into a house across the street. And we didn't know who might be watching, if they had countersurveillance.

We went to the intended victim and told him, "We're gonna get you and your family out of here." He had his wife, two or three children, and grandma in there, and he said, "No one is going to drive me out of my house. I don't care who they are. We're staying." That's how much balls this guy had. So we said, "Well, if they get by us, they'll get you." They stayed. This guy had balls, and his wife had balls. He said, "I'll do whatever you want me to do."

We said, "Okay. We don't know if these people that intend to take you have countersurveillance set up during the day. So what we want to do is get people into your house as discreetly as possible."

So, that day, a couple of our guys met the intended victim away from his office, and we made sure he wasn't being surveilled. And they brought machine guns and shotguns into his station wagon and lay in the backseat. And earlier, two more of our guys came in with the wife in her car, with machine guns and shotguns; they were laying on the floor. They had like a two- or three-car attached garage. So our guys rode in with the intended victims, and once the garage doors closed, they were able to unload the weapons and move them into the house. Then they set up communications and were able to take their places.

I went up and down the street with an attaché case, like I was selling door-to-door. We wanted to get a position across the street. We told them what was going on—everybody in the neighborhood knew about this crew by reading the papers, about what these guys were doing to their victims and torturing them. The people *directly* across the street wouldn't cooperate at all; they said they didn't give a shit *what* happened to the neighbor.

So we went to the next house. When we came to the door and said we were the police and wanted to talk to the guy, the guy who answered the door almost had a coronary because he was a bookmaker. Which we didn't know till after it was all over. We said, "Could we use your house? We think there's gonna be a crime in the area. Could we use your garage?"—it was attached to his house. He said, "You can have anything you want."

So we had three or four guys in the target's house, about three or four of us across the street, and about twenty spread out through the neighborhood.

We had the house under observation. We saw the crew pull up in a rental car. The driver stayed behind the wheel, because he had a crippled right leg and wore a metal brace from his shoe to his knee. The other two got out carrying potted plants. Floral delivery.

As they were approaching the door, I came out of the garage of the house across the street. I had a carbine. I got down on one knee and I was able to take the driver of the getaway car out right away. He was dead.

Bill, the sergeant in the target's house, opened the door. That took more balls than you can shake a stick at. Bill had the machine gun, and he didn't want anybody to open the door except himself. He had the machine gun in one hand—and he opened the door with the other. They came up, he got the machine gun and said, "Who is it?"; they said, "Floral delivery," and he opened the door. "Police. Lay down." They said, "Fuck you." They both opened fire and turned around and ran. And that's when the show was on the road.

Bill emptied the magazine—one guy went back to the car, Bill hit him in the elbow, but the guy got back in the car. Bill dropped the machine gun, it was empty.

And he wound up chasing the other guy down the street on foot, they're shooting at each other as he's chasing him, Bill's using his revolver, and there's a woman watering the lawn, and the sergeant's yelling, "Lady, lady, lady, drop the hose and get the fuck out of here!" She was determined to water the lawn. Finally, she dropped the hose and ran.

Before the guy could turn around and fire again, Bill stopped. You can never hit anybody when you're running. He stopped and took a good aim and put one right through his back. And it came out the front, and he figured he was dead.

When he got up to the guy, he was trying to roll over, because he had another gun in his back pocket, and he was trying to get that out of his pocket. Bill stepped on his hand. And he expired.

This was the guy that had called me on the phone the night before. The barber. I had a lot of coppers call me after that and say, "Jesus Christ, we always thought that guy was a nice guy. He used to cut our hair, he was a good barber." I said, "Where do you think most barbers learn their profession? In the pen.

That's one of the biggest trades that the penitentiaries teach a guy, is to become a barber or a hairdresser."

Now, the driver was dead, but with that brace on his leg, his right foot hit the accelerator, and the car went up over the lawn about seventy feet at least, hit a fireplug on the corner, and automatically went into reverse and started coming back on us. We just kept loading it up with everything we had. It hit the next-door neighbor's front porch, and the show was over at that time. We had to shoot some of the tires out so we could get in to turn the ignition off.

The other guy, the one that got shot in the elbow, had made it back into the car. When I looked in—you assume things you shouldn't—but when I looked in at the guy laying on the passenger side of the car, I figured that with all the bullet holes and everything, we must have pumped hundreds of bullets into that car, I figured he's gone too. I moved away, and one of the old-time dicks called me back, "Hey, Sarge, he's moving." He was still alive. He heard all of us talking, and he heard them saying my name.

He knew me. He was an ex-con and had just been out a short time. I had stopped him once on the street around the Chicago Historical Society about three, four months before this. And at that time, he said he had just come out of the pen. He said, "I'm an ex-con. I just got out. I guess I'm pinched." I said, "Well, just because you came out of the penitentiary doesn't mean I have anything against you. I'm not gonna pinch you because of that. You did your time, you did your time. You go over and buy a newspaper—there's thousands of jobs in there. You get yourself a job and go straight up, I'll never bother you again."

This was the guy I made the street stop on. There was a gun laying next to his hand. He must have had twenty-five guns pointed right next to his head, and I told him, "Don't make a move for that gun, because if you're not dead now, you're gonna be dead for sure."

Then we pulled him out of the car, feet first, he was all full of glass. He said, "Sergeant, please don't kill me. Just turn me over. I'm hurt." We turned him over and at first I didn't recognize him. He said, "Sergeant ——, please. I need some medical help." I said, "How do you know who *I* am?" He said, "Remember three months ago you stopped me and told me I better get a job?"

After it was all over, the bodies weren't even taken away at the time, I looked up from in front of the house where the car was, it had about four hundred bullet holes in it, and I looked up and here are two other guys that I knew were doing the same thing. Home invaders. They came walking by; they were nosy. It was all over the radio and everything; this was fresh news. So I looked up, and I went over and I grabbed them, and I said, "Come here. Take a good fucking look at this. Because the only reason you're not in there is because we got to these guys first. You're next." I later learned both of them soon left for California.

The guy we pulled out of the car made it. How he survived that car is beyond me. He's still a thief. He was afraid to home invade after that, he just went back to stickups and burglaries. Thieves never go straight.

Property Crimes:
Contributing Police Officers

SERGEANT JOHN BURKE, Financial Investigations Unit. Burke, twenty-four years on the force, has been with Financial Investigations since its inception in 1979. Burke spent eight years in uniform in the Second and Tenth Districts, on the South Side and West Side, respectively; two years in Communications as a dispatcher, and three years as a detective in Auto Theft, before coming to Financial Investigations.

DETECTIVE ROBERT HACK, Area Six Property Crimes. Hack came on the force in 1958, spent two years on patrol on the North Side and six years in the old TUF Squad. In this detail, Hack worked various undercover assignments, including robbery decoy, feigning drunkenness in high-crime areas in order to get robbed and make the street-crime pinch on the spot. In 1966, Hack was promoted to youth officer and assigned to Area Five. Hack made detective in 1967, worked the old Burglary Unit in Area Six until 1978, and then was assigned to the Central Investigations Unit, which conducted surveillances on career criminals. In 1980, Hack returned to Area Six Property Crimes.

CAPTAIN JOHN (JACK) HINCHY, former deputy chief of detectives, former commander of Burglary, former commander of Intelligence, former commanding officer of Narcotics, co-founder and co-leader, with former chief of detectives William (Bill) Hanhardt, of the CIU. In addition to masterminding, with Bill Hanhardt, the CIU, a unit devoted to the surveillance and capture of professional criminals, Captain Hinchy, in his thirty-one years on the force, served as a detective and supervisor in Robbery and Burglary. Then-sergeants Hinchy and Hanhardt formed the CIU in 1962. IN 1970, Hinchy, then a lieutenant, formed MEG, the Metropolitan Enforcement Group, whose officers worked undercover on narcotics dealers in the suburbs. Hinchy retired from the force in 1985.

DETECTIVE JACK LAURIE, Area Six Property Crimes. Laurie has been a check specialist for the past thirteen years. He joined the CPD in 1970 and became a detective after one year working patrol in the Twentieth District. He then was assigned to Area Six General Assignment and has worked in Area Six Property Crimes since 1981.

DETECTIVE EDWARD LOUIS, Area Six Property Crimes. Louis and his partner, John Turney, worked on the same surveillance team in

CIU for five years, until CIU was disbanded in 1985. Louis came on the CPD in 1973, worked in the Seventeenth District for eight years, four on patrol, four on tac, and was promoted to detective in 1980 and assigned to Area Six Burglary for one year. Louis then joined CIU and has been back in Area Six Property Crimes since 1985.

LIEUTENANT MICHAEL MAHER, field lieutenant, Fifteenth District. Maher, who joined the CPD in 1961, has worked as a vice detective, a burglary detective, and as an undercover narcotics detective. Maher was one of the first officers assigned to investigate Gypsy crime in 1970. Maher and his former partner, Detective Sal Sorci (in Area Five Property Crimes) are considered two of the preeminent authorities on Gypsy crime and con games in the country.

DETECTIVE LEILAN MCNALLY, Auto Theft. McNally is an auto theft expert, having worked as a detective in Auto Theft since 1971. He joined the force in 1966 and was on patrol for five years in the Third District. McNally was awarded his law degree in 1989.

DETECTIVE SEBASTIAN MUSSO, Area Six Property Crimes. Musso, on the CPD since 1973, has worked patrol, tac, Special Operations, General Assignment, and has been a detective in Property Crimes since 1981. He and Detective Richter have been partners since then, and now work the Pawn Shop Detail together.

DETECTIVE DAVE RICHTER, Area Six Property Crimes. Richter, a police officer since 1967, made detective in 1976, when he was assigned to Area Six General Assignment, which handled everything except murders, robberies, and burglaries. In 1981, Richter came to Area Six Property Crimes. For the past three years, he and his partner Musso have worked the Pawn Shop Detail.

DETECTIVE TODD RONEY, Area Six Property Crimes. Roney has been twenty-two years in the CPD, fifteen of them as a detective, with the Area Six Task Force and Area Six Property Crimes. Roney currently is the hotel crimes specialist for Area Six.

DETECTIVE RONALD SCHUMACHER, Area Six Property Crimes. Schumacher joined the force in 1968, worked tac in the Town Hall District for six years, and has been in Area Six Property Crimes as a detective for the past sixteen years.

DETECTIVE JOHN M. TURNEY, Area Six Property Crimes. Turney has been on the force since 1969 and has been a detective since 1972.

Turney was assigned to Area Five Burglary in 1981, then went to the CIU, where he worked with Louis until CIU was disbanded in 1985. He and Louis were then assigned to Area Six Property Crimes.

LIEUTENANT JOHN C. VOLLAND, Auto Theft. Volland is in his thirty-second year on the force. He started in patrol in Eighteen, went to Auto Theft as a detective, and then to CIU as a detective. When Volland was promoted to sergeant, he worked Robbery in the Detective Division. He then served as a sergeant in CIU from 1972–84, when he was promoted to lieutenant, and headed a tac team in the Eighth District until 1986. Since 1986, Volland has worked as executive officer and acting commander of Auto Theft. The Chicago Crime Commission named Volland "Policeman of the Year" in 1978.

ORGANIZED CRIME

Hitmen wear ski masks and Halloween masks when they go on hits as a courtesy to the citizen. This allows the citizen to stand up in front of the detectives and, swelling his chest with pride, say, "I'd like to help you guys, but they were wearing masks."

This way, the citizen doesn't have to make up stupid excuses like "I was in the washroom when they killed this guy" or "I got something in my eye" or "They all look alike to me."

And that's the only reason hitmen wear them. Absolutely. See, they know that if for some reason, they had to walk into a restaurant and shoot somebody—and these people are smart—they know that you're not going to be able to identify somebody with a one-second look. But let's say things go haywire. And now you've got somebody sitting there looking at them for a period of ten to fifteen seconds, enough to make an identification. They know that they can't kill that person, because if they do, it's gonna bring down unbelievable heat on them.

So the masks are a courtesy. It's a way of saying, "All right, we don't want legitimate people to see this, because we know the kind of pressure the police will put on them. So we'll wear a stupid mask, and now the guy can be an upright Joe, he can go home to his wife and kids and be a hero, and he can describe everything he saw and so what?—Who gives a shit if he saw us shoot the guy?"

**–Detective Ted O'Connor, FBI/CPD
Organized Crime Task Force**

What do you need for an Outfit funeral? One pallbearer to slam the trunk.

–CPD Intelligence Division

"**H**ere's Angelo with a sweater on. They're casual. Casual guys. Sport coats, open shirt, sport shirts, hats. Here's Tony Spilotro—wearing a tie. That's not normal. Good, casual clothes. I never saw Tony Accardo with a tie. He always wore like a suit or sport coat, a dress shirt, but no tie on. They shy away from ties. Sport clothes, sport clothes. . . ."

The longtime intelligence detective is paging through surveillance and arrest photos of members of the Chicago Outfit, a rogues' gallery of the men who like to call themselves "the Boys."

"See? No tie. Good shirts, though. Gold. The young guys go for the gold. Last time I saw this guy, he was counting a fistful of hundreds that thick. This guy's a killer. A casual guy. He drove a Chevette for a long time, a little Chevette; we used to laugh about it, a little *yellow* Chevette. Now here's a guy, Michael Posner, he drove a Mercedes, used to have the jewelry, he was kind of a flashy guy. He's sitting in jail now."

"The last time I saw this guy," says another intelligence detective riffling through pix of the Boys, "he was in an advanced state of putrefaction. Rigidity had set in. Another heartrending story."

Organized crime is not all Banlon shirts and patent-leather shoes. That's the first thing intelligence detectives will tell you. "The problem with organized crime is everybody looks at it as if you're just looking at Italians. But 'organized crime,' just as a general term, is any organized unit that's committing crimes," as Chief Investigator Jerry Gladden of the Chicago Crime Commission puts it. It's divided into what they call traditional organized crime: the Outfit, La Cosa Nostra, the Mafia, the various criminal offshoots of Prohibition that have dominated not only U.S. crime, but unions, businesses, professions, and government for decades; and nontraditional organized crime, the criminal groups coming up in a big way, including the Colombians, the Cubans, the Japanese Yakuza, Jamaican posses, and street gangs that have evolved into enormous criminal enterprises, like the El Rukns, the Crips, the Bloods.

The Organized Crime Division, through its Vice Control Section (including the Gambling and Prostitution Units), Intelligence Section, Narcotics Section, and Asset Forfeiture Unit, and through information the Organized Crime Division shares with other units on what players to watch for, tries to track and trap the men of organized criminal enterprise.

Some organized crime watchers feel having Intelligence deal with both traditional and nontraditional organized crime clouds the picture: "Ten years ago, organized crime among experts was defined as the Mafia," says one intelligence detective. "But now, if you say 'organized crime,' you've got to define about fourteen terms when you're talking to someone—'No, I don't mean the Colombians. I don't mean the El Rukns. I don't mean this cartel, that posse, whatever *60 Minutes* has decided to throw on that week.'

"Organized crime is the Italian Mafia, La Cosa Nostra on the East Coast. And in Chicago, they call themselves the Outfit or the Mob. That's it."

Since 1988, the Joint Organized Crime Task Force, made up of FBI agents, CPD homicide detectives, and State of Illinois agents, have gone after the life's blood of traditional organized crime by investigating both fresh and long-faded Outfit hits. The bite of this task force lies in charging Outfit hitmen and their bosses under the statute that never runs out—murder. Another new weapon, Asset Forfeiture, instituted under the RICO Act, takes the fun and profit out of crime by taking everything away—cars, houses, computers, etc.—used in the commission of a crime.

The Organized Crime Division and the FBI/CPD's Organized Crime Task Force's effectiveness, however, hinges on discovering what the Boys are up to. Finding out about the Outfit has always been a challenge: They've got charts, but they can't get the bosses; they've got bodies, but they can't get the hitmen.

Information comes in odd ways. A big break for organized crime watchers is a botched hit, like the time two hitmen sank three bullets into gambling boss Kenny Eto's skull—and he lived to tell tales on his old buddies under the Federal Witness-Protection Program—or the time a nervous hitman with a .45 walked up to racketeer Al Pilotto on a golf course and failed to make a hole in one.

Investigators get another break when bodies are found that were never meant to be found, like the bodies of the Spilotro brothers, tortured and beaten to death in the Chicago area, transported across the state line, and planted in an Indiana cornfield.

Most of U.S. organized crime itself is buried now, embedded in legitimate business and government. Organized crime lies deep, says one investigator: "The crime syndicate will fall apart the day when you read in the papers that we've walked in and we've served subpoenas on three quarters of the city council and we've gone into the Congress of the United States and we've done the same thing. Because they have somewhere in their political history, passed a law, gotten involved in some transaction, accepted donations to their fund, or shared in insider information that came from the Outfit—some had no idea they were getting tied into the Outfit; others did it *knowingly.*

"And you'll know we're serious when you read that we've pulled these congressmen right out of their seats and then we started in on all the federal courts and the local courts. Then you'll know we're really serious. I mean, really serious that we're gonna do something.

"Because that's where organized crime is at."

Italian organized crime, the bad Boys' success story, shows where a perverse profit motive can lead. As the first and signally triumphant organized crime movement in the United States, the Outfit may serve as a beacon to groups coming up and a distress signal to the rest of us—the worst may be yet to come.

Their mentality on certain things—it's funny, in a sick way.

I had gone into a friend of mine's drugstore on the South Side. I'm looking around, and here are five people in here who are very well connected with the Outfit. There was one fellow in there, he's now deceased, his name was Tony Menza, they called him "Poopie." Well, Poop was an enforcer for the Outfit. Probably one of the most vicious people you ever met in your life. He *had* to be nasty with a name like that.

So when I walked in, they had this big discussion going on. My friend's talking about somebody that owed him five hundred dollars from a bet. And the guy hadn't paid it. I'm listening to this conversation, and I'm looking at the expression on Poopie's face, and he's just standing there, just totally *baffled.* He had this look of utter confusion on his face.

Eventually, Poopie says, "I don't understand what your problem is." And then these words of wisdom come out of Poop's mouth. He says, "I had this guy owed me five hundred dollars. All I did was call him and tell him, 'Hey. I want the money Friday night or your old lady can use it to buy you a nice headstone.' So what is your problem?" What made this so funny was Poopie was dead serious.

I've never seen anybody look so utterly confused.

There was a surveillance guy, a Bohemian. If you know anything about Bohemians, you know they're very conservative about money. This guy was as tight as they come. He always wore the shoes he got in the navy. His oxfords.

One night, they're doing a surveillance on an Outfit wake. He goes in—he's got dark hair, sort of olive skin; he doesn't look out of place. So he's in there and he's sitting on one of the couches in the vestibule of the funeral home with some Outfit guys. And being Outfit guys, they dress accordingly, with their gold and their patent-leather shoes.

They're all sitting there, and John's sitting in the midst of them. They're smiling, he's smiling, he's got his legs crossed—a guy looks down at his shoes, and obviously his oxfords weren't patent leather. He smiles and looks down too. He sees they're all wearing the patent-leather jobs.

They looked at him and he looked at them; he knew what they knew; they knew what he knew. So he gets up. They drew guns on him and chased him right out of the funeral parlor.

Funeral parlors—that's something they like. They own a lot of funeral homes. They bury their own. They bury all the ones found in a trunk.

You would be surprised what they're into. They like to go in on wholesale items, you know discount stores, you know those places that have nothing but discount items? They like that. They can even get rid of their stolen property there. They might come in with stuff they've lifted from a cartage theft—"This is a close-out sale."

Restaurants. Restaurants for sure. They *love* restaurants be-cause they can always entertain and hold meetings.

They come in with their girlfriends; when they want to talk business—"Okay, girls, go to the bar."

Organized crime people, they go for these restaurants at night, they sit down, sometimes they bring their wives. But when they talk *business—then* they meet at Wendy's, at Denny's, at McDonald's.

We follow them and they park, right? Now, they'll meet who-ever they have to meet inside the McDonald's, and then their chauffeurs will go around to take a look at all the cars in the parking lot. They walk the whole parking lot and they look inside every car to see if there's any listening devices or men with binoculars. They just look in every car. We're a block away, watching them with binoculars.

The surveillance guys were bored one night; they were wait-ing for Vito to come out of someplace. So they got some dog doo-doo and smeared it underneath his door handle. Vito comes out, grabs the door handle—"Aagh, ah shit"—he runs in. So then they sneak up and open the door; it was left open, and they smear some more dogshit on the steering wheel. Vito gets back in, touches the steering wheel, and runs back in screaming. Now they go back the third time and get the other handle. Vito's gonna be real smart this time, right?, and he goes in on the passenger's side. "Ah, shit!" They got him three times.

If you asked somebody what your true job description of In-telligence should be—it should be nothing but changing tapes. Have the city wired from one end to the other on organized crime. But we'll never have wiretapping in Illinois as long as we have the Outfit influence in the state legislature. A lot of state legislators are part and parcel of organized crime. The Outfit keeps the wires out. Absolutely.

* * *

True Intelligence just goes out to find out what's going on. And if they find out something's gonna happen, to pass that on to the unit that would investigate that type of crime. Never be identified, never go to court, and never get involved.

Once in a while, you get some overzealous bosses who like to make a splash, so they have their guys make a raid, and they all go to court and they're all identified.

The Outfit brings everybody down to court. You make a raid on gambling? They bring everybody down to Gambling Court to see the intelligence guys that made that raid. They load that court. The courtroom is packed, and the hallway. And you're all pointed out. Or they'll take pictures of you. We take pictures of them. But they take pictures too.

So the next time you go in a restaurant and try to sit down and learn something, you're dead.

If you're in surveillance, don't get your picture taken and don't go to court. Then you're all right. If somebody's panning, you put your hand up to your nose or blow your nose or do something casual. You know what's the greatest cover in the world? If you're sitting in a restaurant and somebody comes in, or somebody looks over, just put your coffee cup up to your face.

There's a lot of bitterness in the Outfit right now. The bosses are greedy and rotten. The guys on the top take most of the money and leave the little guy on the bottom without much.

We *want* them to be greedy and take all the money. Because that's the only way you develop informants.

I'll give you an example. A muscle guy that we know was sitting down at the table with Marshall Caifano, who happened to be a street boss at the time, and two of his close friends. Marshall had a guy in New York that owed him $10,000. Couldn't get the money from him. Both of Marshall's friends said, well, they were too busy; they'd like to get it for him in New York, but they were busy and had their own things to operate.

So Marshall says to the muscle guy, "Well, you go get it then." "Okay. I'll go get it." So he went out and got on an airplane, went to New York, asked the lady at the place, "Who is So-and-so?" She pointed him out, he went over, knocked him right down, drug him in his office, and said, "Give me the ten grand that you owe Marsh or I'm gonna kill you right here in the office. You won't live, so send for it, get it, whatever."

So the guy opened his safe, and he gave him the ten thousand; he walked out, got on the airplane, came back, put it on Marshall's table. And he didn't get a *dime.* Marshall took it all. Didn't even pay him for his airplane ticket to and from, or his expenses.

So that guy told us anything we wanted to know about Marshall Caifano. And the reason he told us, it didn't do a thing for him, but he was that mad because Marshall took everything.

It's almost an axiom with organized crime: They're into everything where there's money.

Gambling is still organized crime's biggest money-maker. Just the sheer volume of business. You got a big football weekend coming up—you *know* there's gonna be a lot of bookmaking on sports betting. Just millions of dollars are spent on sports betting. And horse races, that's the other part of the backbone of gambling, it's just a constant.

And the workers, the guys actually taking bets, they've been arrested, maybe hundreds of times—it doesn't mean anything to them; it's just the cost of doing business, it's just part of the scheme, you know? They get out on bond, nobody gets too excited about it, and they never go to jail.

You know where they have the biggest illegal bookmaking operations? Right on racetracks. You know why? Because people can get credit from their bookie. You can't get credit at the windows; you've gotta have the money.

There are a lot of gambling hits. The bosses might feel the guy's stiffing them on their end of it. They might tell him once, and if he's still doing it, they get rid of him and give the business to someone else.

I remember a guy by the name of Hal Smith a few years back. He was found in the trunk of his car. But anyway, he would meet with his cronies in this restaurant on the Gold Coast every Wednesday afternoon about two, two-thirty. He always had a briefcase with him, and he'd be meeting with these guys and they'd be handing envelopes back and forth—you know, obviously it was a payoff.

He was running a gambling operation is what he was doing, a bookmaking operation. And I told this friend of mine who at the time was a sergeant in the Gambling Unit; I said, "Listen. That goddamn Hal Smith is there every Wednesday. Get over there some Wednesday and grab him." They did. When they got him, he was walking in with ninety thousand dollars in cash in his briefcase and a 9 mm automatic on him.

The strange part was, the guy who was in charge of the Gambling Unit at the time said, "Gee, we've been looking for him for a long time." I mean, if you couldn't find this guy. . . . He would pull up in front of this place in a gold Cadillac, park on the hydrant, and his license plate was Hal 999. If you couldn't find him, you had to be a blind man.

Hal was a very personable guy. He'd always chat, you know, "Hi, how you doing? How's everything?" Very friendly. I remember talking to him about how he had a little heart problem and how he was riding his stationary bike every day for a half hour to keep in shape.

He didn't keep in real good shape. I have some pictures of what they did to him. They burned his tongue off. They were afraid he was gonna be a stool pigeon for the G is what happened to him. And he might have been holding out on them. Burned his tongue. Beat him. He had a lot of bruises around his head. He had twenty or more nonfatal stab wounds—they just took an ice pick and went pick-pick-pick-pick all over him.

With gambling automatically comes juice.

* * *

The average on juice loans now is 5 to 10 percent a week till the debt is paid off. And if you don't pay it, the juice accumulates. They like to call in the entire note every once in a while, then they'll loan it right back to you just to make sure you're not blowing it. So if you borrowed $165,000, your interest per week is $16,500. And maybe you didn't even keep up with the juice payments. So that adds on to the principal, so now you have 10 percent on to whatever adds on. So if you run it up to $200,000, now it's $20,000 a week. And it just goes up. It might be millions. And eventually they just take over your business, and you wind up being a collector for *them*.

Gamblers go to loan sharks. People who can't get money through legitimate sources go to loan sharks. Deadbeats. Some businessmen. High-line burglars. You know, "I want to get into this thing that's gonna get me three hundred thousand dollars. I need fifty thousand dollars to buy equipment." Then they share in the profits.

A lot of Outfit guys go to the juice. An Outfit guy can't borrow any money—who's gonna loan him money? He hasn't got a job. If he wants to go out on a score, he's gotta get some front money. If he just got out of jail, he's gotta spend maybe $10,000 for a new kit and maybe some plans where he can make a score or two. And he's gotta fence through them; he can't fence through anybody else.

They put the squeeze on you. The juice can be any amount, 50, 75, even a 100 percent. It mostly depends on the amount borrowed. There are cases where you borrow $100, you gotta give back $200, those are very short-term kinds of things.

You keep paying. Obviously, they don't have any written contract; this isn't like the General Motors Acceptance Corporation. So even if you've paid it all back, they can come to you, and they do, and say, "You still owe." The guy isn't gonna argue if he's afraid of getting killed. He's gonna keep on paying it. They extend it as long as they want to extend it. So it gets to a point where it's an extortion more than a repayment of a loan.

If the guy has paid off his debt, you know, and they're still squeezing him to get more out of him and he takes off, they probably wouldn't make a great effort to find the guy. But the thing is, if he sticks around, as long as he has money, they're gonna squeeze him.

I would imagine that if you're pretty conscientious about making your payments, they just figure, "Hey, you're so good at it—just keep on doing it."

They used to break your thumbs or break a kneecap with a baseball bat if you were behind in your juice payments.

They don't do that anymore. You have to pay or you die.

Bosses don't want to be in and out of federal court with threatening people, and going back, and by then the guy's wearing a wire. If you've got him up so tight that there's nowhere else for him to go but the government, he's gonna go, and he's gonna wear a wire. If he owes and he won't pay, you want to set an example, you just kill him.

Make your payments.

The Outfit controls pornography. One way or another. Let's put it this way: If you were going to go into business selling pornography, you would certainly be associated with organized crime. If you weren't directly involved with organized crime—if they didn't front the money for you to open the business and if they didn't come to you and try to extort money from you for *doing* the business—then at least you would be associated with organized crime because you would be getting your materials from distributors who are either *controlled* or *owned* by organized crime. Somewhere along the line, through distribution or sales, they're gonna get their piece of the action.

If you take into consideration the fact that there are more adult bookstores in the United States of America than there are McDonald's hamburger stores, you could probably say that pornography ranks among the high incomes for the Boys.

The biggest money-maker for the Outfit in porno is videos now. In adult bookstores, peep shows are the biggest money-makers.

They make the Outfit an incredible amount of money. You go in and just keep paying to keep the show going. They either give you some tokens for the coin-op, or they give you some Susan B. Anthony dollars.

The only use that's ever been found for the Susan B. Anthony dollar is to keep peep shows going—that's kind of ironic.

When Asset Forfeiture came in, and video-store owners knew that everything they had could be forfeited because they were renting pornographic movies, there was panic. All these little Ma-and-Pa video stores—"Vell, vat are ve going to do?"

Well, here's what happened. The old porno boss Mike Glitta saw here's a way to milk these people. So he formed a little coalition and called it something like the "Legal Defense Unit." And he called these people together and said, "They're gonna take your house, they're gonna take your garage, they're gonna take everything you worked and slaved for all these years. We've formed a Legal Defense Unit to help. Kick in some money and we'll have lawyers on retainer for you."

So they had these little video-store owners pay them money. Protection money is all it is. They just figured out another form of extortion.

Of course, the Outfit is involved in escort services, of course they are. There's just too much money for them *not* to be. I've been told by two different services that one of their girls went on a date, got tied up, had a gun put to her head. This girl was told, "You tell So-and-so: Pay or you're going to start losing some girls." The services must have been making too much money and not paying the street tax to the Outfit.

* * *

There was one really good escort service a couple years ago. A guy called them and said, "I want three girls." They sent up three girls, and he put a gun to the head of one girl: "Tell your boss he has a partner now." So now he's a partner.

Contrary to what they *want* to do, the Outfit's in narcotics. Now they don't *like* it, but the money's too good.

At one time I was a strict believer that in the Outfit it was a no-no to even think of going in narcotics. But in the last ten years, the Outfit has become deeply involved. That's why you don't see big jewelry or fur scores anymore; they're making more in narcotics.

Historically, the East Coast families have always been involved in narcotics, especially heroin. But not in Chicago. When Accardo was boss, he wouldn't allow it. I never thought I'd say anything good about a Mob boss, but that's his only saving grace.

It used to be if a guy walked into a restaurant and said offhandedly to some Outfit guy he'd give him a chance to get $200,000—"Are you taking a load? Cutting in on some legitimate business? Fine." But if the guy said it's a smack deal, that guy would be dead within a day for *saying* it—you'd be dead even for *thinking* it. Not anymore. You couldn't keep them out of it. The money's too good.

They have some people that are dabbling in narcotics, and making big money, that start fooling around with young girls and then they will start sniffing themselves, and the next thing you do, you find them in a trunk.

Every one of these men has a wife, has a respectable family, and a girlfriend on the side. The girlfriend knows more of what they're doing than the wife. In some cases, the girlfriend holds the records. The wife is on a pedestal, in the house, taking care of the kids, and given whatever she needs, "But leave me alone." You understand?

That's accepted practice. If you have a girlfriend for twenty years, and some of them do, and all of a sudden you are fooling around with four, five young coke addicts, they're afraid of you. That's when you're signing your own death warrant.

Narcotics, they were always reluctant, because that brings a lot of heat. They didn't stay out because of any ethical scruples. When you can kill people and torture them, and some of the ways they kill people are just . . . If you can kill people like that, who cares about ethics?

There's a made guy now, he was promoted to lieutenant a few years ago, he controls northwestern Chicago, northwestern suburbs: juice, gambling, vice, street taxes. A lieutenant. He's turned into a real chink in the armor for them. He's a coke freak, he likes young broads, thinks he's a big-time guy, a lot of contacts with Sicilian organized crime—a *real* Mafia guy.

But he's bringing something that they *don't* like—and that's DEA heat. They feel they can deal with the FBI and their electronic surveillance, and they're on the phones, and they're watching you—you know, you can deal with that.

But what they don't like to deal with is tax problems. And they don't like the DEA—they're tactical coppers, you don't know where they're coming from; they'll be all over you; they're all over everybody; they heat people up. And this lieutenant is drawing heat from them—they're everywhere; they're all over his people. And that can't help but dirty up everybody else.

They're heavily into arson-for-profit. I remember one guy, Tony Geronda, he worked for the City of Chicago, Bureau of Streets and Sanitation, and he was also a bomber and an arsonist for the Outfit.

I was in Burglary at the time, and we'd go to this little restaurant at Eighty-seventh and Stony. In would come Tony and his crew. Tony talked real loud all the time. He comes in one time, says to me and my partner, "Hey, I'm goin' to Florida. I'm gonna get some heat, you know, relax. I'll be t'inking of you guys all the time." We listened to this all week.

The next week, the paper has a picture of a nightclub in Miami that was torched. Instant vacant lot. Under this is a picture of Tony—"under investigation."

Two weeks later, Tony comes in. *Very quiet.* "Hey, Tony, get a little heat?" "Do we have time to finish our supper?"

They come to *you.* If you're doing anything illegal, they come to you. It's more or less a dogma—you can't operate illegal businesses without paying your street tax to somebody. Gambling, chop shops, anything illegal. Pornography—the people who run pornography seem to think that that's legal because the Supreme Court said so. But the Outfit doesn't think so. So they extract the tax.

You and I couldn't go into business and open a tavern and then start booking horses. Eventually, someone's gonna come knocking on the door. And they *will* find you. They have a better intelligence section than the police department.

One bookmaker downtown was operating for two years; they didn't know about it. They found out about it; they went in and said, "You been open and going for two years. That's twenty-four thousand dollars. Next month. Over on Taylor Street, the hot-dog stand. Drop twenty-five thousand dollars."

Somebody who won't pay the street tax when they tell him to pay, they just walk in and shoot him. Or take him for a ride and stick him in his own trunk. Unless somebody's personally mad at him. Then they'll hang him up and do a few things.

Other organized crime groups in the country think the Chicago Outfit is crazy. The word is, "Stay away from them. They're not normal."

Chicago's always had the renegades. It goes back to Capone. You know, one time two New York guys were sent to kill Capone. They were met at the train and beaten to death. Parts of their bodies were sent back on the train to New York with a note: "Don't send boys to do a man's job."

The Chicago Outfit is *the* Outfit. It's the most powerful individual organization in the U.S. I believe that there's no other monolithic structure with as much power and control and money as the Chicago Outfit.

The FBI right now says the Gotti Family in New York is the most powerful, but the Gottis use power that is borrowed and supplied by the other Families, and they'll have inroads into labor unions, trade unions, and legitimate business and industry, where their in might be one of the other Family guys. Gotti himself is a darling of the news media—he's a good-looking, dapper guy who likes to give interviews. So he would be somebody that even the FBI can discover is notorious.

The secret to their success, which remains a secret today, is when you go someplace and you represent Chicago interests, that's what you do. And I don't care if you stay there for thirty years and think you have your own empire, you are controlled by the Chicago Outfit, and that's where your allegiance goes. And when you forget about it, they kill you.

Chicago has a stranglehold, it has complete, utter domination over major unions—and the major unions we're talking about are groups like the Teamsters and the Produce Drivers. That's Chicago.

The Outfit's union power is incredible, everywhere except east of the Hudson. That's New York Families.

It used to be overt control. Since the federal government was going to bring suit against the Chicago Outfit, you don't have any overt figures who will theoretically hold office in the Teamsters Union anymore. Now this leaves them with about fifty thousand people in various positions in the union all across the United States that owe their allegiance to the bad guys.

It's not so much, "Hi, I'm an Outfit guy, and I want you to do this." It's a personal thing. You'll have a guy call, let's say, the local boss in Houston, Texas, and tell him that Company ABC's got fifty trucks and it's hauling produce from the Salinas Valley to Phoenix, it's not a company that we care to have very successful, and they're not our friends, and "You know, Joey, uh, you know, we shouldn't go along with them." And all of a sudden they might have labor problems—there's all kinds of ways to get a company to toe the line.

That's power.

The Chicago Outfit controls the unions. Because of that, they're into everything.

Chicago controls a big chunk of Hollywood. They don't control the corporations, they don't control the directors and the producers per se, they don't control the actors and actresses. But all the support—all the catering, the lighting, fixtures—the outfit that supplies stuff for the movies is not going to be an accidental supply house. The lighting and fixtures—and everything that moves and walks and talks to cause that movie to be produced— is probably going to be owned outright or by a fictitiously formed blind trust by members of the Outfit.

The Chicago Outfit has never, ever been stuck with a provincial mentality. The Outfit is a monolithic, single-minded structure that has always believed that it didn't stop at the Chicago River. The Outfit's *everywhere.* And there's enough, as we say in Chicago, for everybody.

Organized crime follows a military structure. You've got the bosses, the lieutenants, the soldiers. When they started it in Italy, they formed it after the ancient Roman legions. They thought that was a good idea.

The structure doesn't change; the players change. There's one or two bosses, five or six lieutenants, seventy made guys that we've identified, and about 318 who work for them; that's their sole income; they don't have any other income.

* * *

Each boss has his own bookkeeper. Some are former IRS agents, others are Outfit CPAs.

The only thing they worry about is declaring the amount of income on their income tax that they're gonna spend next year. So they come downtown and they see their tax attorneys. The lawyers say, "What are you declaring? Do you want us to put down where you make your money?" "No." "Okay, so we'll put the word 'Privileged' for occupation." They all put down "Privileged."

The big guys pay the tax. They're just not gonna tell you where they make it.

Then there are some lesser guys who file the income tax, but they don't pay. They can't do anything if you don't pay; all they can do is put liens on you. So what these guys do is, "Yeah, I made a hundred thousand last year, I owe you thirty-two thousand. Hahaha. I *owe* you. If you find something in my name, you can have it." They have no occupation; it's all illegal. So they don't pay.

They subpoenaed Tony Accardo once. They told him to come down and bring his books and records. So he got the Bible and a Beatles record and went downtown with them to comply with the subpoena. "There's my book. And there's my record."

Here's an accurate picture of Outfit soldiers. No matter what you do, or how much money you're making, from the time you get up in the morning to the time you go to bed, you're trying to think up a scam, and you're trying to make a buck. And I don't give a shit if you're on somebody's payroll—when you get up, you're trying to pick up a house on a probate, you're trying to screw somebody in a land deal, you're trying to set up a score for a burglary hit—every waking moment of every waking day. That's true of wiseguys all over.

I used to be in Area Six Burglary. You'd be surprised, the names that we used to chase, the kids, the scatterbrains that we used to chase in Area Six when I was young, are now—not all of them—but a fair amount, are big guys moving up in certain spots. The punk burglars, some of them, are big guys now.

There was a guy they called Legs D'Antonio. Legs D'Antonio always wanted to be a getaway driver when he was a kid, right? He would go out and practice turning around corners. Then he'd run out and feel the tires. "They're still cool—that's good! I did it right." You know. Now, he's handling the gambling and everything on the east end of Grand Avenue.

The whole business of the Italian Mafia and the blood oath and all that stuff, it probably did exist, and it makes great movie copy. But when you get right down to it, the bottom line has always been "Where's the money?"

The Italian Outfit will deal with anybody. They're not so bound by this code that they'll rule anybody out. Wherever they can make a buck, that's where they'll go.

You have a Jewish element involved, you have a Greek element involved—the Greek element is every bit as vicious and cruel as any Italian Outfit guy. It's like the Jews and Greeks are operating in their own territory, but they cooperate—it's like two countries getting along. They're part of the Outfit, and they cooperate because they're a much smaller community. They operate within their community, but they pay their dues.

The way you come up in the Outfit, you earn it. You become an earner. What happens is, if you've been a good worker and an earner, you're allowed to talk to some of these guys and voice your opinion in a manner that's not out of line.

And you kill people for them.

To be a made man, you have to do a successful hit. And you have to be Italian. Until a few years ago, you had to be Sicilian, but that's changed. But you still have to be Italian. The one exception they've made is Greek, Gus Alex.

Organized crime in America *is* Italian. But the Italians in general take a bum rap. It's their tragedy. You know, 99.99 percent of Italian Americans are everything you should be in

America. They're hardworking—they're doctors, they're lawyers, they're policemen, they're FBI agents, they're teachers.
They take the rap for a handful of people.

There are very few Irish in the Outfit; they don't like to have
anything to do with each other.

There was a guy, Red O'Malley, an extortionist, a chop-shop
operator a few years back. I saw him one day, and I said, "Red,
you think you're part of that big family, don't you? You know
what your problem is, O'Malley? The *O* is on the wrong side of
your name."

You can't take over. Or try to take over. The only way you can
ever rise to the top is it's gotta be given to you. There aren't
power struggles. Not in Chicago, just in New York.

They don't kill made guys. That's an exception. A made guy
really has to screw up. And the way they screw up, they get
involved in Family things they really shouldn't get involved in,
or they hold out money that's not theirs, or they mess up on a
killing, or don't do it.

They snatched one guy, Jimmy Catuara, a big guy in the
Outfit, but he had gotten on bad paper with the bosses because
he was holding back from chop-shop profits. They snatched
him off the street, locked him in the trunk of his Cadillac, left
him in there for twelve hours, and then let him out. "Now we
just gave you a message. Why don't you go to Arizona and retire?" They didn't kill him; they locked him in his trunk. This
was out of respect.
    See, they just told him something. What they just told him
was, "Hey. If we want you, we'll get you. Now, we're letting you
out of the trunk—why don't you go to Arizona?" Now you or I,

they'd have told me that, I would have got out of the trunk, drove to the airport, called home, said, "Send my damn clothes out. I'm leaving before they change their minds."

But see, Jimmy . . . you know, "I'm too big a man. They can't treat me this way; I got the power." So they killed him.

The only thing that keeps organized crime strong is that if you don't do what they tell you, they kill you.

Outfit guys—they wait in *line* to kill people. That's the only road to advancement. The only way. You don't get there any other way. You can be a worker and be a highly respected worker, but you can't get in that inner circle unless you go out with them and do it with them. And they'll watch you do it.

When Jasper Campise took this kid Gattuso to hit Kenny Eto, Jasper sat in the front seat with Eto, and the kid, Johnny Gattuso, sat in the backseat. So it was Campise who was going to see that Gattuso did it, and he was going to be a made guy. The kid goofed. Eto survived. The kid got unmade.

You can't kid about it. You can't be an undercover agent and pretend you're something. Because they'll take you right out there and say, "Go ahead and kill him. Let's see if you are what you're saying you are."

Organized-crime murders aren't like ordinary murders. Roughly 70 percent of all murders in the United States are domestic murders, which means it's a husband killing a wife or a wife killing a husband, or a boyfriend or a girlfriend. There's some family or sexual relationship. The killer is known to the victim, and the victim is known to the killer. There's a motivation that's quite clear. Many of them are what we call "smoking guns" in that the terrible passion that led to the murder evaporates at the killing, and the killer picks the phone up and says, "You better get over here. I just killed my husband."

These are very, very easy to solve. They still have to be worked carefully, because you're looking to prosecute someone, but it doesn't take Sherlock Holmes to solve these.

Organized crime murders, however, have all the elements that are necessary to confuse and stymie law enforcement people. One, the killer is probably not personally known to the victim. Two, the motive may not be immediately clear. Three, there's some planning. These are not spur-of-the-moment crimes. Now, there will always be an exception, but for the most part . . . it's something that's planned.

With most *domestic* murders, though, it happens without planning. The murder happens, and *now,* if the individual *isn't* filled with remorse and guilt, the individual wants to get out of this; they now, after the murder, have to come up with a plan.

And that's where things go wrong. That's where you put Mom in the freezer while you try to figure out what to do. Or you drag the wife out of the house and you throw her on the side of the road, you call police up and report her missing. Then they find her, and they're talking to the neighbors, and a neighbor says, "I don't know what happened, but I saw him carrying something out of the house at two o'clock in the morning and loading it in his station wagon. I thought that was kind of unusual." So, trying to come up with a plan after the murder is not a good idea.

The Outfit plans its murders ahead of time.

How good the plan is, of course, depends upon the people who are carrying the murder out. Some of them are quite good and invest a considerable amount of time in their planning. They'll stake the individual out. They'll do a surveillance. They know where he lives, they know where he works, they'll determine his route home, what time he leaves, what time he arrives.

And they're always looking for the opportunity—where is he when he has the least number of people around?—where is he isolated?—where is he out of his car? And if they have the time, they will pick the best time and place. Sometimes, they're pressed for time, in the instance, for example, where the individual may be a threat to them because he's testifying and they think he's an informant, and they decide they've gotta get rid of him fast, then it's kind of hurry-up. Then they'll take greater risks.

So the planning is there. Now the other thing that helps considerably is not only the planning, but utilizing the criminal network to provide them with the things that the ordinary guy can't get. And that's the stolen car that can't be traced except to the legitimate owner. Stolen firearms that can't be traced.

With an Outfit murder, the car can be seen; it doesn't make any difference. If they felt like it, they could throw the firearm down next to the body and walk away. They have a source for weapons, an illegal source that provides them with weapons that can't be traced. And then they have ways and means of destroying the weapons completely. They go to great trouble.

The planning that goes into stalking a guy and picking the spot. Sometimes there's a tail car involved, a driver, a couple of gunmen, walkie-talkies, CB radios used for communication.

There's after-action. There's a place they're going afterwards. There's check-off lists: "Did you get rid of this? Did you get rid of that?" Sometimes the guys immediately responsible leave town. The reservations, the tickets. All that has to be planned. And by the time you find the body, the hitmen may be on a plane to Vegas, or Timbuktu.

It's always a stranger who hits a stranger. They don't hit them very quickly, they find out what time he wakes up, what time he has breakfast, lunch, dinner, who he goes out with, where he goes. They know exactly what his next move is gonna be. What his weakness is, his strong points. That's a good one. A hitman like that will take $50,000 and up. But then if you get a little guy that wants to move up, he'll take $10,000.

A good hit is a piece of art. A lot of crimes are works of art. A good burglary, a good stickup, a good hit. I always tell law enforcement agents, "Don't *ever* underestimate your opponent. You might not like what he's doing, but don't you underestimate him. Because this *is* his business. And he's very good at what he does. He's probably sharper than you are, because he's still out on the street. Don't sell him short."

Billy Dauber. They killed him and his wife out on a lonely road. One of the rare cases where they hit the guy and a family member, his wife. That's very rare. Usually, they try to isolate you, but Billy Dauber was a little too slick for them. The only reason they caught Billy Dauber was he was coming out of court and he was unarmed, which was very rare for Billy Dauber. His wife was killed because she was there. And she may have known the two guys who did it.

They tailed Dauber and Dauber's wife and his attorney—I will not mention his name, but he has very strong Outfit ties—they tailed them out of court one day to a restaurant. Billy Dauber wanted the attorney to come home with him—Dauber had an antiques shop, and it was this attorney's birthday. He said, "Come home with me. I want to give you something for your birthday." The attorney says, "No, that's all right. I have some place I gotta be." He wouldn't go with him.

Dauber and his wife left the restaurant. We figured out later there had to be at least three people on him. We figured that what happened, they had a work car parked about ten miles away from the restaurant, on the way back to Dauber's house out in the country. Very isolated.

The work car pulls in front of Dauber's car, going real slow, and a van comes up behind Billy Dauber. Now as Dauber approaches the car, before he can pass—the car has got him slowed down—the van pulls up alongside of him. Now, they got him boxed in. There's no question at all. They slide the doors back, and the one guy sitting in the jump seat lets loose with a carbine—they got both him and his wife—fifteen shots; we picked up the shell casings out in the road.

The first three shell casings were armor-piercers. That would take out the glass, where a regular bullet would bounce off the glass. The remaining shells were expanding shells, which will literally blow your head right off your body.

Billy goes off the road, hits a tree, they pull the van down in, the work car continues on down the road. They get out of the van, walk up to the car, and shot them—blew them right out of that car. Shot her again, killed her. Got back in the van, drove down about a mile and a half, pulled it over into a soybean field, torched it, got in the work car, and away they went. Now that's a professional job. That is very professional.

There's always a touch of class to Outfit hits. A lot of planning goes into them, unless it's an emergency.

One classic Outfit hit—they were after a wheelman who had a city job. These guys wanted to kill him, and he knew it. He parked within a walled facility at work, so the Mob couldn't get to his car while he was at work. At the end of the day, this guy would charge out of the garage and drive like a Grand Prix driver, always changing his routes and times—he knew they were after him.

But these guys knew he was a greedy son of a bitch. So they waited till Christmastime. Then two cases of scotch were delivered to this guy's work. The note read, "Thanks a million. I won't forget what you did for me."

When he got off work, this guy loaded the scotch into the trunk of his car, zoomed out of the parking lot, drove like a madman, roared up to his house—his wife was waiting, she always waited for him, watching for him from behind the curtains, ready to throw open the door as soon as he pulled up. He grabbed one case of scotch. His wife waited—he came back for the second case.

They knew he'd do that. And as he turned around, with the case of scotch in his arms, they stepped out of the gangways on both sides of his house. They gunned him down. Now that's class.

Another case. A guy in the chop-shop wars fled to Las Vegas. He had an old foreign car that he thought was a classic; he had it for a couple of years when he went out there. The guy's in Las Vegas—he's homesick for Chicago and Rush Street, he keeps calling home, talking to the Boys, bragging about his vintage car. He gets a call saying, "Hey, there's a guy here interested in your car. Are you interested in selling?" The guy's supposedly gonna offer him several thousand for this wreck. So he comes back to Chicago for the deal. He's found in the backseat of a stolen car, shot several times in the mouth.

The greed again. They looked for that fatal flaw in the guy. It was so carefully thought out, how to get him. We're not talking about Ph.D.s here, but guys sitting around saying, "That motherfucker. Let's get him. And we'll get him through that stupid car he's always mouthing off about."

There's no evidence of any kind. Nobody's gonna tell you anything. You might be able to solve it in your own mind, by virtue of having certain information about the person, about his associates; somebody might even tell you why he was killed and who did it, but they're not gonna tell it in court.

In the Chicago Mob, the main reason the murders are not solved is because there's a code of silence enforced by death. If you help us solve a murder and they find out, they'll kill you.

The best way to figure out the motivation behind a hit is whether or not the murder victim was captured first. Did he fall into enemy hands for a period of time or did they shoot him down on the street?

Now, if they shoot him down on the street, chances are that they just want to stop this guy from doing something or they want him dead because of an internal rivalry. If they shoot him down on the street, they don't have any questions.

But when they capture you, they want to interrogate you first. They say, "You gotta go to the meeting. The big guy wants to see you," and then you show up, and they've got you.

Don't forget that even the biggest pooch, I mean, you gotta be a real big pooch, to have somebody say, "Hey, Tony, meet us out in the middle of this cornfield."

So the meeting is probably gonna be someplace where the guy's been before—a warehouse, or the back of a tavern, something along those lines. And they have control over it. Or even a house. I mean, some of these guys have been killed in people's houses.

So now you've got the guy. You start asking him questions. "Where'd you hide the money? What have you been telling the U.S. attorney? Have you talked? If you talked, what did you say?"

You've interrogated him and you've killed him. Once you've gotten information from the guy, it gives you an opportunity to plan, if you can, a way to dispose of the body to hopefully thwart the beginning of a murder investigation. Pretty easy to be a murderer if there's no murder investigation. Like Jimmy Hoffa; he's the prime example of that. Because they're not murders till you find the bodies.

Probably what's happened when the guy's found in a trunk is they've taken him somewhere, killed him, and then put him in the trunk and dumped the car somewhere so there's no crime scene to investigate.

You don't put them in your own trunk. You put them in *theirs*. That's why they're always found in their own car. The hitman don't want to dirty up *his* car.

There's a big difference between the Chicago Outfit and New York's. In New York, they don't want the bodies found. They take the guy to the junkyard, put him in a crusher, the guy is now a little compact steel bale. Then he goes into a smelter or they drop him in the ocean.

But the Chicago Outfit seems to be proud of their work. They *want* everybody to see it.

Usually, someone in the organization is hit because quite often they're found to be cheating. Or there's a criminal investigation and they feel that this guy's cooperating and he's going to jeopardize a boss. Most of the guys that go in front of a federal grand jury and who can't sleep the night before and who are trembling and sweating profusely are not worried about the federal grand jury. What they're worried about is when they get called over to have a chat with someone and the guy sits there and says, "You didn't tell them anything, didju, Tony?"

When we're talking to these people and we're threatening them with two- or three-year sentences—you know, "You better talk or we're gonna put you in jail for three years"—I've had more than one of these guys say, "Go ahead. You got me. I'm going to jail. That's it. Because they'll kill me."

People will kill to send messages. Let's say in an instance where they're moving into a town, they want to get all the bookies in line, and they put out the word that they're going to increase the street tax, or you're now part of our organization. As soon as they meet some real resistance, they have to let everybody know they're not kidding, and so they'll probably kill someone quite openly, and there's no bones about it, the guy's dead. Okay, that's it. Still wanna fight us? It doesn't take too many messages, believe me.

There's different ways to get hit. Basically, having your head blown off is an honorable way to go. An immediate kill shows respect.

On the other hand, you take the Spilotro boys. They beat them to death. "Action" Jackson. Hung him on a meat hook, tortured him. Butch Petrocelli. They tortured *him* to death—poured lighter fluid on his face, on his genitals, and set him afire; burned him with a blowtorch, stuck him with an ice pick. That tells you that he's done something *wrong.* And this is a lesson to people.

But if you're found in a trunk, it's just that you had to go.

If they think the guy's an informant, they do some things. Cut off his penis, stick it in his mouth, let him bleed to death. Kill him with an ice pick. Slowly. Cut him from the ear to the mouth. That's the kind of bodies we find of people that we believe they suspected to be informants. That's the way they were disfigured—as opposed to a guy who just screwed up.

They're kind of getting away from the guns. They seem to be going more for the knife.

Most hits now have gone to throat slashing. I'd say the last half a dozen—whether they're shot or beaten or anything else—they also cut their throats from ear to ear to make sure. . . .

One of my first introductions to an Outfit murder: Two guys were put in a trunk, the typical way they do. I was with the lieutenant in charge at the scene. A reporter came up. "Lieutenant, have you formed any conclusions yet? Any conclusions at all?" And he said, "Yes. I have." "Yes, what is it, Lieutenant?" He says, "They certainly do make the trunks of these cars roomy, don't they?"

It's a business. If they kill you, they don't consider it a murder. This is business. They've only eliminated a weak link of the chain.

You just don't go out and hit people. A hit has to be sanctioned, or you got a problem.

If they give you a job to kill somebody and you don't kill somebody, then you die. That's happened many times. And we tell them each time, "Look, you missed. They're gonna kill you." They laugh at you. They think, Oh no, I've been working for them for thirty-four years. They wouldn't kill me. I'm a made guy.

It's *amazing* that they don't realize that themselves. I just can't understand it. They just think that they're different. And they *all* die. The bodies always turn up within a fairly short period of time. And then you know who did it.

When there's a botched hit, to find out who did it, you just wait and see who hits the trunk.

The guys that did Kenny Eto, they ran away. They didn't make sure. You know, when you think a guy is dead and you want to make *sure* that he's dead, it's always easy to pump three or four more slugs in his head. But these guys just opened the doors and ran away.

The two of them ended up in jail. One who was in there had not made bond; they came and posted bond for him. Now if that had been me, and somebody said, "Come on, somebody just posted your bond," I'd say, "I beg your pardon? Are you a federal agent? Nothing personal, but I am not leaving here." Because— you are dead. And they know it.

When they screwed that up, they couldn't afford to let those two guys, you know, walk around, so *they* wound up in a trunk.

I'm telling you this as a policeman. As someone who's been a policeman most of his life and is a policeman body and soul. I'm telling you that there is no honor. And that is all Hollywood bullshit.

There's no honor—*The Godfather* is all crap—these are a bunch of vicious . . . animals. They don't sit around and say, "Gee, you know, we gotta hit Tony—he's been a great guy. It's really a shame. Let's give Tony a nice send-off. And what we'll do, we'll shoot him right in the head to make it nice and quick."

There are people in this business who are disturbed. There are people in this business who are sociopaths. I personally know of one hitman who I believe to be a serial killer who's simply found a way to vent his homicidal tendencies.

There's no honor.

* * *

I never get too excited when they're killing one another. You know, some scumbag gets knocked off by the Outfit, I can't get excited. You wallow with the pigs, you're gonna get mud all over you.

And they do some horrible things to people. I remember seeing a guy, you know what a catch basin is in a sewer system? They had this guy, he's upside down in it. Head first, his feet sticking up. Some of these things have kind of a grillwork over them. You could see his feet up against the grillwork. They just had him stuffed down, they pushed him down in there, and pushed this thing on top of him. I mean, you think how you're gonna end your life. . . . Apparently, he had been alive when they pushed him in there. I mean, they're vicious people. They're animals.

They can't exist of and by themselves. One of the main reasons they *have* been able to exist is because they utilize middle men. An organized crime figure cannot make a political contribution to an office-holder. That's anathema. He needs a clean middleman to be the guy to make the contribution, to be the guy to get somebody a job. Marlon Brando can't show up with his hair greased back. It has to be the Outfit guy's lawyer or the businessman who's in place.

The Outfit couldn't exist if it couldn't compromise people. They're masters at corrupting. They've never been cheap when it comes to payoffs, to bribes.

So you can't get mad at the Outfit without getting mad at whole other segments of society: at the hangers-on—people enjoy knowing mobsters, they like to be on the fringe. And then you've got to be mad at the corrupt officials, the corrupt lawyers, the corrupt police.

Outfit coppers. Some young kids are told, "Why don't you go on the police department? You get some insurance and it's a good job, and we can take care of you there, we can help you out." And they do that. And then when they get on the job, they try and steer them towards units that they want them to be in, where they can help them: Gambling, Prostitution, Narcotics. The politicians make the clout calls for them.

There've been hitmen on the job. Guys who run gambling. Pickup men, burglars. I'm talking about organized crime burglars who work *in* uniform, with squad cars. And then they take the organized crime regular burglar with them; they bring them, with the tools, in the squad car, and they're the lookout guys while the guy's in rooting the place. But these are rare animals; it's not a common thing.

A lot of Outfit guys are rewarded for illegal conduct with city jobs. We knew a guy who was a bouncer on Rush Street for a number of years. Then he went out with a guy and killed a guy. Thirty days later, he's just sitting, a tow-truck driver, $27,000 a year.

They like to get on the city payroll, the state payroll, for the hospitalization. They're like anybody else; they want their family covered. There's a lot of them working for the city and the state; that's the bottom of the rung, the soldiers. They never show up. It's a hustle.

When Jane Byrne was mayor, she got the word that there were some ghost payrollers at a city repair garage. So she told her driver one day—"Go over here." Eight o'clock in the morning. Nobody knew she was coming, including her driver. She walked in, she wanted a roll call for all the workers, and she got the payroll sheets out. Fifty people were no-shows out of that one garage.

We had an informant over there. We thought he actually worked there. We're sitting talking, he's reading the paper, he says, "How do you like that? They got a sauna over there." I say, "Didn't you know that?" He said, "I never been in that place." I said, "You been on employment there for three years." "Yeah," he says, "I meet the guy in the coffee shop, he gives me my check twice a month, and I give him fifty bucks." Never been to work. Ever. I said, "Did you get fired?" "No. Wasn't I lucky? They just put me down on vacation for that month." He's still working.

You've got them in the news media, you've got them in the state's attorney's office, you've got them in the police department. They're everywhere. They can always reach out to some contact they have. No one's exempt.

Their real power is their influence and their favors-owed formula. Because then they elicit the cooperation of people that are *not* organized crime people. There are Outfit guys *now* that are general managers of major hotel chains; CEOs of major corporations that own hotel chains; they grew up with all these people and took care of them along the way. There is such a huge amount of favors owed.

They talk about the street tax independent illegal operators pay. With the stranglehold the Chicago Outfit has over unions, what kind of a street tax do you think every consumer pays to these same people? What do you think a head of lettuce costs you extra because of these guys? A loaf of bread?

If I could tell Joe in the punch-press room that the thing that he just bought cost him $1,000 instead of the $600 it should have cost *because* of organized crime, I'd make my case. But since we're never able to do that, we have to count on the occasional program on PBS. Who you gonna tell? You know?

And law enforcement's done it to itself. It's easy to pinch the sixty-seven-year-old wire-room operator and call him an organized crime figure. This guy is no more a member of organized crime than you or I are. But we call them that. It suits our purpose. It gives us *arrest figures.* And allows us to say that our part in the fight against organized crime is gaining momentum and we have knocked off somebody who's getting on the phones to major wire-room people, very close to the bosses, and we're getting near the . . . the *top.*

Meanwhile, the city of Chicago gives a ten-million-dollar waste-hauling contract to an out-and-out Outfit-controlled trucking operation. And they've been handling it for the past fifteen years. That adds fifty cents to the street tax we're all paying the Outfit.

Everybody can understand and get along quite well, it seems, knowing that our circuit court judges on the state and local levels can be bought. It doesn't seem to excite anybody. People in law enforcement could give you a list—if you went and just talked to all the people, especially the people that deal with these guys, like the people in the Detective Division—you could amass yourself a long list of the attorneys that pay off the judges and a long list of the dirty judges too. And that's not a tough thing to do.

However, that's just peanuts, and people don't seem to be too excited about it. If they were, they'd demand that something be done about it, and they don't. But if you expand that, then, and show that our government is loaded with senators and congressmen and U.S. judges that are *just* as nefarious, just as crooked—especially congressmen that owe their allegiances to neighborhoods in big cities—you know, that would do some serious damage to the national psyche, I think. If we get away from the Chicago–New York–Philadelphia mentality, put yourself in Iowa or Nebraska, it would, I think, bother people of goodwill if the seriousness of it were really known.

If they wanted to end drugs and porno and organized crime, they could. So what's stopping them? They're politicians, judges, people in law enforcement, businesspeople—what's stopping them?

Money's stopping them. Money. Greed. Kickbacks. Allegiances. Favors owed.

Organized crime could be wiped out. Narcotics could be wiped out. All we've got to do is get together, all law enforcement agencies from the feds on down. If nothing else, wipe out decentralized data bases and put them together. Share information.

I mean, you're not supposed to look at tax returns unless you have a reason. Well, then, get a *reason.* And if you've *got* a reason, get your proof and go before a federal judge and get a court order. And prepare your case.

Follow the money. We just came back from an International Organized Crime Symposium, and everybody agreed on follow the money. That's with any criminal, belonging to traditional or nontraditional organized crime: the Colombians, the Cubans, the Jamaicans, the Japanese. Follow the money. That's how to get them.

Asset Forfeiture is the way to go—civil RICO works well on anybody. The minute a piece of property is used for a crime, it belongs to the U.S. government. So that's how to take the goods and trace the criminals. And the civil application of RICO is much easier to work with than the criminal, because the burden of proof is on them—they have to come up with some proof to defend themselves. They can't stand mute.

But as soon as you get into the banks and the markets, though, where the "legitimate businesspeople" who are thieves are—they're gonna want to do away with that. They don't want RICO used on the Stock Exchange, the Mercantile Exchange. If you start bothering them, they're gonna try to have RICO killed. But RICO can be used on anybody: the drug cartel, the Outfit, bankers—anybody that's a criminal.

Why do all these guys work? To get toys. Asset Forfeiture takes away their toys. It gets them where they live.

We're gonna strike at their heart by going after their murders. We're gonna be successful on these murders. We're *going* to solve some of these murders. There's no way in the world we're not going to do it. And there's going to be some real fireworks when we do it.

Traditionally, hits go unsolved. For a simple reason: In a city that could have as many as eight hundred murders a year, you have to have priorities, and you have to decide how much manpower to allot to an individual case. I can't speak for the department, but some things are obvious on their face. Number one, if a criminal is killed, you're not going to get an uproar from society. But if a child is murdered, for example, then there's an outcry, and policemen will work on their own, they'll come in on their own time, some of them will never forget it, they'll carry the case with them forever.

So there's a real human element in this thing. You know, Joey the Rat gets killed and you'd like to solve it, but you're not gonna lose any sleep over it if you don't.

The PD never gave up on these cases, but they almost always reached a point where they just couldn't invest any more man-hours.

So the way we approach it now is to involve the United States government in the investigation of Outfit homicides. They haven't been involved. Homicide is not a federal violation.

But the FBI now has decided that if they pour their resources into the investigation of Mafia murders, there'll be no cornfield to hide these people in. So now we've got the Joint Organized Crime Task Force: FBI agents, CPD homicide detectives, agents from the state.

All the skids are greased. We're able to cross state lines. We're not worried about our budget. If we have to rent cars and go someplace, we're gonna rent cars. If we have to stay overnight in a hotel, we'll stay overnight. If you have to fly to Las Vegas, you're gonna fly to Las Vegas. This is probably the main weapon in our arsenal now: the budget and the ability to cross state lines, to cross jurisdictions.

It's the same thing as catching serial killers. The serial killer that *doesn't* cross jurisdictions is the serial killer that's gonna be caught. That's why Gacy got caught. Had Gacy been a traveler, he might still be killing people.

If we can charge a Mafia assassin with murder and convict him, there is no way that a parole board would let him out in five years. He ain't getting out. We are going to be telling him, in effect, "You are going to be spending the rest of your life in prison. We're gonna put you in there, and you're never coming out. Is that what you want to do?"

So he is going to be faced with a choice. Is he going to spend the rest of his life in prison or is he going to make a deal?

And the only deal we want is for him to give up his bosses and his fellow murderers. And once that starts, that's when the fireworks start. We are going to put our hands right around their throats.

The other thing that's beautiful about this is that when you're talking about guys in their fifties, they *know* they're going to die in prison. This is not the tough-guy stuff where he says, "I can do five years standing on my head and then they're gonna take care of me when I get out, and I'm gonna be a *real* big guy because I showed them I can hold my mutt." Old Tony's gonna be looking at dying, in prison.

If we get Mob Assassin Number One to flip, he won't want to go to prison. He'll want his own apartment somewhere, U.S.-owned, he'll want the *Reader's Digest* delivered and the *Chicago Tribune.* And I'll have all the questions ready for this guy.

These things don't happen without a lot of planning and a lot of teamwork. They take crews out on hits. Whoever commands the crew will testify against the other crew members and against whoever ordered them to go out and kill the target. It'll bring them all down.

You know what we're saying to them? "You wanna kill people? Go ahead. That's what we're working on. Thanks for providing us with the work."

They're going to go to jail. Or they'll die. They'll start killing each other, and that plays right into our hands. There won't be a cornfield they can hide in anymore.

Unless law enforcement gets their act together, ten years from now, right along with the infiltration of legitimate business and the economic stranglehold they have on unions, industry, infiltration of various other branches, with people running the operations that don't have a criminal record and never did, the only thing we'll be chasing full time, 100 percent, are old wire-room guys. Because that's *all* we'll be able to find.

What else will we do? Ask a big Gold Coast hotel to give us their books and knock out 4 percent of the city-tax levy for that area? And have the mayor fire you? What then will we do when we get ourselves in that kind of a bind?

And we're a microcosm of what must be going on in major cities all *across* the United States.

In a few years, organized crime will be completely buried, completely inaccessible to the local law-enforcement path and difficult for even the feds to get to, even the IRS to get to.

Because they won't have any criminal identifiers. They won't be left over from the Capone era. They'll have MBAs, law degrees, and CPA degrees. And they'll be general managers of major hotels—they already are *that.* They'll be part and parcel of the economic vitality of the area. And how do you get rid of that? How do you get rid of the major stockholders in a Mitsubishi, in a Sony? You can't do that.

These people, they'll be so *cemented* into our economy. Is that dangerous? Yeah. You talk about moral decay now?

Organized crime—it's not the big bad tiger of the jungle anymore. There's other tigers out there—with different stripes.

Some of the nontraditional organized crime groups coming up now make the Outfit guys look like wimps. In their methodology, they certainly do. And some of them have been around a lot longer—the Japanese Yakuza, for example, have been dealing with the *world,* moving money, for more than forty years. The nontraditional criminals make the Outfit look wimpy, in both nastiness *and* power.

Organized crime doesn't usually get you involved in ritualistic procedures that would defeat a law enforcement officer, because you would not be willing to become involved in the ritual. For example, the Yakuza, the Japanese, get into this. They're into tattooing and mutilation. You tattoo your body and cut off one of your fingers. Why would they do that? To defeat infiltration.

Ten, twenty years from now, after the drug thing has run its course, the *big* thing that organized crime will get into—this is both traditional and nontraditional organized crime—will be the selling of body parts. They're already doing it in some countries—they're taking these kids, buying babies, killing them, and selling them for organ transplants. We've started to look into it here.

What will happen is, they'll take the babies, take the girls, take the kids, whatever ages they want, and just grow them like cattle. And then when somebody needs an organ, or a group of organs, from a three-year-old, an eight-year-old, a female white, whatever . . . It's really getting scientific. The fear is that the U.S. is just gonna start buying these body parts from overseas, and that's what we have to protect against. Organ farming is expected to be the next wave after drugs.

Doesn't that scare you?

Organized Crime:
Contributing Police Officers

OFFICER TOM BOHLING, Organized Crime Division, Vice Control Section. Bohling is one of the United States' foremost experts in pornography and obscene materials; in 1986, he testified before the Meese Commission. Bohling joined the CPD in 1968, was assigned to the Fourth District on patrol, served in Vietnam in the U.S. Navy, returned, and was assigned in 1973 to the Intelligence Section, Subversives Unit, for a year, when he went to the Fifth District on patrol. In 1975, Bohling was assigned to the Conspiracy Unit within the Vice Control Section, and has been with Prostitution/Obscenity for the past fourteen years. Bohling has a master's degree in criminal justice.

OFFICER DOMINIC CANNOVA, Organized Crime Division, Intelligence Section. Cannova was assigned to Organized Crime in 1987, with the special duty of establishing the entire computer system for the division. Cannova has been with the CPD since 1970. He spent two years on patrol in the Second District, and two years, from 1972–74, working District Vice Patrol, which concentrated on narcotics, gambling, and prostitution. In 1974, District Vice Patrol was disbanded, and Cannova worked a beat car and served on the tac team in the Eighth District. In 1975, he was assigned to the Mass Transit Unit, where he worked for three years. From 1978–87, Cannova was part of the tac team in the Eighth District, specializing in narcotics enforcement.

SERGEANT JERRY D. GLADDEN, chief investigator, Chicago Crime Commission. Gladden is one of the nation's top experts on organized crime. He's served with the Chicago Crime Commission since January 1987, and was a sergeant in Organized Crime, Intelligence, for eighteen years. Gladden joined the force in 1956, was promoted to detective six months later, served ten years in the citywide Youth Division before being promoted to sergeant and being assigned to Organized Crime, the first two years of which he worked the Gang Unit, before being assigned to the old "Hoodlum Squad."

DETECTIVE JOHN MURRAY, Organized Crime, Intelligence. Murray's twenty-two years on the force have included working patrol in the Thirteenth District for four-and-a-half years, serving as a detective in the old Robbery Unit in Area Six from 1972 till 1978, investigating financial crimes and managing the budget in the Office of

Municipal Investigations from 1980 through 1986, and working Intelligence from 1978 to 1980 and since 1986. Murray has a master's degree in public administration.

DETECTIVE TED O'CONNOR, FBI/CPD Organized Crime Task Force. O'Connor joined the force in 1967 and was promoted to detective three years later, when he was assigned to the old Homicide Unit, where he worked till 1978. O'Connor then went undercover in an operation targeting Outfit-controlled businesses, then into the DEA Narcotics Task Force for five years. O'Connor has also served as the sex crimes analyst for the CPD and as administrative aide to the deputy chief of detectives. O'Connor has been part of the joint task force formed to investigate unsolved Mob hits since 1988.

DETECTIVE BILL PEDERSEN, Organized Crime, Asset Forfeiture Unit. Pederson, who joined the CPD twenty-two years ago, has worked in Auto Theft, the Special Investigations Unit, and for ten years (from 1973–83) as a narcotics detective. Pederson worked as an Area Two violent crimes detective for six years before joining the Organized Crime Division in 1989.

OFFICER DEAN SAKURAI, Organized Crime, Intelligence. Sakurai joined the force in 1981, worked patrol and tac in the Town Hall District for five-and-a-half years, and then was assigned to the Intelligence Unit in 1987 to investigate Asian crimes and Asian gangs.

CAPTAIN BOB SHEEHAN, watch commander, Eighteenth District. Sheehan served as deputy chief of the Organized Crime Division from April 1980 through January 1988. In Sheehan's thirty-six years on the force, his assignments have included patrol officer, homicide detective in Area Four, sergeant on the North Side, lieutenant at Patrol Headquarters, district commander in Eighteen, and assistant deputy superintendent. Sheehan's law enforcement training has included the renowned "long course" at Northwestern University's Traffic Institute and the program offered police by the FBI National Academy.

DETECTIVE VINCE STRANGIS, retired. Strangis's career in the CPD included fifteen years in the high-crime Englewood District, one year on patrol and fourteen as a detective working Burglary, Robbery, and Homicide, and sixteen years assigned to the Organized Crime Division, one in Vice Control, Prostitution and fifteen in the Intelligence Section. Strangis worked on the pilot program for the FBI/CPD Joint Organized Crime Task Force, and was one of five intelligence officers originally detailed to it.

CONNIE FLETCHER developed an interest in crime during a typical Chicago girlhood, when her father, James T. Fletcher, took her every holiday to visit the site of the St. Valentine's Day Massacre and to finger the bullet holes left in the stones of Holy Name Cathedral, where Little Hymie Weiss was gunned down. Like her father, Fletcher was educated at Loyola University Chicago, where she is now an assistant professor in the Department of Communication, teaching journalism. She has a doctorate in English Literature from Northwestern University. Fletcher lives with her husband, Trygve, her daughter, Bridget, and her son, Nick, in Wilmette, Illinois.